The Stump's On Fire And I'm Naked

J. Donald Oakes

August 20th, 2005

To: Herbert Jones

Best wishes

J. Donald Oakes

D1218387

The Stump's On Fire And I'm Naked

©J. Donald Oakes 2003

ISBN: 0-9742161-8-6
Library of Congress Number: 2003115069

Published in 2003 by
Global Authors Publications
*Filling the **GAP** in publishing*

Edited by T.C. McMullen
Cover Design by Kathleen Walls
Author Photo by Steve Thornton Photography - Atlanta
Book WebSite: www.stumpsonfire.com

Printed in USA for Global Authors Publications

The Stump's On Fire And I'm Naked

A Global Authors Publications Book

I dedicate this book to Mama, Daddy, my brothers J.P. and Red, my sisters Ruby Lee, Inez, and Marilyn. Dedications are in order for my daughters Donna, Michelle, and April.

I also dedicate it to Sandra in a very special way for putting up with me during the "lean" years.

Acknowledgements

I would like to thank my collaborator, Gerald G. Griffin, for adding a new dimension to my story with his knowledge of Shakespeare and other fine poets. His experience and knowledge in psychology also was of great benefit to this book.

I would also like to thank my editor T.C. McMullen and all the G.A.P. staff members that offered support and assistance in making this book the best that it could be.

This book would not have been possible without Dr. Nancy Engle. She planted the seed for it and never gave up on me.

Foreword

*F*IND THE SPRING that controls your own Universe.
These words, whispered by some unseen presence to Donald Oakes as a young boy, begin Donald's arduous healing journey as he struggles to survive in an environment fraught with unspeakable poverty, both material and spiritual. At the end of this journey, one that takes him to the darkest places in his soul, there is a wellspring of hope that enables Donald to come to terms with the question: what is the meaning of my existence? And in his search Donald leads us, the reader, on a journey to find an answer to a similar question that has hounded mankind since the beginning of time: what is the meaning behind human suffering?

As a Licensed Professional Counselor who has worked for over fifteen years with children who have suffered a variety of abuses at the hands of adults, I was stunned and humbled as I read *The Stump's On Fire And I'm Naked*. At first glance, the title seems lighthearted, humorous even, but from the beginning of the book we find that the content is far from funny- it is by turns appalling, disturbing, moving, but ultimately touching and triumphant. Beginning with a paranormal experience that will stay with Donald for the rest of his life, we watch with sadness and humility as the life of an innocent child unfolds before our eyes, a child who is abused, neglected, and tormented yet who, with the help of these otherworldly figures, finds within himself the grit and determination to survive.

Whether the abuse comes in the form of enduring his mother's irrational fear of storms or overhearing his parents incessant fighting at night, Donald begins at an early age to exhibit classic symptoms of a child who is in the throes of a full-fledged emotional crisis. He suffers from enuresis (bedwetting), encopresis (involuntary bowel movements), and debilitating anxiety attacks. He develops asthma so severe that at times he digs through the family's fireplace in search of discarded cigarette butts, thinking that inhaling the smoke will help him to breathe. These stress-related ailments leave him so incapacitated that he is unable to help his family pick cotton in the fields, prompting them to label him "lazy" and accuse him of faking his illnesses in order to get out of the work. He is so ashamed of the stained bed sheets his mother hangs out to dry while he is at school that he distances himself from other children, thereby increasing his sense of isolation, because he doesn't want to bring peers home to see the soiled sheets or the dilapidated, crowded shacks that the family lives in from the time Donald is born until he leaves home.

Dreams are a useful window into the psyche, and children who suffer from consistent trauma are known to have routine and disturbing nightmares. Donald's sleeping life is similarly tormented by a faceless man with deep black eyes who continually and silently taunts him, never answering the boy's frightened pleas of "who are you?" . The faceless man only laughs a demonic laugh as Donald's father burns in the fires of hell while Donald stands by, powerless to save him. In this metaphorical dream we witness Donald's all-consuming desperation to save himself from the living hell of his waking life.

When Donald leaves Alabama as a young man he naturally thinks that he is escaping his parents and the memories of his childhood abuse and destitution. He joins the military and there learns for the first time that he is intelligent, gifted, and talented. But even though he is given envious assignments and has his pick of attractive young women, he soon learns that he has not escaped from his past as he so desperately needed but rather, as we all do, he has brought it with him. With mounting horror, he realizes he is beginning to act out on his own family many of the torments reaped on him by his mother. The fundamental realization that one cannot run away from one's self is at the heart of many therapy sessions, and it is with great sadness that most adults come to understand that just by leaving their homes physically they have not left their "baggage". Donald comes to this understanding with equal trepidation and sorrow. His past is inside him, a part of him, and he is forced to face the hardest fact that any human being must confront- that we are our own worst enemy.

Against all odds, broken and disheartened, Donald struggles for many years to conquer his demons. When he finally does, this triumph spares his life and that victory illuminates the theme of this book. Returning to his childhood home in Pea River Swamp, Donald once again sees the ghostly apparitions he had seen as a young boy, only this time he understands their message. And therein lies his peace, his hope for a better life for himself and his children, and his ultimate victory.

Donald's journey is one that we all take, in some fashion, and it is the brave few who can bring their own personal pain to a level of healing that Donald has done, who can transform their suffering not into perpetual violence and hatred but transcend it for personal and spiritual growth that others can learn from.

What is the meaning of existence? It is a question we must each answer for ourselves. Donald poses it to himself at the end of the book and discovers the answer in the final place he searches- inside his own heart. All of us would do well to heed his lesson.

Find the spring that controls your own Universe. Donald Oakes, in *The Stump's On Fire And I'm Naked* gives us hope that we can.

Kelly L. Stone, MS, LPC

Kelly L. Stone is a Licensed Professional Counselor who has worked with children and families for over 15 years. She has published essays on the experience of transforming pain and loss into personal growth. Contact her at kellystone@kellylstone.com

CHAPTER 1

D USK, UNUSUALLY QUIET, the sky awaiting its carpet of stars. Below, a thicket of pines began its fade into tall shadows. Then suddenly an eerie sight moved toward the trees. Ghostly forms. Floating. Then the forms disappeared, vanishing into the thicket.

In those few moments the seeds of destiny, not only eventually changing my life dramatically, but also rescuing thousands of others, like myself, wallowing in the wrong Universe.

I was only five years old, minutes before, in our dilapidated shack, waiting with Mama and my three sisters—Ruby Lee and Inez, older than me, and Marilyn, younger—for Daddy and my older brother, Red, to return, off helping to sell our landlord's crop recently harvested. Suddenly, all five of our hunting dogs outside began barking, quickly working to loud, ferocious growls. Then just as suddenly their growls switched to unnatural howling, that peculiar whine, primitive chilling sounds of retreat. Soon every dog in the neighborhood joined in the barking frenzy.

Ruby Lee cocked a brow, blanching grim. "Oh, my God!" She shuddered. "What's happenin'?"

Inez's face was just as ashen with fright, and the two sisters rapidly became unnerved, heaving their heads and shoulders, shouting, waving their arms wildly.

"Lord have mercy, ya girls!" Mama scolded, frowning impressively. "No sense in such a fit. That racket is probably over nothin'." But a certain reedy timber in her voice betrayed her uneasiness.

Still frowning, Mama scrambled for the door, my sisters and me right behind her, the five of us rushing jerkily out onto the porch, greeted by a strange chill in the air and a sight curling our spines.

A long string of vivid ghostlike figures, hands joined, dreamy in appearance and movement, floated quietly a few feet off the ground at the edge of a peanut field across the road in front of our shack. Though we could see them clearly, the figures appeared both to be there and not to be there, as if functioning in two planes at once, showing visible from another dimension. Their shapes kept changing back and forth from an irregular mass to surrealistic cloud-like forms, suggesting pulsation, varying from dull grayish-white to luminous transparency.

It was an eerie sight, with no reference to experience, eliciting chaos among those on the porch. The wide-eyed stares of Ruby Lee and Inez disintegrated into screaming, raspy disembodied screams rivaling the barking of the dogs. Mama uncorked right along with them, and their fright became little Marilyn's fright. I was the only one on the porch remaining quiet, motionless, not making a sound, caught up in some calm of vibrations obscuring my eyes with a filmy gaze.

I wasn't afraid. I didn't feel threatened. Whatever the ghostlike figures were, to me they seemed empathetic. I knew they meant me no harm. Then for an instant my mind seemed to become ageless, boundless, sensing oddly that the appearance of the apparitions was for my benefit. An effort to communicate in some subliminal manner, enciphered and unidentified. But I could make out no message, feeling only that there was one.

Mesmerized, I watched as the last ghostlike image in the chain disappeared, overcome with a cryptic sensing as I did so. A sensing momentarily uplifting. Something about the future. The unveiling of a secret. A mystery to be revealed. Then the sensing vanished along with the apparitions.

From the glow of his lighted cigarette we spotted Daddy approaching the shack; and as he drew nearer we all scampered out to the road. Mama, Ruby Lee and Inez swarmed around Daddy and Red with obvious discomposure, the three of them, almost incoherently, attempting to inform them of what had occurred.

Neither Daddy nor Red believed a word of their ghost story, laughing at it with resonant amusement.

"Yer all crazy!" Daddy exclaimed, his tongue deftly flipping his cigarette across his mouth in a wad of spit. "Seein' things. Sure, somethin' spooked them dogs, but it was probably a bobcat. Now jest calm down."

Mama eyed him with a hard look of dreamy terror floating through her inside out, all the way from the bone. "No blame bobcat is gonna scare them dogs like that!" She snapped. "I know what I seen!"

As much as Mama, Ruby Lee and Inez insisted upon the truth of the ghost story, no one believed them and after awhile they no longer discussed it. As for me, I never mentioned the ghosts from the beginning, though puzzled as to why Mama and my sisters had been so frightened by the apparitions. Why hadn't they sensed what I sensed?

And what I sensed later came true. There was to be an unveiling of a secret. A mystery revealed. Something I had to share. But this secret, this mystery, would come only after I was ready to receive it. The right time. The right place. The right apparition. I was to see those ghostlike figures again, the second encounter prompting the writing of this book.

In 1984, almost three years before that encounter, I was sitting at my desk, ostensibly a successful executive in Atlanta, highly paid, highly respected by those in the organization employing me, charged with the demanding responsibility for implementing special computer software accounts nationwide. All at once my life up to that point caved in on me. My feet suddenly became cold and numb. My body stiffened. My shoulders knotted. My face became a grimace of stone. Then my ears buzzed with a frightening roar. I was stunned, disoriented, debilitated, the room spiraling, a pain of darkness engulfing me, terrorizing me, slumping me in the helplessness of my own finality. I was convinced I was suffering some fatal attack.

They say when you're dying your life flashes before you. Mine didn't flash. It crept by slowly. An emotional stocktaking. Agonizing gulps of memory.

My first remembrance was more of a conclusion; a summary of memories: all I ever wanted was just to be normal. A normal kid. A normal adult. A normal life. But from the moment I was born that wasn't to be, that moment around 11 o'clock on a cold and rainy night, February 5, 1944, the place a sharecropping shack in the sticks of southern Alabama, 20 miles northeast of Troy. My Grandma Oakes delivered me. Following the death of Grandpa Oakes—he died in agony after being kicked by a belligerent mule—Grandma Oakes, to keep herself busy, took up midwifery and busy she remained delivering hundreds of babies in south Alabama, not too few of them now either impoverished paupers, drunks, uneducated dolts, perverted misfits or flirting with the funny farm. Or murdered. Or dead at their own hands.

Such were my likely prospects coming into this world. A world of trauma. Ravaging trauma. Psychologically, trauma takes many forms, the most acclaimed the Four Horsemen of the Apocalypse—war, famine, pestilence and death. My four horsemen were privation, depravity, turmoil and torment. And there was no waiting for them. Like vultures pursuing a sure carcass they were hovering around at birth, ready to pounce and consume, the inevitability of being born into the rock bottom, austere, ne'er-do-well setting of the sharecropping lot.

My two brothers and three sisters shared this legacy with me but never displayed the revulsion to it that I would. Apparently Mama and Daddy preferred their babies in groups of two. My brother J.P.—That's all he was ever called, J.P., I suspect after my paternal grandpa, James Phillip Oakes—was born first, followed two years later by my sister, Ruby Lee. After another three years my brother, Red, was born, followed a year later by the birth of my sister, Inez. Then there was an interval of nine years before I popped into the world, and two years later my sister, Marilyn, slid through, mercifully bringing an end to this untidy progeny.

My parents, Joseph and Anna Oakes, certainly were no love story. Some kind of bond existed between them but it was too primordial to grasp, possibly having something to do with the caveman mentality for survival. I don't think my parents knew what love for one another was all about. Nor did they have time to find out, too preoccupied with the pressing tasks of enduring a mean existence.

Both of my parents—my father I always called Daddy, my mother, Mama—were born in Alabama, and if ever there was an odd couple they were it. He was 20 and she 14 when they married, and it didn't take long for whatever affection existed between them to sour on the vine, replaced by animosity and ill feelings, particularly on Mama's part. The two no more belonged together than did a rattler and a bobcat and I often wondered how they ever met and became man and wife. My best guess is that they eyed one another in some honky-tonk place, smiled bewitchingly at one another long enough to start their hormones gushing, and Mama became pregnant with J.P.

Unlike Mama—totally predictable, Daddy was a paradox. Though in many ways he epitomized the essence of the sharecropper's legacy, completely captured by its unyielding setting, in other ways he was impervious to it, unaffected, living as if he harbored some secret enabling him to look upon those who took life with any weighty import as silly fools.

In keeping with the rock bottom aspect of the legacy, Daddy never attended school. He couldn't read or write, making his signature with an X. A sharecropper by trade, a moonshiner by necessity, sometimes working in a sawmill during the sharecropping off-season—October through March, daddy wasn't much on motivation. Not caring for material things, he had no need to be enterprising acquiring them. But when it came to common sense he had few peers, empowering him to deal easily with people while being highly regarded in return.

A good-looking man, slim, six-two, 190 lbs., square jaw, square chin, long pleasant weathered face, Daddy was easygoing and friendly, liking his fun. He was also an alcoholic, but a happy drunk, more the impresario when he was drinking, better natured, his face creased with a smile, or beaming gigglish, ready to joke, ever the prankster, ever seeking out jollity wherever he could find it. For Daddy, enjoying life was never to take it seriously. Things never upset him. He never worried, even when things were tumbling down about him. He simply took his woes in stride, smiling and laughing them away with another swig of moonshine.

This waggish disregard carried over to his dress. Daddy's trademark was overalls. That's all I ever saw him wear—old, worn-out, faded overalls full of holes, never buttoned down the sides, a faded shirt tucked inside of them. He never wore socks, and his shoes—old high top brogans, were as worn out as his clothes, holes in the ends and sides of them, his sockless big toes sticking out, revealing the corns and calluses on his feet. If he had ever dressed up he would have looked impressively debonair, but he never did so, not even when he journeyed into town to a dance.

And his appearance wasn't helped by his tobacco habit. Incessantly, he smoked roll-your-own Prince Albert cigarettes, slobbering spit each time he smoked that was absorbed into the mouth end of the cigarette, a nasty, disgusting sight. And while smoking he continually switched the cigarette from one side of his mouth to the other with his tongue, at the same time reaching his hand down to his crotch, fiddling with a bad hernia rupture, uncomfortable and bothersome, constantly keeping him toying down there to keep his rupture in place, caring not who saw him.

Unpretentious, caring for little more than his fun, his moonshine, his drinking buddies and a roof over his head when he needed it, Daddy was the happiest member of the family.

With the exception of myself, Mama was the unhappiest, opposite in disposition from Daddy and as pretentious as they come, maintaining a prim facade around those outside the family. Naturally nervous and fearful, she was superstitious, domineering, overly protective and cautious, keeping herself uptight, and she took everything much too seriously, seemingly suffering every breath she took when isolated with family members. But it was the intensity in which these states possessed her that best characterizes Mama. Most people strive for the best in life but she had a compulsion for the worst.

With memorable exceptions, I seldom saw Mama smile or laugh. Whether real, imagined or the unreasonable product of her fears, Mama was too prone to worry, too prone to frustration, too negatively over reactive to everything, too ingrained with the misery of her lot, too engrossed with magnifying events of horror, to smile or laugh with her family, or to be happy around them. And being unhappy she made certain everyone else was unhappy by keeping the household in a constant uproar.

An eye-catching woman when she was younger, Mama was tall, five-nine, 125 lbs., a high energy person with beautiful cascading long black hair, her face smooth complexioned, set off by emerald eyes and fluttering lashes when she wanted them to flutter. Having a third grade education she could manage simple reading and writing, and unlike Daddy she attempted to dress herself neatly, though her attire was limited mostly to a shirt with jeans or khaki pants. But on her visits to town she'd spruce up her appearance by wearing a simple flower patterned dress.

Mama's lot was a hard one. She worked like a slave. Not only in the hot sharecropping fields chopping and picking cotton along with Daddy, Red, Ruby Lee and Inez, or picking peanuts or corn, but also taking care of her wifely duties at home, including tending our vegetable garden and hours of canning for our winter consumption.

She had the stamina of a bull. Rising every morning before daylight, Mama built a fire in the stove, and then prepared breakfast. Following this early meal she washed the dishes, then scurried off to the field with everyone else. There Mama worked as hard as anyone until 11 o'clock, then hastened back to the shack, gathered wood, built a fire and cooked lunch. After the family ate, she again washed dishes, and then scooted back to the field with the working members of the family, laboring there until sundown. Then back to the shack, build another fire, cook supper, eat, wash dishes, bring on an uproar within the family, sleep a little, then start all over the next morning, managing through all of this to wash clothes using an old black pot and scrub board, carrying the water herself from a distant spring, all the while exacerbating the problem of varicose veins in her left leg.

By the time I was five years old, the family had moved into what I refer to as Shack 1. The period of my childhood from the ages of five through seventeen is most easily chronicled by the sharecropper shacks we lived in, seventeen in all, located in Bullock and Pike Counties in south Alabama, Shack 1 through Shack 17, all of them located within a six mile radius of one another. With the exception of one, all of these shacks were almost identical, right out of the set for *The Grapes of Wrath*: small, old rundown houses, poorly constructed out of pine lumber, a dilapidated porch in front, the outside finish having that sickly, weather-beaten gray color look. Inside, there were three cramped rooms—a kitchen, one room serving as a living room and bedroom and a third room used just as a bedroom. All of we kids slept in one bedroom, in two separate beds, Red and I in one, Marilyn and Inez in the other after Ruby Lee was married and gone.

Each shack was no more than a flimsy roof over our heads, a skimpy roof, and a sheet of rusty tin that leaked. The walls and floors inside were distinguished by large, wide cracks that Mama plugged up with rags. The windows were often broken and had to be plugged up by rags as well. Shabby-looking fireplaces heated the shacks, and smoke not only came out of the top of the chimney but also billowed out of its sides. There was no plumbing or air conditioning in any of the shacks and most of them had no electricity. We used kerosene lamps to light the darkness—it wasn't until I was thirteen that we moved into a shack with electricity. Water had to be carried in from either open springs or from a neighbor's house—or, if we were fortunate, a nearby well. There was no insulation, so it was miserably hot in the summer and extremely cold in the winter. The floors would creak when you walked on them, and animals were always living underneath, usually dogs and chickens, sometimes pigs.

We never had a telephone. Our bathrooms were outhouses and we used corn cobs to wipe ourselves. As an outhouse filled up with urine and feces the stench became unbearable, so when this happened, if it wasn't raining, we hightailed it to the woods to relieve ourselves, or to the nearest cotton or corn patch.

Summer evenings in the shacks offered at least the comfort of cool breezes. But winters offered no relief, day or night, the air so bitingly cold that it stung through you with shivering pain, freezing the water in our kitchen wash pan and bucket to the hardness of brick. Mama put linoleum rugs on the floors to keep the frigid draft out, helping some, but not enough to keep us from feeling like polar bears on Arctic ice skinned of our fur. The only thing that saved us in the winter was the thick, heavy quilts Mama made, and we needed no prompting to crawl shivering under them for precious warmth.

And at times in the winter all we had to eat was "lardy gravy," made by melting hog lard in a skillet, adding flour and cooking to a brownish texture, then adding water—when it wasn't frozen, causing a loud searing noise to form the gravy. The gravy, along with the biscuits, would be the total of our meal. But during the warmer months we had fresh vegetables grown in our garden, and at certain times of the year we had fresh hog meat from the hogs we raised and slaughtered. We experienced stretches of little food, and what there was wasn't nutritious. But at better times we'd eat fish that we caught and small game from hunting. On varied occasions we had chicken and eggs to eat from the chickens we raised. Sometimes we ate fried mackerel from a can made into patties, and salt fish— a mullet that's been cured and packed in salt.

We seldom went to the grocery store, then only to buy cornmeal, flour, sugar and salt. Now and then we had a cow to provide us milk and when we did we made our own butter. When we were without butter or eggs we'd visit our neighbors—other sharecroppers or landowners—and buy these foods from them rather cheaply.

Our family income from sharecropping, moonshining, off-and-on work at the sawmill and an occasional sale of livestock was under five hundred dollars a year, thus we never owned much of anything—mostly just old worthless furniture, a few simple clothes, a mule, an occasional cow, some chickens and a few pieces of worn-out farming equipment. Nor did we ever own an automobile. Daddy had no desire for one, quite contented with his mule and simple one-horse wooden wagon to get him around in.

By the time we had moved into Shack 1, my oldest brother, J. P., had flown the coop, and my oldest sister, Ruby Lee, 19, was champing at the bit to follow suit. Five-ten, 120 lbs., pretty face, pug nose, shapely and big bosomed, Ruby Lee took after Mama. Outgoing, flirtatious and lively, she was juicy ripe and ready for plucking. And the plucking was near.

Inez, 13 was less attractive, and less shapely. Five-seven, light complexioned, rather skinny, her hair was long and strikingly red, and her face was plastered with deep red freckles, a warning of her spunk.

Red, the middle son between J.P. and me, was 15 at Shack 1. A stocky, muscular five-six, light complexioned with red hair and freckles like Inez, only the freckles not as pronounced, his hair always slicked back from a good-looking oval face, Red was as strong as an ox and worked like one. As with Daddy he didn't take things seriously but was without Daddy's hilarious disposition, viewing life instead from aloof indifference. You never knew what was going on in Red's mind, but even at five I could see that Red was a lonely and troubled person, as I was becoming, only he dealt with it differently. Having dropped out of school in the third grade, Red, like Daddy, couldn't read a lick.

Marilyn was only three, little more than a wisp of meat and bone, as yet not too cute with her straight brown hair and flat nose, but a healthy frisky kid who, as she budded with age, would fight with me tooth and nail.

Along with Mama, all the kids, when they became old enough, worked with Daddy in the sharecropping fields. Daddy insisted upon it. Needing them as field hands, Daddy never encouraged his children to go to school—in fact; he dissuaded them from doing so. And they didn't go to school, not for long anyway. With the exception of Marilyn, who managed to go as far as the eighth grade, my other brothers and sisters never survived beyond the fourth. That suited them, fine, precluding any Nobel Prize winners in the family.

My agonizing, slowly creeping memories before the age of five were rather fragmented and unclear, consisting more of feelings and images than of events and incidents. And what I remember most of those feelings were that they were already in a flux of turmoil, confusion, uncertainty and insecurity, enough to suggest to me that it was no great favor being given life.

The only positive memory I have before five was the first time I caught a fish. I was at a lake, accompanied there by Daddy and a man name Hubert Singleton. While they were perched on a hill in back of me, talking and drinking moonshine, I waded knee deep out in the water, fishing with an old cane pole. While doing so I became caught up in the isolated beauty of the surroundings, distracting my attention to gaze at the wonder of the scenery and to watch the birds swoop. When I glanced at my pole again it was heading at an angle out into the lake in tugging, jerky movements.

"Daddy . . . Daddy my pole's moving! I got a fish! Come help me!"

"Hot a mighty!" Daddy grinned. "You sure got one on there. Reach out and git it."

"I can't. It's over my head!"

"If yer gonna fish, ya gotta catch 'em yerself."

As sensitive as I was, I took this as a threat: if I didn't get this fish on my own, Daddy wouldn't take me fishing again, this fear becoming greater than my fear of the water. Immediately I scampered awkwardly into the deeper water after the jerking pole, and soon the water's resistance slowed me to tiptoeing. Before I knew it the water was up to my neck and I was jerking my head back, my chin barely above the water, at times my mouth gulping water. Finally I was close enough to the pole to make a desperate grab for it. Success. With my hand clutching the pole I pulled it back to shore. Hooked on the end of the line was a tiny, flouncing fish glowing in the sun, barely bigger than a quarter. Soaking wet, smiling proudly, I held the fish up for Daddy and Hubert to see. They both burst into laughter.

"Hardly worth drownin' over," Hubert bellowed.

Sensitive as I was, vulnerable and fragilely pliable, Hubert was to be one of the major torments beginning my road toward emotional destruction.

A well-heeled carpenter, married, Hubert Singleton was a skinny man of six foot and as sneaky as a weasel. With a pointed face and pointed nose, he even looked like a weasel, a weasel wearing horn-rimmed glasses. He wasn't a close friend of Daddy's—though Daddy got along with him, as Daddy got along with everybody. But Hubert was very close to Mama. He was her lover.

Mama and Hubert were lovers since I can remember, a relationship of unending anguish for me. Startling are my memories of being hauled around in the back seat of Hubert's car, he and Mama up front, Marilyn and me in back. Mama's captive, I felt mighty uneasy about these rides. I'd sit up in the back seat, lean forward, and then study Mama and Hubert in the front seat with confusing alarm. He was always fingering one hand over Mama's legs as he was driving, she giggling girlishly and fluttering her lashes in return. The instant she became aware that I was watching, Mama gawked at me with a frowning grunt and abruptly pushed Hubert's hand away. Then she skittishly straightened herself up, assuming a sedate expression of propriety.

But too late. I'd seen enough. Enough to become angered at Hubert for doing something to Mama that wasn't proper, and becoming infuriated at Mama for being a part of it, for permitting it to happen, though confused as to what was happening but unable to dismiss that is was some sort of abomination.

But I could do nothing; say nothing, overwhelmed with a sense of helplessness; my anger was not helpless in tearing me apart. Quickly I repelled a retaliatory urge to tell Daddy. The strain between he and Mama needed no more added to it. A hefty portion of this strain was Mama's furious contention with Daddy over his drinking, producing never ending, drawn-out verbal battles between the two of them which we kids were forced to witness with shattering impact. Moreover, she held Daddy responsible for turning Red into an alcoholic.

When Red was about twelve years old, Daddy took him to his moonshine still and, as a joke, an amusement, gave him a drink of moonshine. It was like introducing a duck to water. Red developed a taste for the "stuff"—Mama's term for moonshine, falling in love with it, a gift of good feeling in the midst of poverty and hardship, and he kept on drinking it, and drinking and drinking, until at times he began acting like some loon with his brain fried out on hash, making him a frequent object of Mama's yelling and wrath.

She hated liquor, especially when Daddy and Red drank it. Never touching a drop herself, her choice of escape from her miserable, lonely, bleak life was clandestine sexual affairs, primarily with Hubert. And I feared that if Daddy found out about Hubert and Mama something dreadful would happen. He'd hurt Mama. Or break up the family. Or there'd be some other awful outcome. So I kept their abomination to myself, at the price of warping my emotions. This secret about Mama and Hubert strangulated me night and day, producing such immense guilt and shame that I couldn't look at Daddy in the eyes. Always I was fearful he'd read my secret. Then Armageddon.

This fear became a horror, terrorizing me, keeping me tense, tight, on edge. Adding to this sufferance was my escalating fury with Mama for continuing to see Hubert; continuing to shanghai Marilyn and me and hauling us around in the back seat of his car; continuing to giggle as he ran his hand over her legs—and elsewhere. She never giggled like that with Daddy. And I never saw Daddy run his hand over Mama's legs.

I knew nothing about the fidelity binding husband and wife. Yet I knew Mama was violating some trust to Daddy. Outwardly my fury was silent. I had no choice. Inwardly, it was devastating. I had no conscious escape from it. There was no one I dared speak to about it, even if I knew how, the harbinger for keeping all stressful feelings and emotions tightly contained within myself, not daring to let them out.

I was hapless, helpless, having nowhere to go with the torment of my guilt, shame, fear, anger and fright save to keep it within myself, letting it continue its silent warping process until my agonizing could no longer be contained, bursting out in the inevitable physical disorders of psychosomatic disaster, symptoms masking psychological trauma that would deepen into an even more insidious and self-destructive unconscious life operating outside of my awareness.

The first of these symptoms pounced on me shortly before I turned five. Mama and Daddy sometimes socialized with Hubert—Mama and Hubert arranging for these threesome get-togethers, without Hubert's wife. On one such infrequent occasion, Mama and Daddy, along with Hubert, attended a dance at a schoolhouse, leaving Marilyn and me in the back seat of Hubert's spanking-new 1949 black Ford sedan. He had parked it near the schoolhouse, blaring inside with the hubbub of Saturday night country music.

In spite of the loud noise, I managed, somewhat sullenly, to fall asleep, and while sleeping I urinated in my pants, the beginning of my bed-wetting horror. I woke up, at Marilyn's prodding, in wet, cold, miserable shock, immediately wanting to flee but paralyzed with a new version of shame.

Mama and Daddy were still in the schoolhouse and, feeling wretched and abandoned, I began whimpering, then crying, and then bawling loudly. "Come out! I want to go home. I want to go home!"

After a long howling fit, a stretch of tears frightening Marilyn, Mama finally moseyed up to the car, Daddy and Hubert behind her, Mama dead sober and quiet, Daddy dead drunk, grinning, laughing, enjoying himself—Mama was maintaining her facade to the hilt, refraining from jumping on Daddy for his drinking when people outside the family were around.

"Mama, can we go home?" I whimpered timorously as she opened the car door.

She ignored my plea with a sudden disgusted sniffing of her nostrils. "Good God Almighty!" She recoiled, her face souring at the strong stench of urine, both in my jeans and on the back seat. "Ya pissed yer pants! All over yerself! All over Hubert's car . . . Messin' it up. Lord have mercy! Smells like an outhouse in h'ar!"

"Aw, don't worry about it," said Hubert, but his eyes frowning at the urine stains on his shiny back seat covers, "It'll be all right."

"What's all the dang fuss about?" Daddy laughed. "Jest a little piss. Won't hurt nothin'. Leave him alone."

I began washing my anger away in bed-wetting.

Up until shortly before I turned five, I was healthy and bright, a rather vibrant youngster, babied by my older sisters and aunts. But with the dawn of my bed-wetting, I came to be viewed as some sort of freak and the babying ceased, leaving me to fend for myself. And with that the vibrancy of my spirit began to wane. And it wasn't just because of the bed-wetting, which was mostly just humiliating. It was also because of a new psychosomatic symptom springing itself upon me, one that would mushroom into something more physically devastating. I began developing asthma.

But Daddy didn't find out about Mama and Hubert, mainly because he was too busy with his own escapes, meaning escape from Mama. After working in the field all day, often Daddy disappeared from sight, drifting off into the sunset to make and sell moonshine. Or, if it was during the sharecropping off-season, and he wasn't working at the sawmill, and he was cooling it on the moonshining because the authorities were too close to sniffing him out, Daddy scrambled off possum hunting or vanished on a fishing outing, his covers for relaxing, laughing, joking and boozing with his drinking buddies.

It was during these times while Daddy was away that Mama did her own disappearing act, fetching Marilyn and me, her traveling bags, and hustling us off to meet with Hubert, leaving Ruby Lee, Inez and Red—if he wasn't off with Daddy—to occupy themselves.

As I approached five, the longer I had to keep the secret of Mama and Hubert from Daddy, the more my fear and fury boiled inside, ransacking my emotions not only to produce psychosomatic symptoms, but affecting me physiologically in other ways, pounding me into a puny, ailing, sickly, unhappy kid. Suffering this, and occupying such a hapless, helpless pecking order in the hierarchy of things, my mind, in addition to my emotions, began undergoing some warping itself. I needed a safe object on which to at least vent a fraction of my vexation. Marilyn was the safest object, but being my constant companion in the back seat of Hubert's car, I pitied her too much to use her for this. I chose Inez, the next safest object, and we began fussing and fighting over everything. On one notable occasion we began arguing over which of us was going to cut a watermelon. I had the knife by the handle and Inez had it by the blade. "Let me have the knife," I yelled, indignant. "I want to cut the watermelon."

"I'm doin' it you little twit, so let go!" Inez screeched.

"No, I'm doing it!"

"Yer not. Let go or I'm callin' Mama!"

Suddenly I wasn't tussling with Inez but with Mama. And with Mama in my sights I yanked the blade from Inez's grip, slicing a deep cut in her hand. Immediately the blood gushed forth like the fast sssssshhhhh of air out of a blown tire, a deeper red than the freckles on her face. Then realizing it as Inez, not Mama, I became aghast, stunned at my action leaving her screaming and bleeding profusely, certain that I had cut off her fingers. I hadn't, but still I was scared senseless and feeling hideous. And Mama, enraged out of her head, looked upon me as hideous, giving me one of the worst switch whippings of my life.

CHAPTER 2

WHY IS THIS happening to me?
Many people, once they reach age 70, reflect back upon their lives with disillusionment, feeling discarded, left embittered, depressed, afraid, lonely, protesting that life had treated them so unfairly, too harshly, then abandoned them to a pain of prolonged blackness entombing every facet of their being.

I felt that way when I was five years old.

And in reflecting back, remembering, none of the impact is lessened. I've always possessed an astounding memory, and from Shack 1 on, by the time I was five, my memory is vivid on events, incidents, times, places—and dreams.

Shack 1 was located just southeast of Josie, Alabama, a small rural town in Pike County, about a mile from where I was born. Barely a speck on the map, consisting of little more than a cotton gin, three country stores and an aging structure passing as a cafe, Josie was where farmers brought their cotton to be processed and where people from miles around, traveling over rutted, dusty dirt roads—there was no other kind, did their shopping and congregated on Saturday nights, finding their entertainment in noisy music, boisterous drinking, and outlandish dancing.

I still recall a sign on the front door of the Josie cafe that read: NO COLOREDS ALLOWED. GO TO THE BACK DOOR. When I first read that sign at the age of eight, I was sad and confused, and deeply bothered, reacting out of step with all the other white kids—and white adults. I knew how badly the blacks were being treated, and being so sensitive to unjust treatment, I empathized with their plight, identifying with it.

This was but one instance underscoring a shortcoming of mine by the time I was five: I was too sensitive. Super sensitive. I perceived things differently from others. And this sensitivity, especially to the defeating despair of my surroundings and circumstances, was so keen as to make me feel cursed.

What am I doing here? With these people? These conditions? I don't want to be here. I don't belong. Always the question: Why is this happening to me?

If I didn't know the why I certainly knew the what. And my chagrin over Mama and Hubert wasn't my only distress. Of equal if not greater trauma were the frequent, almost daily violent verbal clashes between Mama on one hand and Daddy and Red on the other over their drinking of moonshine. Mama hated their drinking with such a passion that it flared with messianic zeal, bursting her into relentless screaming-hollering-shouting tirades shaking the entire shack on its foundation.

Unsettling, scary, deafening, these frays were downright knockdown, drag-out verbal blitzkriegs, with no holds barred, no quarter given, none asked, especially by Mama. They were shattering explosions, reducing us kids to trembling fear and unleashing more havoc than all the cock fights within Alabama combined. Mama could immediately smell moonshine whiskey—"stuff"—on either Daddy or Red's breath, and that's all it took. Bedlam!

"It looks like to the good Lord ya wouldn't come home in that shape," was one of Mama's pat beginnings to her tirades. "I'm gonna git me a stick of dynamite and blow myself to Kingdom Come!"

Then she'd proceed, verbally, to blow Daddy and/or Red to Kingdom Come.

It was a tense moment for me whenever those two returned to the shack from somewhere. Anxiously I'd scamper out to meet them—inspect them, really—to see if they were staggering. If they were, or if I detected other signs that Daddy and Red had been drinking, I'd begin shaking and trembling helplessly, white as a ghost, my throat tightened and my heart trip hammering out of control, scared over the hell that would be erupting from Mama when she saw them.

As if Hubert wasn't enough.

But Mama didn't let the turmoil end there. When a small girl she was trapped in a house during a terrorizing storm that ripped the roof off and blew it away, this fright shackling her with a lasting insane fear of bad weather, even a hint of it. So each time we moved to a new shack, Mama's number one priority, her number one obsession, was to have Daddy build a storm pit for the entire family to flee to upon the slightest sign of bad weather. To Mama, bad weather was a cloud in the sky, making her jittery and nervous. Extremely so. And God forbid if it thundered. This threw Mama into an emotional state of raging hyperbolic panic.

Under a melodramatic threat worse than eternal damnation, Mama, upon her slightest whim of foul weather, would hustle the entire family out to the storm pit, forcing us to remain there until the weather cleared to her satisfaction. And sometimes this meant clearing to perfect conditions.

We kids, realizing that this was crazy, strenuously objected to being so holed up when there was no reason for it. But our objections were no match for Mama's indomitable insistence, serving only to invite her wrath down upon us harder. We hit the pit whether we liked it or not.

And Daddy, when home, knowing the futility of objection, went along with Mama's insistence like some drunken diplomat, squeezing into the storm pit with the rest of us moles, dealing with its craziness in a more subtle manner. Nor did he complain when he was instructed by Mama to build the pit, no small labor.

First, Daddy dug a hole into a clay bank, six feet deep and eight feet wide. Then, cutting down trees for wood, he laid the logs on top of the pit to form the roof, then spread tin over the logs, plastered around the tin's edges with dirt, and packed it down so the wind wouldn't pick up the roof and blow it away, making the pit airtight. But it wasn't watertight.

Day or night, no matter what the family was doing, regardless of where we were at, or what time it was, all of us had to make a mad dash out to the pit upon Mama's slightest perception of bad weather.

The nights were the worst. During the day, while working in the fields, or doing other chores in the off-season, Mama, able to see the sky more clearly, would order us to the storm pit only if she saw solid evidence of bad weather approaching. But during the night the weather was much more difficult for her to ascertain. She was uncertain of how dark the clouds were; and more uncertain of the state of the weather—how rapidly it could be deteriorating. So she took no chances. At the slightest sensing of gloomy clouds, or the sensing of approaching foul weather, to any degree, real or imagined—and often her bad weather was imagined, we hit the pits, literally and figuratively.

And since many of these trips were decided by the whims of Mama's imagination, it was impossible to predict when she'd haul us off to the pit. But it seemed always to be when we didn't expect it. Mostly when we were asleep. Then—bang! Mama's feet slammed to the floor, her voice a drill sergeant's piercing bark, but unhinged, fearful; ruled with stark panic:

"All right, ya'll git up from thar!!"

Her crazed command charred through us like bolts of lightning, each succeeding word a larger dose of volts.

"Whassawharra?!" We'd object, staggering out of bed in sleep-rusty mumblings. But Mama paid us no heed. Quickly, frantically, she'd herd us—groggy, disoriented, confused, and still mostly asleep—and corral us outside and into the pit.

Why is this happening to me?

Being forced into the pit with Mama was nothing but traumatic shock, similar to jumping into a bomb shelter during a bombing raid only to find the enemy inside with you, subjecting you to psychological torture.

I hated the pit. Hated being forced out there at any hour of the night, particularly when the weather didn't warrant it. To be holed up in the pit was abject misery—cramped, cold, dark, dreary; always damp or wet; and always a putrid, suffocating musky smell. And there were the spiders crawling all over you. And sometimes snakes. It was impossible to relax or sleep in that horrid place, not with the threat of an unseen serpent crawling up inside your pants.

If Daddy wasn't around when we packed into the storm pit, Mama panicked even more, screaming her lungs out, fearful of his welfare; or that of Red's; or that of anyone in the family who wasn't there, certain they would meet their doom in the calamitous storm fancied in Mama's mind.

"Oh, God Almighty! Have mercy! Spare them!"

God was sparing them—from this torture. Now how about us? Get us out of this pit and away from Mama.

It was disconcerting enough being jarred awake in the middle of the night, but to go sit for hours, sometimes days, in an uncomfortable, cold, wet, dark nauseating hole just because of a routine cloud burst or less, listening to Mama's ranting and raving maundering soliloquy ventilating her fears—well, that was not exactly the best exposure for a five-year old from which to spawn any sense of normalcy about the world.

The most traumatizing time of all, though, was when Hubert, the fighting over Daddy's or Red's drinking, and the storm pit all struck in one day. This happened often, more frequently during the off-season when the family didn't have to work in the fields and Daddy was away during the day.

Dragging Marilyn and me along with her, Mama would meet Hubert and we'd be off on a riding jaunt in his car. Then returning home, she'd wait for Daddy, and usually for Red as well. Finally seeing them walking toward the shack, Mama's eyes glared, studying their gait, knowing by their movements whether they had been drinking heavily. If intoxicated, and they usually were, Mama slowly worked herself into a tizzy, growing more agitated by the second.

"I want ya to look comin' yonder," she hissed to anyone in the shack who could hear, her voice piercing, attention-getting. "Looks like they wouldn't do that to me every day. I'd rather be buried and dead over there in Ramer graveyard than keep puttin' up with this!"

Her face drawn, Mama then scooted out to the front yard for a face-off with Daddy and Red, the confrontation beginning.

"I thought ya said yesterday ya weren't goin' to do this no more," she grimaced to Daddy, her voice pained and totally stricken.

Hair rumpled, cheeks stubby, his complexion the color and texture of old leather, Daddy gave her a why-don't-you-let-me-be? Look. "Damn, Anner. I'm not drunk," he shot back, swishing his cigarette across his mouth, voice mellow and pleasant. "I'm all right."

"Yer so blasted drunk ya can't walk straight! Look at yer blasted eyes! Just smell of ya!"

"Aw, damn, Anner, I ain't botherin' nobody." The voice dropped an octave, becoming more authoritative.

This was the warm-up to the fierce verbal battle to erupt, lasting until 10 or 11 o'clock, or until midnight, or into the early morning hours, continuing even after Mama and Daddy retired to bed, keeping everyone in the shack awake.

How desperately I prayed for them to shut up. Let me at least get one hour's sleep. Knowing that a bad cloud or Mama's imagination could herd all of us out to the storm pit at any moment, I needed some sleep, no matter how little, to endure the ordeal. There was no sleep in the pit.

And more than not, while they were fighting, we'd end up in the pit, that dreary, spider-infested hole of damp blackness where Mama and Daddy prolonged their violent arguing within inches of our ears.

But once in the hole, their fighting never lasted long, at least not continuously. Daddy saw to that. He just couldn't sit still for too long in the pit. It was too uncomfortable for his hernia, the discomfort causing his hands to clinch and work tightly against one another. Over Mama's vociferous objections, he'd leave, on the pretense of going to the bathroom, toying with his crotch to comfort his rupture as he departed.

"Joe, don't be gettin' into anymore of that stuff!" Mama tongue-lashed.

"Good, God, Anner, I'm not goin' to do that!" Daddy quipped, knowing full well that he was, but the voice tight, the look grizzled, "Seems like a body could take a piss in peace!"

"If ya didn't drink so much, ya wouldn't piss so much!"

Daddy would be gone for about ten minutes, time enough for a good swig of moonshine deadening his senses to the reality of the pit, then he'd return for a short time, argue some more with Mama, then leave again, maintaining this schedule of come and go until Mama gave the all-clear signal, which sometimes didn't come until the early pink rays of the sun peeped forth at the horizon. Then she knew for certain about the weather.

Hubert. Mama fighting with Daddy and Red over their drinking. The pit. Continuous. I could never adjust to this madness. A great desolation chilled my being, and I felt dead like the empty windows of an old abandoned shack.

I needed relief. Any kind of relief.

One day, Sid Phelps, an acquaintance of Daddy's drove up to Shack 1, bringing with him his son, Kommer Lee, 10 years old. Mama let me ride with them in their car. While doing so, Kommer Lee nudged me. "Pssssst," he whispered secretively. "I wanna show ya somethin' when we git back to yer house. It's really neat!"

My eyes lit up. "Okay. What?"

"A surprise. Somthin' that feels good! Wait til we git thar. I'll show ya."

I was excited. Between Hubert, the fighting and the storm pit, I was ready for something that felt good.

As soon as we returned to our shack, Kommer Lee jumped out of the car, motioning, "Follow me."

Eagerly, I did so, in step with my newfound benefactor as he led me around to the back of the chicken house. He took out his penis and urinated. I did likewise. Then I asked, "What's the surprise?"

"I'll show ya it. Somthin' that feels real good!"

He walked toward me, holding his penis, grinning. Then, to my astonishment, he touched his penis to mine. I stood there motionless, waiting for something magical to happen. It didn't.

"That's it?" I frowned, a clipped, strangled tone.

His crooked grin widened, his penis still touching mine. "Yeah. Don't that feel good?"

"No," I grimaced. As young as I was, I knew this wasn't the proper order of things, male with male. Then he began rubbing his penis against mine and suddenly I became nauseous. With not another word, I tucked my organ into my pants and ran petrified into the house, feeling heinous for being part of such an activity, my face coloring with shame and guilt. Kommer Lee came in behind me, but I felt such self-loathing that I couldn't look at him. I never had anything to do with him again.

That incident, though, was "good times" compared to what was to come—my introduction to real terror.

Shortly following the penis debacle, Mama and Daddy held one of their infrequent parties at the shack, inviting several guests. The party, loud with chatter and music, was at night, thankfully a calm, clear cloudless evening, the moon big like some hanging ornament, the stars twinkling bright so Mama had no difficulty assessing the weather. Otherwise, in the middle of the party, we could have been dragged off to the storm pit.

If guests or overnight company were present when bad clouds approached, or Mama's fearful imagination popped into play, it made no difference. We still went to the pit. Only Mama, straitjacketed by her social facade, was much calmer about it. She simply and politely announced that the family was going out to the storm pit, and then left her guests or overnight company to shift for themselves.

While the party was in full swing, I was asleep in one of the shack's three rooms used as only a bedroom. Mama and Daddy's room. Suddenly: "YAAAAAAAAAiiiiiEEEEEE!!!"

It was the loudest and most bloodcurdling scream I had ever heard, jarring me awake with a startle. The tumultuous commotion. A sunken feeling hit the pit of my stomach. Dazed, shocked, I jumped out of bed and scooted to the door, peeking around it. My eyes bulged at what I saw, a man lying prone on the floor, his face squashed in a pool of blood, the oozing plasma squirting outward from him. Instantly my mind and body were frozen from thought, paralyzed by mind-bending terror. I gagged; having difficulty breathing, and my heart pounded and raced, and seemed to throb inside my throat.

William Stuart, married to my Mama's sister, Aunt Gladys, a man six-four and weighing over two hundred pounds, one who had killed one of my uncles, had smashed this man over the head with a singletree—the swinging bar with which you hook a mule up to a plough—when he made a pass at my Aunt Gladys. The man came close to dying.

From that night's incident terror was to be with me every day. A new alarming trepidation was added to everything else, and all I could see in the days and nights to follow was the frightening image of that man lying in a huge puddle of blood, his head cracked open, causing my fear of William Stuart—already known for being as mean as a deranged rattlesnake—to escalate. It also brought with it another fear. I now visualized Hubert or Mama in that pool of blood if Daddy ever found out about them, this fear leaving a constant, unspent, agonizing plea stuck deep in my throat.

Why is this happening to me?

Then came that bizarre dusk at Shack 1 when the ghostlike figures appeared, as if summoned by my soaring emotional turbulence.

Why is this happening to me?

It had to happen.

CHAPTER 3

"**I** KNOW WHAT I seen! . . . I know what I seen!" Mama kept hollering, curdling piercing screams, the ghost incident igniting her into such an uproarious fit that she wouldn't come out of it until we moved. There was no way she was going to expose herself to the possibility of another terrorizing encounter with the eerie apparitions. Daddy didn't want to move, not because he didn't give the ghost story any credibility but because he didn't want to build another storm pit. But Mama prevailed. We moved. Pronto.

Our new residence, Shack 2, was just over a mile from Shack 1, above John Henry Ingram's house, thus was known as the Ingram place. As always when we moved, the very first order of business was for Daddy to build the hated storm pit, which he grudgingly did, easing the pain with plenty of moonshine.

After moving, Mama ceased mentioning the ghosts to Daddy or Red, but she kept my ears full about them. Her talk of the ghosts shaded into a more encompassing theme, adding a new constant of fear and anxiety to my already existing torment.

As if the frightening images spooking me from the night of the shack party weren't traumatizing enough, Mama began talking to me continually, scaringly, every day, about how William Stuart, my uncle, had almost killed that man in Shack 1. She was in her glory magnifying the smallest aspect of any fearful story into utmost horrors. And this story about William Stuart invariably led into the ghastly detailed tale of how he and the rest of the Stuart clan had killed my Uncle Gus, married to Aunt Chellie at the time, sister to Mama and Aunt Gladys.

Impulsive natures inviting feuding, William and the rest of the Stuart bunch locked horns with Uncle Gus and the resulting argument left long simmering ill feelings calling for eventual vengeance. About two years after the argument, the Stuarts caught Uncle Gus in the woods, off guard, alone, and settled the matter. While the Stuart boys, including William, held Uncle Gus down—struggling, begging for his life, their father shot him in the buttocks with a shotgun.

"That mad died a horrible, painful death!" Mama dramatized. "The whole Stuart clan needed killin' for doin' that!" But instead of the death penalty for his part in the murder, William was sent to prison. After his release he married Aunt Gladys, sister to the woman whose husband he had a hand in killing. Just as weird, he was accepted into the family, though I could never bring myself to call him "uncle".

Mama described Uncle Gus's murder constantly, obsessively dissecting it with electrifying emotion, especially since the murder occurred close to Shack 2. She wouldn't let up about it, describing it so vividly, making it so real, and forcing me to listen in drugged horror. Each time she painstakingly told the story

I not only could visualize it, but I could smell it, touch it, and hear all the agony, my skin crawling in goose flesh.

"Mama, quit! I don't want to hear any more!"

"Shaddap! Don't talk back, ya hear! Ya gonna listen! Ya need to listen!"

I was her captive.

That turned me into the captive of something else. Nightmares! The beginning of terrorizing dreams.

The murder of Uncle Gus, with all the bloody details Mama described, became my first nightmare dream, so terrifying that it awoke me in the middle of the night in a muffled gasp, my body trembling and shinned with cold sweat.

But one killing, one nightmare, wasn't enough for Mama. She began describing another ghastly deed, a local murder taking place a few years before I was born. The victim, known as the "Wavey Man", was from Barbour County, just across Pea River from Pike County. As Mama told the story, over and over, four men brutally butchered the "Wavey Man" with an axe, then sadistically mutilated his body before dumping it into Pea River from a bridge—hearing that, I could never approach a bridge without extreme apprehension and caution.

Mama told the story so clearly, and in such grisly detail, I was actually there, horrified as I watched the mangled body being tossed over the bridge, then splash into the river below, dispersing into grotesque pieces as it hit the water, blood gushing out of each piece upon impact; some of these chunks of corpse then snagging on overhanging tree limbs as the rushing current moved the chunks swiftly downstream.

What I envisioned carried over graphically into my dreams. As with Uncle Gus's murder, I began having horrid nightmares about this murder as well. But the nightmares intensified, becoming more gory, move vivid, more haunting, until I began awakening in the night with sudden indrawn gasps, my mouth dry, my heart pounding, my eyes wide and staring into the darkness, burning like melted steel as drowsy terror stole through my veins, muting the terrorizing scream behind my lip I couldn't release.

Every night now became terror. The terror of nightmare dreams.

Then, in the midst of these nightmares of murder, I had an odd dream; a neutral dream out of context with the rest of my life. I was in a strange lighted hallway, standing before an impressive table, a young man sitting behind it, dressed in some kind of foreign garb. His face was expressionless and undefined except for the eyes, shining like black marbles.

The dream, unlike my other ones, wasn't frightening, therefore I could speak. "Who are you?"

The young man made no answer but seemed to be pointing at something I couldn't see. Then he faded and the dream ended, replaced by the ongoing nightmare of the "Wavey Man" murder. The terror was back, continuing every night.

And Mama continued every day. In addition to her murder horror tales, she kept repeating things like, "I'd ruther be in Diddy Wah Diddy"—a frequent saying of Mama's and her euphemism for some foreign, barren desolate place like hell—"than keep livin' in this mess!" Or, "I'm gonna git me a stick of dynamite and blow myself to Kingdom Come!" Or, "You're gonna kill me Red!" Or her oft repeated saying, "I'd ruther be dead and buried over yonder at Ramer Church graveyard than keep puttin' up with this!"

But "this" and "this mess" kept continuing on for Mama, and her repetition of these sayings referring to her wish for death rather than put up with "it" repeated so frequently, and so intensely, equaled in my young mind to the reality of her death, a reality pounding away at my psyche with such frightful impact that, to me—to the warped frailty of my five-year-old emotions, her death had to be imminent, adding one more nightmare to those I already had.

The agonizing constants of Mama's running around with Hubert, her verbal battles with Daddy and Red over their drinking, and the storm pit, with Mama's inimitable frantic screaming, yelling and crying, all continued—the anger, fear and anxiety caused by these constants backing up in my throat in bitter waves, at times boiling into such rage at Mama that I could not speak. And now, lumped on top of this emotional chaos, was the effect of these nightmares—Uncle Gus, the "Wavey Man", Mama's imminent death—awakening me in the night, terrorizing me then and during the day, the knowing that these nightmares were coming my daytime horror.

At five, I was being terrorized the way a five-year-old shouldn't be. At five I was asking myself alarming questions that a five-year-old shouldn't have to ask: Why was living so cruel? So throbbing with fear? Was there any other reality? Was this the truth of existence—squalor, harshness, hard living, deceit, fearful fighting, storm pits, murders, nightmares, terror, torment, craziness, and bleakness?

It was too much. The question, why is this happening to me? Now became: How am I going to keep on surviving what is happening to me?

Only one answer. Escape. Escape Mama. Escape the house. Escape like Daddy escapes. At least try. At least attempt to find some offsetting comfort, however small, among the meager opportunities of an isolated world.

My only hope.

The first possibility of such escape came when Ruby Lee got plucked, marrying Franklin Riley, a fellow like every other in my isolated world, a sharecropper and moonshiner caught up in the legacy; a hard worker in the field, but a heavy boozer, always drunk on his time off—his daddy and brothers pursuing more moonshining than sharecropping.

Marriage was Ruby Lee's escape, and she and her husband moved into a shack about a quarter of a mile below ours. Great! I could spend time with them; get away from Mama.

One morning, early, I sneaked down to visit them, suffused with a new breath of freedom. When I arrived both were still in bed and I heard faint mumblings—little moans and grunts. Then more clearly, "Ooooohhh . . ." It was Ruby Lee, sighing breathlessly. Was she sick?

I made a noise. Ruby Lee peeked up and saw me, looking not at all sick.

"Ooh . . . uh . . . co . . . Come in, Donald," she stammered, surprised, quickly jerking up in bed, hastily slipping into an old white nightgown patterned in pink flowers. "Uh . . . Old lazy Franklin hasn't got up yet."

But old lazy Franklin was awake. About five-eleven, 180 lbs., wavy jet black hair, upon seeing me his eyes took on a devilish glint. Yanking the covers back off of himself, he exposed his naked body, a hairy mat of glistening muscle. Then, grabbing his huge hardened penis like he was arm wrestling with it, he shook it at me, chuckling:

"Here, Donald, what ya think of this beaut? Ever seen one this big?"

My mouth gaped open speechless, my face all startled eyes. I bolted out of there as if dashing for the storm pit during a real storm, outrunning the devastation of a hurricane, the rich rolling tones of Ruby Lee and Franklin's laughter roaring hilariously behind me.

Some escape. I was so embarrassed, feeling so ashamed, that I though it impossible to ever face them again. And I might not have if I hadn't tasted Mama's fresh homemade lye soap. I didn't know what it was but it looked so creamy and inviting that it had to taste delicious!

"Yeccchh-h!" I screamed the moment the soap hit my mouth, my eyes bulging to the size of oranges. The burning taste clawed through me like one of Mama's blistering whippings, blistering the inner lining of my mouth so badly that I had to run to Ruby Lee's shack for water. There was none in ours.

Shortly after this, Ruby Lee and Franklin moved to Phenix City, Alabama. My brother J.P. lived there with his wife and Franklin obtained a job in the cotton mill where J.P. worked.

J.P. was another escape—sort of. He occasionally visited us and when he did I was joyously happy. He was the only sibling with whom I shared a positive relationship. Tall, six-three, a skinny 175 lbs., he was the spitting image of Daddy and similar in disposition—mild mannered, easygoing, always a smile on his face, a smile for everyone, a warm friendly smile, infectious. And like Mama, J.P. never touched a drop of liquor.

From the time that I can remember, there were two stories of great humor surrounding J.P. Seems like he was forever looking for ways to escape the wrath of Mama. Once he crawled under the house thinking he was safe until she cooled off. Unbeknownst to him, Mama started a fire in the stove, filled a large pot with water and brought it to a boil. She then poured it in the gaping cracks commencing to flush J.P. out. He not only had a few burns, he also received a memorable whipping.

The other time that he tried to avoid a thrashing he decided to climb a tall pine tree to escape her. She merely fetched the axe and started chopping away at the tree. J.P. stated several times that he was coming down but failed to do so until the tall pine gave way. He received several scratches and bruises but still got the personal thrashing promised by Mama.

But J.P. wasn't around that much. I needed an escape that was. An escape, I realized, not involving people. One of my own.

I discovered that by throwing files up into the air in a certain way resulted in them making a loud humming noise as they zoomed around in unpredictable patterns. This seemed to offer a good escape, and I enjoyed hours at a time throwing this one particular file—old, worn-out, almost smooth at the surface. This one day I had the file zooming exceptionally well, much like a boomerang. Now, there were always chickens running around loose in the yard and on this day one of them, Mama's prize Domineker hen, was unfortunately in the path of the file's flight pattern as it sailed through the air and zoomed its way back on its return path to the ground. The file hit the old hen in the back of the head with such force that it lifted her right up off the ground, breaking her neck instantly. She flounced around for the longest time in a crazy, mindless death dance. The dance was over.

When the last sign of life was gone from the old hen, I reluctantly told Mama the bad news. Very bad news for me. Grabbing me by the neck, she yelled, "Whaddaya throwin' those files for, anyway?" Then blistering me with one of her infamous switch whippings—I'd rather take twenty lashes at sea any day—she uncorked on an even harsher high-decibel diatribe on being so careless, ending with, "Now stop throwin' those dern files! They're dangerous!"

So much for that escape.

Mama cleaned and dressed the old hen and made a big pot of tasty chicken and dumplings for supper. At first I declined to eat it, feeling so guilty; and the switch whipping didn't leave me in the greatest of moods—as if such were possible around there.

"Ya gonna eat it!" Mama screamed. "Die bust a gut!"

I wondered if that was worse than dying of nightmares. I ate. I didn't enjoy it.

Still feeling guilty about the old hen, I adopted my own chicken, a pet, as an escape, raising her from a freshly hatched biddy after its mother died. I caught and killed flies for her and grabbed her attention by tapping on the hardwood floor with one finger. No matter where she was at the time, she'd make a beeline to me to fetch her treat. I came to love that chicken.

One day she was across the road scratching in the dirt for food. An old black Studebaker, one I'd seen many times before, came speeding down the dirt road toward us. Just as the car passed in front of the shack, for some reason known only to chickens, my pet chicken attempted to cross the road.

Blam-Squash!

No more pet chicken—crushed under the Studebaker's tires, the old ugly car not even slowing down afterwards. And no more escape. I ran into the woods devastated. My pet chicken, one of the few comforts I had, was gone.

Next, I tried a dog as an escape. Rabies was quite common in our neck of the woods, and one day a rabid coon attacked one of Daddy's hunting dogs. Daddy penned the dog up to see what would develop. Several times a day I scurried to peek at him from outside the pen—I was forbidden to go inside, each time praying that the dog was okay. After several weeks of these "peeking" inspections, the dog looked as normal as ever, boosting my confidence in his continuing health.

Then one day, when my confidence was certainty that the dog was just fine, I opened the door to the pen without peeking in first. A mistake. One glance at the dog and my heart sank. I could see that he was finished—foaming slobber at the mouth, the wild raging look in his eyes. I slammed the pen door shut and ran into the house to tell Daddy what I had seen. The poor dog had to be shot. It hurt—all the way to the bone. I had so prayed that the dog would make it. So hoped.

A chicken and a dog I had taken a loving interest in had both bitten the dust within a span of a few months. I was running out of escapes.

But Mama wasn't running out of torture. In between focusing on William Stuart and the murders of Uncle Gus and the "Wavey Man", Mama talked endlessly of people being sick or dying—relatives, neighbors, people she'd heard about, turning these tales into horror stories. And when not concentrating on this or the murders, she'd dwell on anything negative. Her whole outlook on life was negative, causing her to complain relentlessly about life in general, things in particular, and the motives of mice and men. A major complaint concerned sonic booms from jets. Mama thought the sonic booms were bombs dropping and they would scare her into the pit. Other complaints had to do with military aircraft flying low overhead—unnerving her, and people of means.

"That Green family is just too highfalluntin . . . Thar noses stuck in the air! If truth be known, they got thar money illegally. Financin' moonshine. Big! So ya youngins stay away from them crooks—ya hear! Don't go lettin' me see ya around them."

And Mama would remind me of the time Daddy—in his younger years, before he approached 40 and mellowed into nonviolence—knocked her down when she was pregnant, during a fight over his drinking, killing the unborn baby. Squaring off dolefully at me, she'd exclaim, "That could a been you!!"

I thought: the baby was lucky.

On top of everything else, Mama was a highly superstitious person, having more superstitions than a truck load of cats have lives. If lying on the ground working, resting, whatever, no one could ever step over her. If they did they had to retrace their steps backwards. Certain work could not be done on Sunday. Food couldn't be cooked on Sunday—leftovers from Saturday had to be eaten. Meat couldn't be bought on New Year's Day. If a black cat crossed Mama's path, a certain ritual had to be observed to undo its curse. And no one could be idle. If Daddy took a moment to relax on the porch during one of the rare times he hung around the shack, Mama would say to him, "I wouldn't lay on the porch, Joe. Git up, if ya can, and go to the woods somewhere." And if any of us kids sat down and rested for more than a few minutes at a time, Mama said to us, "Ya better git up and move around a mite, else ya'll come down with the dropsies."

She never explained what the "dropsies" were, but I envisioned them as being frozen in a state of immobility, and that thought, sometimes, kept me from sitting in one spot for too long—except, of course, when we were in the storm pit. There, instead of the dropsies, we got the "pitsies."

By far, I preferred the dropsies, but got more of the pitsies.

On one occasion in Shack 2, the pitsies was really rammed down my throat. After two days of a strong wind, the wind accelerated even more, building up fiercely, blowing sand with such force that when it struck you in the face it clawed at your skin with unbearable biting stings. A sand storm. Mama became all confused as to what was happening. She had never been in a sand storm.

"Lord, I don't know what this is all about, but we're goin' to the storm pit to be safe!"

For a change, Mama was rather calm about it. Only thunder and lightning uncorked her into an insane panic of frantic screaming, yelling and crying.

We walked to the storm pit rather than ran because Mama wasn't scared, just cautious. But we couldn't run if we wanted to, the wind was blowing that furiously against us. Even walking was difficult.

It was the calmest I'd ever seen Mama in the storm pit. She knew the sand storm was no threat to her in terms of her fear, thus regarded it as harmless. But, as usual, she was taking no chances. Because she was so calm, we kids pushed her to get out of the pit.

"Why can't we go to the house?"

"Well, we're jest goin' to sit here to see if it clears up," Mama replied.

After another hour of dawdling, "Why can't we go to the house?"

"You might as well hush. We're goin' to sit here jest a while longer. It's not gonna hurt anything."

An hour later, "Mama, it's not that bad. Why can't we go to the house?"

"We'll see. We'll jest sit here a mite longer. Might as well hush."

We squirmed in that squalid storm pit for three days and three nights. The sand storm lasted that long.

Not much of Mama's energy was diverted from her pessimism to teach us kids what was good or positive. Everything had to end up being analyzed by one of Mama's negative "laws" to determine "safe" behavior.

One day this huge black stray bull, looking as mean as a frustrated rhino, came trotting and bellowing up the dirt road. Red, about half drunk, decided all of a sudden that he was a matador. Rushing into the house he returned with this bright red handkerchief.

Mama, seeing what was taking place, became alarmed and yelled, "God Almighty, Red! Don't mess with that thang! He'll stomp ya into that ground and make a bloody pulp out of ya!"

"God dang, Mama!" Red yelled back—God dang being the closest thing to cursing Mama would tolerate from any of her children. "No he won't. I jest want to have some fun with him."

Leaving Mama begging and pleading, Red galloped to the road, wildly waving the handkerchief, but smart enough to remain inside the old hog wire fence stretched across the front yard. The red handkerchief perked the bull's attention as if it was a harem of overheated cows, and it took only two smashes into the fence with the animal's long menacing horns for the fence to give way. Red did an instant about face, and then scrambled in a mad dash to outrun the bull to the porch. A photo finish to the steps, Red winning, the bull left in front of the porch snorting and hoofing the ground, making one ungodly racket.

During the time Red was racing toward the porch, Mama's facial colors grimaced through varying shades of white. Once Red was safe, Mama glared at him disdainfully, her eyes circled with the white of shock.

"Yer gonna kill me, Red!" She screeched. "Don'tcha have any sense?" Then, her eyes glassy and intense, she blasted Red with every derogatory denouncement she could think of, raising more ruckus than the bull, repeating feverishly:

"I'd ruther be hung up by my heels in the middle of Pea River Swamp than keep puttin' up with ya youngins like this!"

Later I said to Red, "I didn't know you could run that fast."

He gave me an inane grin. "A bull breathin' up yer ass does wonders fer yer speed!"

The bull and the rabid dog incidents, like everything else, were pounced on by Mama to formulate "laws" to preach. In these cases two more "behaviors" to be added to her "don't do" list:

"Don't go in any pastures with bulls." Which meant don't go in any pasture since they all have bulls.

"Don't go around any dogs." But since dogs were a way of life with us, Mama had to modify that law to: "Don't go around any dogs without being at all times on guard and watchful."

Mama wanted us to live in her berserk bubble; one molded by her superstition and fears, and the chaos resulting. But near the end of our stay in Shack 2, approaching nine months, with no escapes, I didn't know how I could keep on surviving in her bubble. One fear kept being piled on another, an endless onslaught, deep and dreadful, bringing counterfeit sleep leaving the blood thumping thickly in my ears.

The chaos never slowed down. The fighting with Daddy and Red over their drinking began increasing; and as it did, Mama insisted upon repeating the tales of the nearby murders more frequently. My asthma became worse and I'd awaken at night to smell my own urine, voided in the extremity of my terror: and I'd stiffen in horror, for a moment thinking it was the pungent sweet sickening smell of decaying flesh come with me out of my nightmares.

"Why ya so lazy ya can't piss outside like regular folk?!" Mama admonished fiercely. "Nobody else pisses in bed. Lord have mercy!"

For me, the Lord had no mercy.

In torment, tired, clasping my jaws together, poking the muscles out in my cheeks, my eyes far away and cloudy, feeling the blood in my temples, I'd sit and agonize over the unyielding dilemma twisting away at me. In my agonizing I'd occasionally stare at the old Liberty National Insurance calendar on the wall, wondering what all of those numbers and letters said and meant.

One day, for some reason, I asked Mama what they meant. For a change, during a rare peaceful period between her emotional outbreaks, Mama did something constructive with me: she taught me the elementary basics of word structure. I grasped it quickly, hungrily, and before long I was reading and counting, sensing the opening of a new world, that world holding me spellbound, enticing me to devote all of my spare energy to learning to read. A beckoning out of desperate unhappiness. The great escape.

But not an escape for now.

The day before we moved from Shack 2, I had that odd dream again: the strange hallway, the impressive table, the expressionless, undefined face of the young man sitting behind it with the black shining eyes.

"Who are you?!"

Again he motioned his finger, saying nothing, pointing to something. This time I could make it out. Vaguely. The outline of a huge, dark portrait of some kind.

Then the dream ended.

CHAPTER 4

HUBERT. FIGHTING WITH Daddy and Red over their drinking. The storm pits. Morbid obsession with William Stuart and the murders of Uncle Gus and the "Wavey Man". Undue, ongoing preoccupation with sick and dying people. Fixed, superstitious negative perceptions of life and living, resulting in negative "laws".

By the time we moved into Shack 3, these were Mama's six juggernaut constants, perpetual with her, all consuming, shack after shack, their impact perpetuating in me veiled constants of my own, unceasing and intensifying, constants I dared not reveal: shame, guilt, anger, rage, fear, torment, terror—and nightmares, the horrible, horrible nightmares.

Shack 3 was located a little further southeast of Josie, below the residence of S.E. Green, a wealthy landowner in the area owning the shack, giving Shack 3 its name, the S.E. Green place. We moved there during the winter of 1950, the off-season from sharecropping, when the family wasn't working in the fields, and as soon as Daddy built the storm pit we settled down to our normal routine of chaos and turmoil which, for me, meant trying to deal with my much-maligned emotions under constant attack. But feeling alone, isolated, bitter, much too depressed, feeling much too awful, frail and ailing with asthma, bed-wetting and physical puny growth, coping with my emotions was almost impossible.

Most dismal and disheartening was that there was no relief. Like a finished animal in some vicious snare, I was trapped. I had no escape. There was the promise of my reading, the great escape, maybe sometime off in the distant future, but that future was of no use to me now.

The only thing that saved me in the present was the vague remembrance of what I sensed as I watched those ghostlike figures floating off into the woods: some day all of my misery would go away. Vanish. Something magical.

Was it true? I had no choice but to accept that it was. But what? How? When? Could I last until then?

I had to. Somehow. The remembrance gave me the will to keep on struggling; to keep on kicking no matter what. Without the remembrance it was bedtime for Bonzo. Permanently.

When we moved into Shack 3, almost before we could resume our habitual sorry state of disorder, the family problems had sunk to a disarray of desperation beyond normal. There was no sharecropping; and Daddy wasn't working at the sawmill; and he hadn't had time to build his moonshine still and get business moving there. Nor, as yet, had we had time to hunt or fish.

In short, we were without income and totally without food. We were starving. And freezing.

One night I overheard Daddy and two other down-and-out sharecroppers planning to steal and butcher a neighbor's fat pig. Something had to be done—but stealing? Daddy?! Hearing their clandestine plot deepened my shame, sinking it to a new low.

As planned, the following night Daddy and the other two conspirators stole the pig and butchered it in Pea River Swamp close by, then buried the pig's entrails and other discarded remains so as to prevent them from being discovered by buzzards.

That night we had food to eat, and food for the next week or so as well. But a couple of days after they slaughtered the pig, Mama spotted a group of buzzards in the morning circling close by and immediately became unglued, panicking herself into a frenzy.

"Lord have mercy, Joe!" She blared at Daddy, face frowning and puffy. "They found those pig guts ya buried down yonder like I knowed they would. Now what in the world are we gonna do?! What, Joe?!!" Her chin was visibly sagging.

Well on his way toward inebriation, Daddy smiled slightly and chewed his cigarette thoughtfully, his face still red from alcoholic slumber. Then, "Good God, Anner, I'll be damned if I know!" He replied, furrowing his brow, scratching his crotch. "But let's be sure what those buzzards are buzzin'."

Daddy, his old, worn, ragged overalls looking as though they we only half on him, moseyed off in the direction of the circling congregation of buzzards to investigate. Mama right behind him, walking as though she were constipated, her mouth a frantic motion of screaming noise and panic with every step she took.

"I'll swanny if I know what we'll do if they send him off! I jest don't know! It looks like they wouldn't've done that to that old hog! What's people gonna think? Lord, this is gonna drive me crazy! It looks like the good Lord would take me out of this!"

She repeated these sentences over and over, as if they were a superstitious ritual. Focusing on part of it, "… send him off!… send him off! …send him off!", my breath caught, my chest tightened, the idea of Daddy being sent off to jail petrifying me. But when he returned from his inspection, the lackadaisical grin on his face conveyed good news before he opened his mouth.

"That jest about beats all I've ever seen," he said, the words rolling out in a pleasant southern country drawl, loosening every line in his rugged leathered face into a wide smile. "Them old buzzards were after some cow that died while havin' a calf."

I sighed in relief, but the relief was only temporary. The news didn't prevent me from later walking around on edge, my nerves tense and singing like wires. Daddy's theft could still be discovered. He could still be hauled off to jail.

Every day thereafter, feeling dubious and uneasy, I ventured outside to see if I could spot buzzards circling anywhere. When I saw one circling my heart panicked, jumping into my throat, my eyes rigidly fixed upon it until the buzzard flew out of sight, my anxiety taking temporary flight with it. But with the next buzzard the anxiety was back.

A stupid buzzard could make my Daddy a jailbird.

This thought haunted me all the while we were in Shack 3. I wanted to leave. So did Mama. But we couldn't move. We were broke.

Daddy was unbothered, his calm unruffled, ready to steal and butcher another pig if necessary. While we worried he simply laughed, getting on with setting up his moonshine still to bring in money. Using 55 gallon drums, he made the still at a creek not far from the shack. His moonshine, called Shorts, was made from bran flakes mixed with sugar and water, then allowed to ferment until "ripe." The moonshine to be sold was then placed in clear five gallon jugs, sometimes one gallon, and hidden in the woods so the revenuers wouldn't find it. The first place they'd hit during a raid would be the shack.

Normally, Daddy saved most of the moonshine he ran off for himself—for him and Red to drink, moonshining only about eight gallons for money. But during bad financial straits, like now, he'd run off much more, as much moonshine as he thought he cold sell while keeping enough for his own stock.

Moonshining was much more lucrative than sharecropping, but Daddy didn't do it for the money. He did it for the fun. His fun led to him being caught several times by the revenuers, who promptly escorted him off to jail, leaving Mama throwing a fit, near cursing. "Lord, I'll never live this down! I'd ruther be buried over there in Ramer graveyard than keep putting up with this!"

Whenever Daddy ended up behind bars for moonshining, the landlord, or one of Daddy's brothers, or whoever was convenient, would bail him out. Then he'd appear before a judge and be fined, with the judge warning him:

"If you're caught one more time moonshining, I'll send you to prison."

"Aw, don't fret yer honor. Ya won't see me no more!"

Daddy kept on moonshining and kept on being caught. But the judge never sent him to prison, just threatened each time to do so.

Everyone in the shack neighborhoods was moonshining. And everyone, including the judge, knew that Daddy was only a small time dealer. It was only those dealing in high volume moonshining, when caught, who were sent to prison. Daddy never made it to this league.

During hard times, the winter months, when there was no sharecropping, Daddy and all of the other sharecroppers couldn't have survived financially without making moonshine. And without this moonshining to survive on, there would have been many more times the killings and thefts and other crimes. The authorities knew this, and because they did they weren't as hard on small time moonshiners. However, if the revenuers ran across your still they'd bust it up, no matter its small size or how small time you were or how much you were starving.

Moonshining was illegal. Starving wasn't.

I turned six years old in Shack 3, and as kind of a birthday celebration Daddy introduced me to hand fishing. Along with Red, and an ample supply of moonshine, he took me to hand fish in Pea River Swamp—the network of woods and sloughs adjacent to the Pea River.

Pea River Swamp was within easy walking distance of Shack 3—and several of the other shacks we were to live in. The area of the swamp we journeyed to was a big timber marshland section with a slough. Pea River flooded in the winter and spring—the rainy seasons, and in the summer the main river receded, leaving isolated patches of still water behind, sloughs, and the fish trapped in the sloughs were easily caught, especially as a slough became smaller. But no matter the time of the year there were always sloughs.

The slough we hand fished in was about 30 feet by 60 feet of still water, each of us sticking our hand blindly under a rooted bank, stump or log and feeling for fish. Once we felt one the trick was to grab the fish and pull it to shore, much like a grizzly would do salmon fishing with its mouth.

I was so excited I couldn't stand still. Noticing this, Daddy instructed, "Careful. Look out for their fins! They can slash ya!"

When I grabbed a scaled fish, such as a bream, its touch to the hand under water was rough. But a catfish was slimy and slick, except for the fins, which were sharp and could cut your hand badly if you didn't work it around them. The fins I made certain I didn't grab hold of.

Once I got the hang of it, hand fishing was easy. And fun! I never knew what I might "feel" next. I jumped on this sport like a bass after a June bug. Finally, something uncontaminated by Mama. Something challenging and delightful. A saving distraction from the chaos and turmoil of home. An escape. A burst of sunlight suddenly pouring through many darkened windows, now open.

For the first time in my life I felt a surge of happiness.

We caught several good-sized catfish and bream. My pile of fish kept getting higher as I'd catch a fish, return it to my pile, then scamper back excited to the slough again to catch another one. On one such trip, bringing a fish back to my pile, I found that a large, poisonous, rusty-colored water moccasin had coiled itself on top of it, one of my large bream in it mouth.

Who invited you?! The moccasin, an unwelcomed intruder, butting in on my rare fun, was trying to rob me of it, reminding me of Mama. Infuriated, I found a stout piece of wood nearby and beat the snake as viciously as my puny body could manage, enough to kill the moccasin. Tossing the dead snake and mangled bream aside, I eagerly returned to my fishing. Nothing was going to spoil my fun. Nothing! It was a gasp of air to a drowning soul.

On the way back to the shack, carrying our fish with us, Daddy, mellowed with moonshine, managed to say to me soberly, "Whatever ya do, don't tell Mama about the snake. She'll raise holy hell!"

I didn't tell Mama. I wasn't about to share a moment of my pleasure with her. I knew better. She'd only say something negative about it. Even if I was so inclined, I wouldn't dare mention the snake. Mama was always cautioning me to watch out for snakes, and before we had left for the swamp she had warned me: "Watch out for snakes! If ya see any, stay away from 'em. And watch for clouds. If ya see any, come right home to the storm pit!"

I loved Pea River Swamp. There I was free. My refuge. My place of peace.

Me escape.

The swamp was Nature's wonderland. Bear, bobcats, leopards, host owls and crane roamed there. Because of the river, the soil was richly fertile, giving root to undergrowth and ferns, and to big, big timber—thick masses of oaks, beech trees, poplars and pine. In the spring and summer months the swamp was lush greenery; in the autumn a wheat-colored like golden expanse, glistening, suggesting the luminosity of a masterwork oil painting; in the winter a panorama of browns, interspersed with the white bark of oak and beech trees, and the flight or robins. In the hot summer months of July and August the swamp took on the stink of dead water, but in late March it ushered forth with the quickening smell of spring freshness.

It was in the spring that the swamp was alive! A deep lively green landscaped with a picturesque array of flowers and colors—the dazzling whiteness of magnolias, the yellows and pinks of honeysuckles, honeysuckle sweet shrubs with their intoxicating fragrance of reddish-brown blooms, a few scattered dogwoods gracing the swamp with their greenish-white blossoms set off by bright-red drupes. And the birds with their chirping sweet melodies—blue birds, mocking birds, whippoorwills, morning doves, and the song of bob white quail calling to one another to organize back into coveys, and the blue jays and crows that were in the swamp the year round.

It was magical. A monument to life giving new life, offering something new to me. Standing in the presence of the swamp, I could savor life rather than curse it. And in my savoring I thought of the ghostlike figures, as though they had something to do with it.

The personality of the swamp changed with the seasons, each season bringing to it a different and distinct character: spring—serene, inviting, pleasant: summer—calm and peaceful: autumn—breezy and restless: winter—still and cold. Whatever the personality of the swamp, it was nirvana compared to the abyss awaiting me at home. And now that I had tasted the pure beauty and freedom of the swamp—and Pea River, I wanted to escape there from that abyss whenever possible. But at six years of age my escapes were limited.

One of these few escapes, an escape within an escape, was the surprising time Daddy took me cane-pole fishing at Pea River, just him and me alone. It was surprising because Daddy seldom ever took me fishing with him and Red, much less take me by myself. And adding to the surprise, Daddy didn't care much for cane-pole fishing, preferring instead hand fishing and seining. But he knew I needed to get away from Mama, though he never put it into words.

"Watch out for snakes!" Mama cautioned me as we left, her eyes flitting nervously. "And for clouds. If ya see any, come right back!" Then turning to Daddy. "Ya hear that, Joe? And don't be drinkin' any of that stuff!" She added in heated warning.

"Damn, Anner, I won't," Daddy replied, tongue in cheek.

At Pea River, while we fished, Daddy, guzzling down his moonshine, got as drunk as a sailor on a one night binge after a year at sea. But this provided me no anxiety. Daddy's presence, being with him alone, seemed to prohibit anxiety. Besides, I was too animated by the river to be anxious; too enthralled with the fishing; too exhilarated dashing about the shore, watching the quiet rippling of small circles on the water where fish would surface, then dart away, back to the deep.

I was too vigorously alive to waste it on anxiety. I was free. Savoring fresh breaths again. Rare moments.

We fished until dark then Daddy said, "We better git home, else I'll never hear the end of it."

My freedom ended. Under the night's bright moonlight, we rolled up our cane poles and headed up an old logging road toward home, walking side by side. As we did I was thinking of the hell in store from Mama because Daddy was so drunk, slowly transforming my earlier vigor and happiness at Pea River into rage and helplessness. The anxiety was back.

Suddenly, out of the corner of my eye, I saw Daddy hurriedly drop his cane pole. Then quickly, with the swift movement of a big cat, he walloped me with his powerful arm across my chest—"AAAUUGGHH!!!", sucking out my air, sprawling me backwards, my eyes crazily orbiting in their sockets.

Daddy's gone crazy!

Then, with furious motion of movements—swift, highly nimble for a man of his size, a fast moving blur in the night—Daddy grabbed a big fallen tree limb and commenced ferociously beating the ground with it, as though a mad phantom in a fit of rabies.

He killed the largest, most menacing, meanest looking rattlesnake I've ever seen, anywhere, even up to this day. The gigantic snake was stretched across my rut of the logging road, and there's no way I could have lived if that monster had bitten me. We were a mile from the shack, where there was no transportation anyway, and twenty miles from the nearest doctor.

It wasn't so much the length of the rattlesnake that was so frightening, though it was well over five foot, as much as it was its diameter—immense, as thick as the lower part of a man's thigh, like a python.

In spite of him being so full of moonshine, Daddy had spotted that snake in the dark and saved my life. I could have become a ghost right there, joining those I had seen floating off into the woods.

Dropping the tree limb, Daddy let out a long shuddering sigh. Then, his eyes crinkled, he said calmly, flat and joyless, "Don't tell yore Mama you nearly stepped on 'im cause she won't let you go no more."

How a man could sound and act so sober, move so quickly, react so alertly, be so coordinated in his actions, yet be so drunk, was mystifying. From that moment on Daddy became an enigma to me. There was much more to him than he let on—to anyone, his inner being belonging to the mystery of the stars.

After the snake, as we walked home that night, Daddy's mood remained sober, obviously concerned for me. Yet, inwardly, I couldn't help but somehow sense that he was laughing; laughing at me for letting life become miserable by taking it so seriously.

"Daddy, do you believe in ghosts?"

"Ya been listenin' to your Mama again?" Then he added strangely. "Don't matter what I believe. If they exist my belief don't change it."

I never mentioned ghosts to him again.

That fishing trip was my last escape from Shack 3. I returned to misery; to anxiety and buzzard duty.

Our neighbors whom Daddy had stolen the pig from had a son in his early teens who was deaf and dumb. When I was around him I felt uneasy, fearful that his parents might ask me about their missing pig, the crime still unsolved. So I kept away from him, studying him from a distance, mostly as he sat under an old oak tree. I couldn't help but wonder what he was thinking. Did he miss his pig? Had the pig been his pet?

Red, not sharing my uneasiness, would approach him and attempt to carry on a conversation. The boy smiled at Red, then perked up with a bland, awkward laugh. He enjoyed Red's visits. Red was one of his few friends. But to me the boy was another buzzard. Another reminder that we should get out of Shack 3 while we were still ahead.

Mama shared this view, and as soon as Daddy made enough money from his moonshining, she saw to it that we moved.

CHAPTER 5

OUR STAY IN Shack 3 lasted only three months. Though I wanted to get away from the place, I left with misgivings; with bittersweet feelings. It was at Shack 3 that I was introduced to the saving escapes of Pea River and Pea River Swamp, and now I was leaving that wonderland. Shack 4, our new residence, was a few miles south of Union Springs, Alabama, six miles from Shack 3, six miles from Josie, and out of walking distance to Pea River and Pea River Swamp—Daddy had no car to drive me to those invaluable sanctuaries.

We moved into Shack 4 as the off-season was approaching its end. Located in the Corinth community—an area top-heavy with big time, bigwig moonshiners, and close to the site of Daddy's next sharecropping job. Shack 4 set atop a hill, the highest elevation in the area, thus became known as the Top of the Hill place. Less than a quarter of a mile away, at the bottom of the hill, lived Grandpa and Grandma Dease, Mama's parents, whom we kids called Popper and Mommer.

After building the storm pit, Daddy's very next move, as well as Red's was to acquire work at Mr. Dunn's sawmill in Josie, where Daddy sometimes worked during the sharecropping off-season. But this time Mama gave him extra incentive. There was to be no more starving leading to stolen butchered pigs, the buzzard watch, and tense moments waiting for Daddy to be apprehended. Mama had had her fill of that.

And I was back to my fill of Mama. All of my escapes—Ruby Lee, file throwing, the pet chicken, the rabies dog, Pea River and Pea River Swamp—kept being taken away from me. But that which I as trying to escape, Mama and her unyielding constants, all remained, all intensifying. Each time I lost an escape I was thrown back into the clutches of uninterrupted despair, but the despair after the loss of my latest escape was especially shattering.

The remembrance.

Daddy and Red rode the six miles daily to the sawmill in Josie with Junior Culpepper and another sawmill worker. Every night, if they were a minute late arriving home from work—and often they were more than a minute late, Mama's face took on a horror look and, working herself into an emotional tizzy, she'd shout:

"Somethin' bad has happened!"

I heard this every evening. Something bad was happening alright—but it was happening to me.

The worst were the continuing nightmares! Then something peculiar began occurring in my dreams. The expressionless, undefined face of the young man from that odd dream began popping into my nightmares—just his head, his black eyes glowing. His appearance made no sense to the dreams. He took no part in them. He was just there. A vague, fleeting face observing me. Observing my terror. Then he was gone, leaving me with the horror of my dream.

One night, a rarity, I was spared from my nightmares. My only dream was that odd dream again. I was back in the strange hallway, standing before the impressive table, the young man—his appearance as indistinct as ever, except for the eyes, and ethereal blackness—sitting behind it. Again he was pointing to the huge dark portrait. This time I could make it out. A portrait of Daddy. I froze, and the dream ended.

The next day, as evening approached, Daddy and Red were unusually late arriving home from the sawmill. "Somethin' bad has happened!" Mama screeched. When more time elapsed, and they still weren't home, Mama's ritualistic tizzy metamorphosed into near panic. Then a strange car drove up to the shack. Red exited from the car and dashed to the porch, blood pouring from his nose, a brown splatter of it across his chest.

Incredibly intense and jumpy, Mama rushed out to meet him. Upon seeing his disheveled condition, the oozing blood, she became delirious. "Lord have mercy, Red!" She screamed. "What in the world is wrong?!"

Red was shaking, grief-stricken, his face wrinkled in tears. "Mama, we've been in a wreck and they think my Daddy is *dead*!"

The news crushed through us. First disbelief, then wave after wave of shock, reducing us all to zero at the bone.

No, not Daddy. Not Daddy. Anyone but Daddy. My mouth was suddenly dry and sour, my eyes hot, my heart trip hammering, my throat frozen—like in the dream.

"Oh, Jesus God no!" Mama pleaded, her face a pasty gray, her breath stopping in a harsh gasp, squirting the panic from her mouth like bitter poison. Her eyeballs began moving disjointed from side to side, then she totally broke down and took off running, deranged, no semblance of rational thought guiding her. She galloped down the hill toward Popper and Mommer's place, her shape quickly becoming a dark blur of silhouette in the night's moonlight. But I could hear her dreadful bellowing, derangement beyond delirious panic, screaming and hollering as though she were frying in hell.

"Joe's dead, ya'all!!! *EEOOWWEERRRR*!!! *Joe's dead*!!!

She kept repeating this, over and over, her screeching a piercing wailing ripping up the evening air, echoing and reverberating, causing the flesh along the back of my neck to suddenly tighten. I was petrified again, certain that Daddy was gone. Dead! The thought diffused my mind, terrifying me even beyond the terror of my nightmares, leaving me horrified and confused, more traumatized than ever. Mama had made us so terrified of death and now that terror was closing in on me full force, ripping me apart.

All I could see was Daddy in hell. During their innumerable fights over his drinking, Mama, during each fight, invariably screamed at Daddy:

"Yore gonna die and *burn in hell* for the way yore treatin' me!"

That sunk in. And that hell Mama graphically detailed for me so that now, below the turbulence of my terror, below the flux of my emotional horror, was a tumbling locked with doom and desecration. All I could envision was Daddy in Mama's hell, standing on his head in stinking human feces up to his hips, shackled in chains, flames leaping all around him, eating at his flesh, scorching the meat on his bones down to black embers, but leaving him alive to agonize, screaming in excruciating pain throughout eternity.

Weeping for Daddy in the pain of this hell, its vision burning away at my insides like hot rivulets, I scampered down the hill after Mama, unable to catch up with her, my breath racing, my body twitching and jiggling beneath my clothes, the tendons of my thighs and calves and ankles burning and trembly, the running sounds of Red, Inez, and Marilyn behind me.

When I finally reached my grandparent's house, Mama was still screaming and hollering; still piercing the night with her deranged wailing, dogs barking, everyone in an uproar. If Popper and Mommer's house had not been at the foot of the hill, Mama would have ran until she dropped dead.

Uncle Nig—Mama's brother, and his wife, Aunt Pearl, were living with Popper and Mommer at the time, and Uncle Nig, who owned a car, readily volunteered to drive Mama to the hospital in Troy, thirty miles away, where Daddy had been taken.

The family packed into Uncle Nig's car, and with tires screeching, Mama screaming, we roared off toward Troy on one of the few paved roads in that part of Alabama. There were no other cars on the road, so Uncle Nig—slightly younger than Mama, very light complected, a boozer, bloodshot eyes poking out on their stems—pushed the accelerator to the floorboard and drove down the middle of the road in a squealing smolder of rubber, the white center line hurling at us and past us in whizzing splashes, keeping time with the horrible lurching beat of my heart causing the flames of hell to lap at Daddy all that much faster.

Then flashing lights and the loud, ubiquitous "pull-over" scream of a siren, an Alabama State Trooper patrol car bearing down behind us.

Mama, her energy spent, her face quieted to that pinched deathly look, let loose with a pathetic cry. "Lord have mercy, Nig. They're gonna pull ya over!"

"We gotta stop!" Nig drawled nervously. "Don't want the tires shot out! Shee-it!"

He brought the car to a stop at the side of the road. But even before the State Trooper approached us, Mama had her window rolled down and her head sticking out.

"Pleeeaaasseee, Mister, let us *goooohhh!*" She yelled frantically to the trooper. "My husband's been in a bad car wreck and he . . . He—he's dead! Or they think he's dead!"

Overtaken by the panic in Mama's eyes, the trooper immediately responded with empathy; "All right, Ma'am. Ya'll folks follow me!"

Once more the road's white center line rushed toward us with whizzing speed, as did the lapping flames.

The trooper escorted us to the hospital in Troy. But to my disbelief, Mama, claiming we weren't dressed well enough to go in—I was dressed in my usual garb of ragged jeans and a ragged shirt. Marilyn in a ragged plain dress that Mama had made out of a flour sack, made Marilyn and me sit in the car and wait while everyone else rushed into the hospital.

For most of the night I sat with Marilyn in the car, waiting for news, visualizing Daddy dead, already burning in Mama's hell, the fear of Daddy's death, leaving me alone with Mama, causing my heart to leap into my mouth like a scalding cob of corn.

Then Red returned to the car, looking mighty disheartened. "He's dead—right?" I blurted.

"No, my Daddy's not dead . . . Not yet." Red breathed glumly, a formidable expression altering his face. "But he's in real bad shape with head injuries!" He shook his head and grimaced, on the verge of tears. "Real bad ones. The doctors don't give 'im a chance to live—not even through the night."

But most important—he was still alive! Immediately my visions of Daddy frying in hell eased off. Don't die! Don't go to hell! I prayed silently, an odd feeling within me.

Red informed me how the car accident happened. It was after work and they were driving home. Junior Culpepper behind the wheel. Daddy in the front seat with him. Red and the other sawmill worker in the back. Junior's car was following behind another auto of sawmill workers heading toward the Corinth community when the fellow sitting next to Red in the back dared Junior to pass the car in front on a tricky, curving dirt road full of ruts. Junior accepted the challenge, gave it an ill-fated try, lost control of the car, ran off the road, plunged down a bank and slammed into a huge oak tree. Daddy was thrown through the windshield, hitting headon against the tree. Junior thrown from the car as well, into another tree. Red and the other fellow, sandwiched in the back seat, escaped with only scratches and cuts.

"They busted into those trees awful!" Said Red. "I don't know how they weren't killed right off!"

Mama wouldn't leave the hospital, nor would Red or Inez, so Marilyn and I ended up staying with Popper and Mommer. That night I didn't fall asleep for the longest time. When I did, the odd dream again. I could now see a mouth on the young man, a smiling mouth beneath those shining, glowing, ethereal black eyes. As before, he was pointing toward the portrait, Daddy. Then the portrait began glowing, becoming redder, hotter, until it just exploded, disintegrating into fire as far as my eyes could see. The hot inferno of hell! And in the fire was Daddy, ablaze, locked in chains, screaming, trying to escape. He couldn't.

The young man began laughing, loud throaty sounds, laughter at Daddy so pathetic and trapped and burning alive; laughter at me looking on so horrified and so helpless.

"Help me, Donald!" Daddy screamed, his flesh burning to a blackness matching the young man's eyes. "Help me get out of here! Please—help me! Help me!"

The young man's laughter became louder, harder.

"I'll help you, Daddy!" I yelled, running toward him. But the wall of fire engulfing him stopped me. It was too hot, too intense.

"Donald, help me! Help me!"

"I'm coming Daddy! I'll help you!"

Infuriated by the laughter, I dived through the wall of fire with new found strength, grabbing hold of Daddy, putting my arms around him, feeling the flesh slip from his bones as I attempted to pull him from the fire raging around us, all the while the young man continued his laughing—piercing gurgles, then deafening howls, reverberating echoes of hell.

Then I awoke from the dream, trembling, agonizing in a hot sweat on my skin, laughter still ringing in my ears. "Daddy, I'll help you! You won't die!"

The next morning Marilyn and I returned to the hospital with Uncle Nig and Aunt Pearl. The doctors had predicted that Daddy would be dead by now. He wasn't. He was still alive; barely hanging on with a smashed jawbone, a severely fractured skull, his face caved in, a dangerous loss of blood. The doctors' new prognosis: Daddy couldn't possibly live through the day.

Mama still wouldn't let Marilyn and me go in and see Daddy. Drawn and tired, I'd look at her with eyes both frightened and accusatory, feeling an acid rage enveloping me, leaving the blood beating loudly in my ears, then sit through hours of waiting in the car, going through the torture of waiting for news but hearing nothing.

I was taken back to Popper and Mommer's house. Bordering around their 60's, respected in the area, Popper and Mommer's dispositions were quite unlike Mama's. They seemed to be normal people, particularly Mommer—bubbly, pleasant, very energetic, wearing spectacles and keeping her gray hair all balled up on the top of her head. But they were of no comfort to me. During the crisis all anyone talked about around Popper and Mommer's place was the terrible condition of Junior Culpepper and Daddy, speaking of them with troubled expressions and cloudy eyes.

Popper—a light complected, practical man, still working as a sharecropper, always wearing a hat—expressed the sentiments of others when he said hollowly, "I don't know how either one of them can still be livin' in that kind of shape."

Hearing statements like that didn't help my mental and emotional states, my body already a fragmented mishmash of nervous impulses. That evening, in anticipation of a long night's stretch of nightmares, before drifting off into sleep, I said aloud, my mouth a tight bloodless slit:

"I'll help you Daddy! You won't die! You'll see. They'll all see!"

Oddly, that night I slept without nightmares. I didn't dream at all.

The following day Daddy was still alive, leaving the doctors befuddled and baffled, egg on their faces, now encouraged to alter their diagnosis, deciding that maybe he had a chance for pulling through. Daddy was delivered to surgery to relieve pressure on his brain. After surgery his condition improved. Critical but better. A few days later he regained consciousness for the first time since before the accident.

His first words: "Where's Donald?"

Now Mama had to let me see Daddy. She bought me a new pair of pants and a new shirt. Marilyn a new flower print dress, and took us to see him.

The sight of Daddy upon first walking into his hospital room was frightening. His head was all wrapped in bandages except for openings at the mouth and eyes, the wrappings as huge as a washtub. He looked like an Egyptian mummy.

"Hi, Dunk!" Daddy yelled to me, a sudden spurt of vigor. It was the first time he had ever called me by that name. "How ya doin'?"

I let out a long exhale, then felt the pulse beating thickly in my throat, tingling with excited thanks I couldn't express. Speechless, I rushed over to Daddy. Immediately he wrapped me in a hug, gazing at me warily from shadowed sockets, a wistful expression about him, pouring out from his tenacious constitution. He had beaten off death as he beat off rattlesnakes. I touched his flesh to see if it was solid—and still sticking to his bones. It was, as whole and as inseverable as rugged granite. No more hell. He was going to live!

I felt the elation of Pea River Swamp, the only feeling I could equate with happiness. The only feeling I knew as happiness.

"Ya been lookin' after things for me, Donald?" Daddy said, mustering a grin.

I nodded eagerly. "Yes."

"I know."

That night the young man returned to my dreams, his black eyes a peculiar glow, as though I owed him something.

"What do you want?" I asked, remembering his horrible laughter.

Now I could see his mouth. Smiling. He pointed at the portrait. But it wasn't a portrait of Daddy. It was a portrait of me!

CHAPTER 6

DADDY REMAINED IN the hospital for several more weeks, until his bandages were removed, disclosing a badly scarred face, very ugly scars, looking awful, reminding me of his face from hell that I'd seen in my nightmare dream with the vague young man and all the mocking laughter. Then Daddy came home where, much to his chagrin, he was laid up in bed for six weeks, his appearance pallid and grizzled, the prominent facial scars dramatizing his hollow sickly look.

But my thoughts were on the latest dream with the young man, where I saw the portrait of myself. That dream didn't make sense. It didn't fit my feelings. Daddy was alive, and at the moment I as happy. In fact, the six weeks of his convalescence in bed was the most peaceful time of my childhood. There was a welcomed lull in the fighting between Mama and Daddy—mainly because Daddy wasn't able to get out of bed, roam about outside the shack, and plaster himself with moonshine. And preoccupied with Daddy's care, Mama's trips to see Hubert and our trips to the storm pit were reduced drastically, as was my bed-wetting, asthma and nightmares.

I couldn't have felt better. But in the dream the portrait revealed me as wretched and pathetic. A being without substance.

I shrugged it off. Just a dream. Another nightmare.

Still, it wasn't all peace and quiet at home. There was no lull in the fighting between Mama and Red. My brother continued his heavy drinking. He also continued to work at the sawmill in Josie and was the sole support of the family while Daddy was laid up.

Red spent most of his free time at Thad Green's country store, within walking distance of Shack 4. Thad had a slot machine there and Red thoroughly delighted in feeding it quarters. One night he became so drunk that he fed his entire sawmill paycheck to the guzzling machine. When Mama found out she rocked the shack on its foundation.

"Why would anyone slave like a nigger all week long and throw thar money away like that?" Mama slashed at Red.

"God dang, Mama, it was my money!" Red slurred hoarsely, his voice pettish, petulant. He didn't care what he said when he was drunk.

"It's *not* yore money! It's all we have to *live* on! Now we have nothing'. Lord have mercy, Red! Why do ya do this? I work my fingers to the bones and jest look what I git for it!" Her ire activating her melodramatic instinct. Mama then blurted out her oft repeated prophecy. "Yore gonna *kill me*, Red!" Her voice was violent and at the same time despairing. "The day's gonna come when ya'll look back on this and regret it! We have enough grief with yore Daddy without ya addin' this! I'd git down on my hands and knees and pray to the good Lord if I knowed it would do a lick of good!"

From there Mama went into her own impersonation of hell, verbally frying Red to a crisp.

Daddy was held a silent captive to these continuous fights between Mama and Red, but they never bothered him. What did was the frustration of his immobile life laid up in bed, though a mellowed frustration, enabling him to carry his suffering with nobility and enjoy the many visits from his drinking buddies, a cigarette always jittering between his fingers.

After six weeks in bed Daddy's sallow expression took on color and his eyes became lighter and he finally got up and began walking around, wandering outside, playing with the fork of his crotch and stealthily finding opportunities to begin drinking moonshine again, the smoke of his cigarette raftering away lazily beneath the open sky smiling down upon him once more. It would require ten more weeks of recovery before he was back to his full routine of activity, but just being out of bed made him more sanguine.

Because of his accident and convalescence, Daddy missed out on spring planting, crucial to his sharecropping, thus missed the season sharecropping for himself. When fully recovered the best he could do for the remainder of the year was to hire his services, as well as Mama and Inez's, out to other sharecroppers while Red finished out the season working at the sawmill.

When Daddy was up and about, adequately mobile, Daddy, Mama, Marilyn and I were invited by a friend of Daddy's—a man called Rube, whom Daddy had known for years—to go to the Troy drive-in theatre with him and his wife. When they picked us up in Rube's car for the trip to Troy, Daddy was inebriated. He had been drinking moonshine most of that day, with the usual fussing from Mama over it, the two gradually working back into their inevitable fighting routine. And with the reestablishing of this routine, Mama was gradually working back into her trips with Hubert, her trips to the storm pit, and her obsession with nearby murders, all of which was gradually reactivating my bed-wetting, asthma and nightmares.

As soon as we seated ourselves in Rube's car, Mama ceased her fussing at Daddy, never fighting with him over his drinking in the presence of non-family members, instead holding it off until such people weren't around. But there was another problem. Ever since Daddy was up and about he was peculiar about how he rode in automobiles. Whenever riding in the front seat of a car he sat about half sideways facing the side window, with his hand gripping the door handle, ready to leap out of the car if he saw another accident coming. To avoid this nervousness, to put Daddy at ease, make him feel more comfortable, it was arranged that he sit in the back seat with Rube's wife, Marilyn and me while Mama sat in the front seat with Rube.

The most distinguishing feature about Rube was that he had only one arm. Otherwise, he was on the homely side, skinny face, plain looking and thinning hair. What he lacked in looks, though, his wife—attractive face, beautiful black hair, big bosom, curvaceous figure—more than made up for.

We arrived at the drive-in movie and began watching the motion picture, some slow developing western where the hero never kisses the girl. Daddy and Rube's wife were sitting next to one another in the back seat and it didn't take long for Daddy to begin looking at her with mock-machismo. Then, grinning roguishly, be began fondling her, and soon the two were embraced in passionate cuddling and caressing, kissing one another like two adolescents on their honeymoon.

And there I was sitting right next to this amorous clenching, red-faced with embarrassment and wanting to crawl under the seat. Not only was I flustered over Daddy's Don Juan antics, but I was apprehensive and taut, expecting Rube to jump all over Daddy at any moment. But whether he was so engrossed in the movie, or what, Rube didn't say a word.

The back seat oohing and cooing kindled hotter and the next thing I knew Daddy had reached in his overalls and whipped out his penis, erect and as huge as a rail spike crawling with veins. Then in brow-arched expression he waved his organ at Rube's wife, gurgling wantonly:

"Look at this, baby! Wouldn't ya like to have some of it?!"

I was stunned enough to shit acorns. But Rube's wife wasn't. Wide-eyed with an expression on her face saying, "Ooooohhhhh, that's a nice, long, big devil, isn't it?!" She giggled and squirmed, sneaking in a quick glance at Rube up front to see if he was watching.

He wasn't, but Mama was, finding much more action in the back seat than in the movie. And Daddy wasn't quiet about what he was doing; nor did he seem to care about any of us being in the car with him, as if since his close call with death he had resolved to live every moment, every opportunity, to it fullest, no matter what.

But the fullest for this opportunity had just expired, with the what coming next.

As with his drinking, in the presence of non-family people, Mama always held her cool regarding whatever Daddy did. But on this occasion her cool was a little slow in coming.

"*EEEEKKK!*" Mama squealed upon seeing Daddy's penis in his hand and pointed at Rube's wife. Her squeal of unveiled disgust grabbed everyone's attention, preventing Rube's wife from saying a word. But then, struggling to compose herself, Mama uncomfortably attempted to sound as cool and calm as a preacher wishing someone a good top of the morning, her tone though betraying her deep-throated, drill sergeant toughness as she put a cold, still, unfathomable gaze upon Daddy, sputtering thickly:

"Joe, please don't do that! Please don't do that, Joe!"

It ended up sounding as if she were reprimanding him for picking his nose rather than for waving his phallus around at another woman, ready to gird the old loins and hop to it.

Her words didn't set well with Daddy. Becoming less jaunty, agitated at

Mama for interrupting his romancing, Daddy, his neck bulging, his face darker, growled in hectoring pitch, "Damn any sonofabitch that don't know how to have a good time!"

With that laconic pronouncement, and with grunts of strained effort, Daddy opened the car's rear door and staggered off into the darkness, his penis still wagging in front of him. We waited a couple of hours for him to return but he never did.

During those two hours I didn't once look at the screen. I was too ashamed of what Daddy had done, at the same time so worried that something bad would happen to him. Mama, never the diplomat, didn't help my vexation by blurting:

"Somebody will wind up knockin' him in the head before the night's over!"

So I worried myself sick about exactly that happening until early afternoon of the next day, when we were informed that the Troy police had picked Daddy up the night before and tossed him in the slammer to sober up.

Mama went on the warpath over Daddy's behavior that night, triggering back chaos and despair in full swing. I needed escapes again. I had none. I went searching. Since Mama forbade me from throwing files, I began throwing rocks, throwing them and hitting them with sticks, becoming so proficient at the throwing that I could usually hit a sparrow sitting on a power line.

But the rock throwing would be little match in countering the turmoil Mama again would create.

In the idiotic nature of their relationship, Mama and Daddy declared a truce to their fighting every Saturday night; long enough to slip away together to a rowdy honky-tonk place within easy walking distance of the shack. Owned by Bud Youngblood—a short potbellied man, and one who had a reputation of his own. Bud and his wife Mable were well known for their fussing and fighting. On one occasion, their fight escalated to the point where Bud packed his clothes and stormed out of the house. He proceeded to the well and tossed his clothes in first. He then jumped into the well himself. Mable summoned some of the neighbors who rescued him.

Bud was also well known for his ass-kissing episode. He asked Otis Arrington to loan him five dollars. Otis was at N.C. Green's store in Josie at the time. Otis told Bud that he would give him five dollars if he would kiss his ass. Bud told him to drop his drawers and bend over. Bud then proceeded to kiss Otis's ass and collected the five dollars.

Bud's honky-tonk was one large room with a small wooden bar, a few tables and chairs, a dance floor and a big silver and gold Rockola jukebox that never remained silent.

Mama and Daddy went there to dance and socialize, or as Daddy put it: "To raise a little hell!"

Mama didn't drink but she needed the dancing and mingling with the men, the reason for her truce. And taking advantage of her silence when he drank around her in the presence of other people, Daddy didn't hesitate to quickly become sloppy drunk. Then after they returned home they'd argue all week until the next Saturday night over who did what to whom at the honky-tonk—Mama's complaint perpetually centering on Daddy's excessive drinking there; Daddy complaining about Mama becoming too friendly with the other men, though this really didn't bother him but was simply used as retaliation against Mama for making such an issue of his drinking.

Remembering too vividly the near killing at Shack 1 involving my infamous uncle, William Stuart—that remembrance still terrorizing, I remained on pins and needles the whole time Mama and Daddy were at the honky-tonk place. Many rough people hung out there and it was commonplace for somebody to be stabbed or hit over the head with a lead pipe. And among the rough people hanging out there were the notorious "three musketeers", William Stuart, Leon Golden and Ralph Riley—brother to Ruby Lee's husband, Franklin Riley. They were the main fighters, and any one of the three, at the drop of the hat, would just as soon kill you as look at you.

The three of them never failed to show up at Bud Youngblood's honky-tonk place on Saturday night, and when not fighting among themselves they fought with anyone else dumb enough to dare cross them. Because of their undue attention to Mama, which she invited, I was terrified that Daddy would become involved in a row with them and, as with that man in Shack 1, I visualized him ending up on the floor, his head busted open and his disfigured face in a hot pool of blood, his soul burning in a hotter hell. Mama's hell.

So each time Mama and Daddy visited that honky-tonk place I sat on the porch, or laid in bed, crying, fearful of the disaster waiting to strike. But it never did, primarily because Daddy never made an issue of Mama flirting and dancing with other men. As I was to learn, it never bothered him. But I didn't know it then. And too, as I was to learn, Daddy, with his instinct for character, an observant eye, always the diplomat in tough situation, sober or drunk, was one of the few persons able to get along with William, Ralph, and Leon.

This began to dawn on me one night when the three came to the shack for a social visit. William Stuart, a slumbering type man with blond hair, big and bulky, over 200 lbs., six-four, was the meanest of the three. He had the huge round face of a gentle giant but wasn't gentle at all when he became drunk. Then he was prone to violent outbursts at the slightest provocation when in the wrong company. Ralph Riley, rather stocky at 200 lbs., had a fat face, an elephantine ego, and the cocky, arrogant disposition of a 25-year-old youth thinking he ruled the roost. Leon Golden, the smallest of the three at five-nine, 195 lbs.—And the best-looking, was a big moonshiner and dangerous speed demon on the roads, and was just plain mean, wild and volatile.

On their social visit, the three of them, along with Daddy and some other men, were outside in the yard and I overhead them talking about sex, the subject perking them up with amusement, then laughter, as they passed a moonshine bottle around amongst themselves. Daddy was laughing the most and the loudest. The more he drank the more became a garrulous impresario. I didn't understand sex, but their discussion of it sure perked my curiosity.

From what I heard, Daddy, William Stuart, and Ralph Riley had taken this woman, Jewel Singleton—Hubert Singleton's cousin by marriage, and also a sister of my Aunt Pearl Dease, to a nearby neighbor's house for "sex" purposes.

"Geee-zus, her thing smelled so bad I couldn't touch it!" Daddy chortled. "It smelled jessst awful! Enough to gag a maggot! . . ."

I knew he was talking about the human body but I couldn't imagine what part could smell so badly.

". . . And ol' William here said," Daddy continued, now laughing to tears, enjoying the story immensely. "Oh, hell! Git out of my way and I'll show ya what to do with it." When William jumped on her and into that awful thing, me and Ralph had to leave 'cause the smell got so bad. I mean baaaaaad! . . . Ugghhh!!"

That wasn't the only story I heard about Jewel Singleton. Later I heard another one from Mama, but this story more morbid. And more disturbing, introducing me to another nightmare in my sleep.

Jewel had been married to Colin Culpepper, a man much older than her, and they had lived about a half mile from Shack 4. And, in spite of Jewel smelling so badly, she was having a heavy affair with Bradley Singleton a man much younger than her. According to Mama, the two of them couldn't wait for her husband, who had cancer, to die.

"So they killed 'im!" Mama dramatized. "Now he's dead and those two heathens are married! Lord have mercy! The way they killed 'im! Those two…"

Mama reached the zenith of horror magnification in telling me the story of how Colin was bizarrely murdered, the abhorrence of her words slicing through me, remaining with me, embedded in my brain for years, terrifying me.

Colin and Jewel had lived next to Thad Green's lake, which had a small drain pond just below the dam. According to Mama the pond played a terrible and key role in Colin's death, and I began waking from my sleep at night terrified by a recurring nightmare in which Colin popped to the surface of weird-looking, acid hot water dissolving the flesh off of his bones while he screamed futilely for help.

These nightmares were so graphic, so intensely traumatic, seeming so real, that they were much more frightening than the nightmares of the other murders Mama kept harping on, causing me to awaken with severe asthma attacks and discover that during my nightmare dream my urine had broke in greater quantity than usual, pouring effortlessly from me.

About the time the Colin nightmares began occurring, Mama decided I was becoming old enough to "notice things", so she stopped hauling Marilyn and me around with her in Hubert's car, from then on seeing Hubert alone, without us. She usually took off with him when Daddy was away possum hunting or moonshining. If it was during the week, Mama snuck off from the field where she was working for another sharecropper and disappeared for several hours with Hubert. Or if on the weekend she'd vanish for several hours and nobody knew where she had gone. But I knew who she was with. Hubert always seemed to know when Daddy was away—and that's when he'd show up near the shack in his car. Each time Mama left with him, I'd go off looking for her, crying, knowing something wasn't right. Many times when she'd disappear Marilyn and I were left at the shack alone to take care of ourselves.

My nightmares begin hitting me full force—Uncle Gus's murder; the "Wavey Man" murder; Colin's murder, sometimes all three nightmares coming in one night, leaving me with no sleep. My bed-wetting intensified. So did my asthma attacks, now constant, becoming so bad that I became bedridden with them. But this didn't prevent Mama from disappearing. She'd leave me alone for hours sick in bed; leave me crying, tense, confused, beset with sullen self pity and resentment, showered with impetuous rage and inarticulate misery.

Life became a blackness. I felt worthless. Abandoned. And I never felt so alone.

Red and Inez knew what was going on between Mama and Hubert. But it didn't bother them as it did me. They seemed to accept it. I was the oddball. Different. And none of us talked about Mama and Hubert with anyone, least of all me. I didn't talk about anything with anybody, I didn't dare!

Whenever Mama came home after a spree with Hubert, my skin would boil and I'd glare at her furiously. But quickly my fear collapsed the fury, imprisoning it inside of me, and my gaze at everything around me would turn vacant and unseeing.

The only thing I could see was that portrait of myself in the dream with the vague young man. I now felt like the portrait. A being without substance.

CHAPTER 7

IN 1951, AS the new sharecropping season approached, we moved out of Shack 4 and into Shack 5, the two shacks within easy walking distance of one another. Shack 5, owned by the man Daddy was to sharecrop with that season, was located not far from the foot of the hill on which Shack 4 was perched, and across the ditch from Popper and Mommer's house, thus was called the Across The Ditch place.

Though ugly scars were still evidenced on his face, Daddy was recovered from his auto accident, now with enough energy and vigor to begin his crop planting. And reinvigorated, he also was able, as never before, to go toe-to-toe with Mama in their verbal fighting, triggering back into full play her outspoken references to the cruel hell Daddy was doomed for. And once she started, she never stopped, screaming at him:

"Yore gonna die and *burn in hell* for the way yore treatin' me!!"

Hell again. The old terror resurfacing.

I had no shortage of nightmares. An evening didn't pass without one. And most horrifying was the nightmare of Colin Culpepper's murder. One night I was fully into its grip. His corpse—disfigured, mangled, horrible-looking—had popped to the surface of that awful, bubbling, hot acid water, screaming for help, his flesh dissolving from his bones, when suddenly the face on the corpse was no longer that of Colin but that of the vague young man of my odd dream. And instead of screaming the young man was laughing. Laughing at me. That loud, horrid, gurgling laugh.

Just as suddenly the face and laughter disappeared, immediately throwing me into another nightmare; Daddy burning in hell, ablaze in flames, his mouth twisted all over his face in blood curdling screams, his body chained neck high in feces, feces all over his charred, dissolving flesh, unable to wipe them off, unable to escape their burning stench.

"Help me, Donald! Help me!" Daddy agonized.

But I couldn't move.

"Help me! . . . Help me! . . . Help me! . . ."

I instantly woke up. In a shudder. A hot sweat. Petrified. An agonizing plea unable to escape my throat. Then a stinking smell. A messy, queasy feeling substance under me. I had defecated in bed. The smear of feces beneath me, all over the sheets and quilt. Then came the self loathing, nearly unbearable. I literally wanted to die. Take Daddy's place in hell.

When Mama discovered what had happened, my shame and embarrassment knew no description as she annihilated me with scorn. "Ya'd think pissin' in bed was bad enough," she screeched, grinding her teeth, her eyes a blast of exasperated, fed up revulsion, "but now yer *shittin'* in it!! Why in tarnation don't ya *git up* and go?! Lord have mercy!"

"Mama, I… I don't remember doing it." I trembled, my voice a tomblike tone, my apology in my tears, drowning me in shame. "I did it while I was asleep."

I never told her, or anyone, about my nightmares.

"How can anybody lay there and do it and not *know* it?!" Mama's eyes rolled ceiling wards in disgust. Then glaring back at me, "I think yer jest *plain out lazy*!!"

The sting of her reproach burned through me like hot rivets, battering me to awkward silence; a doomed, empty feeling of unconscionable misgivings. I slithered off somewhere like some feral creature, looking glassily about, crying, plagued with the heat of smoldering doubts and an anguish no name could describe.

My nightmares of Daddy in hell, screaming for my help, me unable to help, continued. And so did me defecating in bed. And so did Mama's wrath and scorn. I was becoming a joke. A bad joke. An outhouse joke. Mama never let up.

One morning, when Daddy was gone, Mama left Inez with Marilyn and me while she scooted off with Hubert. We were about to eat and I wanted a big plate for my food. But Inez snapped, "Ain't no sense messin' up a big plate." Then holding out small coffee cup saucer to me, she ordered: "Eat off this!"

I wasn't about to eat my biscuit with syrup, along with my streak-of-lean, off that tiny dish. "I don't want to eat out of that little saucer." I objected steadfastly. "I'm going to get me a big plate."

"No yer *not*! So *hush*!"

"I *want* a big plate!" I persisted, throwing a little tantrum.

"I told ya there's no need for ya messin' up a big plate that somebody's gonna have to wash!" She admonished snootily. "It's enough yer messin' up yer bed and the whole place with *shit* every night!"

Her added gratuitous remark infuriated me, the fury stifled in my throat. But as soon as Inez turned her back, I climbed up on the hutch with two doors that swung out—and was almost to the top, where the big plates were, when my weight tipped the hutch over. Every piece of dishware Mama owned—plates, bowls, cups, saucers, glasses—came flying out and crashing to the floor, smashing into a million pieces.

Inez screamed, jumping three feet off the floor. "You little *twit*! I'm *tellin'* Mama when she gits home!"

Right then I knew I was condemned with no reprieve.

And when Mama got home, seeing the shattered mess in the kitchen, her face knotted so startled that I thought it would snarl right up over her skull. She cut a limb off of a tree, Inez gloating right behind her, and gave me the worst thrashing I'd ever received, worse even than the clobbering for killing her Dominecker hen.

"Ya wanna shit yer pants?! I'll give ya somethin' to make ya shit all night!"

But I didn't need Mama, or Inez—or anyone, to continue shaming me for defecating in bed. I did that for myself, feeling monstrous enough. And I had other reminders. Whenever I'd see the quilts on the clothesline Mama had washed, see the hotchpotch of yellow and dark stains on the quilts from my feces, my humiliation suffocated me, and I never felt more worthless.

No amount of shame, though, stopped those nightmares of Daddy in hell.

It was a time of raw humiliation for me, coming in large, nasty lumps, and even Daddy added to it. One evening, my brother J.P. and his wife, Doris, were visiting us from Phenix City, and they brought with them Doris' brother, Junior, and his heavy set wife, Mary Francis. Mama had prepared fresh cream corn, a dish she had a special culinary knack for cooking, and Marilyn, Inez, Red, Daddy and I were sitting at the supper table with our company, ready to eat. When Mama served the dish, in a pot straight from the oven, Mary Francis, always hungry, became all goggle-eyed, drooling voraciously.

"Ummmmmmmmmmmm-ump!" She emoted. "Boy does that *look good!* Aahhh . . . oohhh . . . mmmmm!!!"

She couldn't wait to sink her teeth into that delicious pot of corn. But unfamiliar with how scalding hot baked corn is when it's first taken out of the oven, Mary Francis, blinded by savory expectation, hastily gulped a huge mouthful of the steaming hot delicacy. The moment she did her eyes popped to the size of cantaloupes. Instantly, in crazy movements of survival, she pushed herself back from the table, as if ready for any emergency dash to the outhouse, but too late. Then, looking like a blowfish in its death throes, she commenced with a long, strong, frantic blowing out action of breath from her mouth, jerkily grabbing her glass of tea and gulping it down in desperation, then blowing again, her eyes popping weirdly in their sockets in a life of their own.

The sight was both pathetic and hilarious, and the hilarious element ignited Daddy. Falling back in his chair, he erupted into loud, bellowing, leg-slapping laughter lighting up his scarred features, great gurgling sounds, seizures of laughter, laughing so uncontrollably that he nearly fell out of his chair; and laughing so self contagiously—one laugh triggering the sheer exuberance of yet deeper one—that it brought him to tears, impossible for him to calm himself or to speak for the longest time.

"Good God Almighty, Junior," Mary Francis gulped, frowning, gasping in between words, "is that stuff *ever* hot!"

"You orda knowed it was hot," Junior replied above the roar of Daddy's laughter. "The stuff was steamin'!"

The continued goofy look of Mary Francis—still blowing, eyes bulging, tears streaming her cheeks—made Daddy laugh with harder hilarity. Finally the scalded insides of Mary Francis' mouth cooled down enough to allow her to sit back down, and that quieted Daddy's laughter to snickering, then snatches of snickering. In between snatches, Daddy exclaimed, "Geee-zuss! I ain't never seen nothin' like that in my life!"

Daddy began eating, still snickering in between bites, unable to help himself. Then his control broke down and he started laughing again. And as if he wanted the hilarious show to continue, he picked up the pot of corn and held it out to Mary Francis, laughing as he cajoled, "Here, Mary Francis, this stuff has cooled off by now. *Have* some!" Then his laughter became uncontrollable all over again.

I not only felt sorry for Mary Francis, but also I was dreadfully embarrassed and ashamed over Daddy's laughing fit at her painful experience. Her mouth was burnt so badly that she couldn't eat for several days. And I couldn't face her. My humiliation wouldn't allow it.

But there was more to the incident disturbing me than shame and embarrassment. For a few moments Daddy's irrepressible laughter sounded identical to the horrid mocking laughter of the young man popping into my dreams.

I thought of the ghostlike figures; the sensing with them that things would get better. They didn't. Things became worse. Daddy's drinking increased as did Mama's battles with him over it. There were more middle-of-the night trips to the storm pit; more of Mama's running around with Hubert; more shame, embarrassment and humiliation; more tales of violence and murder; more nightmares, more bed-wetting, more defecating in bed, more asthma attacks. The torture and torment seemed endless, threatening to destroy my young, shaky sanity. And throwing rocks couldn't cut it as an escape; it could in no way begin to offset my emotional chaos. Deepening.

I needed another escape.

After moonshine, dirty jokes and practical jokes, Daddy's greatest enjoyment was cock fighting. He owned some of the best fighting roosters in the Corinth community area, and finding other roosters to fight them was no problem. Not only were Daddy's game roosters superb fighting birds, they also were strikingly beautiful, no two alike, each unique in its own bright array of colors—shades of shiny sparkling blue, mixed with black and streaks of yellow. Exquisite in their long red combs and their long razor sharp spurs, when they strutted about the roosters struck an awesome pose of powerful majesty that at times could be breathless.

Cock fights were the big attraction on Sunday, and took place at someone's shack. Daddy's or whomever else volunteered their yard. The crowds at the fights were always large, noisy and rowdy, with heavy betting, drinking, shouting, cheering and jeering, the air reeking with the lust for blood. A mad, maddening hullabaloo.

Being territorial birds, fighting roosters hate other roosters. There can only be one of them around, so there's no problem getting them to do battle. The two participating birds in the fight, before it begins, appear as immaculate as if they had hopped off a page of National Geographic. That beauty is short lived.

As the cock fight begins, the two roosters kind of circle each other, a hated, locked in look to their eyes, vigilantly feeling one another out like feathered boxers, deadly sharp spurs protruding menacingly out on each foot, ready to strike at the first advantage. Suddenly one of the birds makes a lightning move with its powerful spur at the other's head or exposed body, and the fight is on, a violent bouncing and flowing and flinging of spurs, feathers ruffling, loose feathers flying, blood sputtering, picking up momentum, the roosters blurs of movement, flashes of speed back and forth, hitting and missing, the crowd going wild, egging them on, the maddening frenzy of a hornet's nest cut loose.

The fight lasts from one to ten minutes; lasts until the losing rooster runs away from the battle—fleeing for its life, the other rooster chasing it, or simply lies down, too bloodied and mangled to run. At this point the fight is stopped, the battered roosters gathered up and the bets paid off. The losing rooster frequently ends up dead, and the winning bird is so badly mangled that it would be better off dead.

In my desperation for an escape, any escape, I began helping to nurse Daddy's severely injured roosters back to health, their suffering prolonged for weeks until they recovered. But this escape wasn't an escape, proving too much for me to nurse a rooster back to health only to have it torn to pieces, mangled or killed in another fight.

"Daddy, why do you have these birds fighting?

"Jest to have fun!"

I soon became an effete observer of the cock fights, no longer able to watch, or able to nurse the birds back to another round in the sharecropper's coliseum.

I turned seven years of age in Shack 5, meaning I was old enough to enter school come fall. With my escapes exhausted, Pea River and Pea River Swamp no longer available, school was my much awaited salvation. The great escape. The only escape. The only hope keeping my sanity together.

To prepare for school—some months off, I immersed myself in reading, becoming more diligent in the learning of word structure and the meaning of words, persistent in asking questions, grasping quickly, reading anything I could lay my hands on—maps, calendars, newspapers, magazines, and precious, precious books. Shack 5 not exactly being the public library, I had to beg, steal or borrow these materials from others. Anyone. Anywhere.

One such source was my ten-year-old cousin, Carolyn, daughter of Uncle Nig, who loaned me some of her books. Very tall, much taller than me, and skinny, but with an attractive, freckle scattered face and long darkish hair, Carolyn was an avid reader and her intelligence appealed to me.

One day I became attracted to more than her intelligence. Trailing behind Daddy in his old overalls and tattered appearance and tobacco-stained fingers, I followed him across the ditch to Uncle Nig's house. Since Daddy had no car—he couldn't even drive for that matter—it was common for him to ask other people who did have cars for a lift to the store. It always embarrassed me but, every now and then, I'd tag along with him to enjoy the ride, a small escape of sorts.

Uncle Nig agreed to take Daddy to the store, and Carolyn jumped into the car and rode with us. Carolyn and I in the back seat, Daddy and Uncle Nig up front. Carolyn brought a blanket with her and I wondered why. The weather was hot and sticky.

Suddenly, "Pssssssst!"

I gawked at her, wondering why she was being so secretive.

With the disposition of a diplomat, Carolyn whispered, "Say, have you ever played camera?! Her eyes were very vivid, a sly, almost impish grin tugging at the corners of her mouth.

I looked at her startled, having no idea what she was talking about. "No," I found myself whispering, dumbfounded but inquisitive, instinctively glancing over the seat to see if Daddy of Uncle Nig were looking at me. They weren't, both engrossed in one of Daddy's jokes.

Cozy like, Carolyn curled up under the blanket and motioned for me to join her. I did. Then whispering and conspiratorially, she said, "Let me have your hand, I'll show you."

I offered her my hand, looking at her with strange and growing curiosity. Taking it, she guided it under her dress and, to my astonishment, pulled it upwards, placing my hand between her pantiless thighs. Then sliding my hand over the pearl color of her skin, she placed it up against the soft, delicate silky hairs of her pubic triangle. My hand began trembling. She squeezed it more firmly, guiding it implacably to the spot she wanted touched, the juicy wet rawness of the slit between those hairs, hairs the color of taffy, the touch of her slit warm, inviting, exciting, its tender moistness causing me to tingle all over.

"Click!" She whispered with verve, writhing just a bit, then emitting a long sigh of satisfaction.

I sighed as well, in a grand state of mesmerization, experiencing the most fantastic, sensational feeling imaginable; an inspiring, delicious feeling, as though the sun was birthing into a new bloom and opening the heaven to me with new light.

"We can play camera again," she whispered, her eyes sparkling with secrecy and hidden joy. "But don't ever tell anyone."

I gulped. "O...O...Okay." I whispered back, my heart in my throat, my nostrils scrambling helter-skelter, invigorated by the pungent, sweet-sweaty odor vibrating the air under the blanket, the enthralling smell from between her legs. Suddenly it dawned on me; maybe school wasn't *the* great escape!

"It's to remain our secret."

"Y-E-A-H!"

Then Daddy heard us, "Hey, ya kids, what in tarnation's goin' on under that blanket?!"

"No... Nothing, Daddy," I shrieked in passionate falsetto, hastily coming out from under the blanket.

He saw my misplaced look and a peculiar smile flickered across his lips. "Better not be messin' with that sweet girl."

Carolyn giggled innocently, like Rube's wife.

I was to play camera one more time with Carolyn before school started. Then the time for school arrived and I was ready, chomping at the bit to go.

On my first day of school I dressed up in a brand new pair of overalls Mama had bought for me and scooted across the ditch to where I'd be picked up by the yellow school bus, beaming exuberantly and carrying with me a new notebook and pencil, and my meager lunch in a paper bag with a big grease spot.

I waited for the bus across the road from Uncle Bill and Aunt Martha's house, staring at it, wondering if they were drunk or sober. Having a habit of being inordinately reclusive while inebriated, they spent weeks at a time holed up in their house while the two of them lay drunk. It was embarrassing for everyone since Aunt Martha was Mommer's sister. The family was continually concerned over the welfare of their neglected dogs—several of them—while they were on a binge, but no one dared pay them a visit, the understanding being that when they were in the grip of one of their "spells," no one showed up.

While pondering the fate of their poor dogs my school bus arrived. Eagerly I boarded it, livened with excited expectations and hope. My first glimpse of the bus driver, Mr. Oz Dykes—tall, light complexioned, thin hair, false teeth, in his 60's—didn't do much for my hope, though. But he did catch my attention.

Funny looking in bedraggled khaki pants and khaki shirt, wearing an old beat up gray hat, his false teeth out and laying on the dash, Mr. Dykes was chomping fiercely and noisily on a gigantic wad of chewing gum, an entire pack of Juicy Fruit—the whole bus smelled like Juicy Fruit. Each time he shifted gears and put the bus in motion, he smacked on the chewing gum even more wildly and noisily, as though the frantic motion of his mouth kept the bus running. When he tired of chomping and smacking, he took the huge gob of gum from his mouth and stuck in on the sun visor. There were about ten globs of the stuff stuck there. Then, as he drove, from time to time the bus's engine would act up, sounding as if it were ready to blow, and he'd reach up, pull off a chunk of gum, jam it in his mouth, and noisily began chewing, chomping and smacking again.

Miraculously it seemed, the bus managed to make it to the Corinth School, a big white wooden building with endless windows, located about a mile from Shack 5. Mr. Dykes not withstanding, I exited the bus ecstatic, ready to begin the first grade; ready to satiate my yearning for learning, improve my reading, my counting, my arithmetic. My great escape. Deliverance. A driving obsession with me. A reason to live.

In addition to being ecstatic, there was also an undercurrent of nervousness and apprehension. A lot of uncertainty here—unknowns, new people, new environment, a new society foreign to the one I came from. Nevertheless, I was determined to master it. I had to. I would.

The white schoolhouse, a palace compared to our shack, consisted of two large, airy rooms. In one was located the first, second and third grades; in the other the fourth, fifth and sixth. For each grade there were eight to nine students, mainly a mixture of sharecropping and landowner kids.

In our room the first grade was on the left hand side, the second grade in the middle, and the third grade on the right. The same teacher, Mrs. Ethel Dykes, wife to the "mad gummer" bus driver, taught all three grades. She rotated amongst the three grades, attempting to keep all of the student's busy learning, each of whom was assigned a wooden desk, with a desk top and a compartment underneath for books, our school books the first day already piled neatly on our desks.

The school morning began, as every day, with a devotion. The students in our rooms were huddled over to the other, joining the fourth, fifth and sixth graders in a pledge of allegiance to the flag, followed by reciting the Lord's prayer. That first morning of devotion, without thinking, all excited, in awe of my new surroundings and the opportunity it represented, I absent mindedly took my books and notebook and pencil with me over the other room, the only kid to do so. Subsequently, when the other students gave the pledge of allegiance, I was unable to. My arms were full and I couldn't cross my heart, causing me to turn red-faced with embarrassment as the other kids gawked in my direction, regarding me as some kind of misplaced buffoon. Not exactly the most auspicious of beginnings.

I was still red-faced as we returned to our desks and the first grade began. Right away we opened our books, very easy for me to read. I had learned all the words reading at home. The teacher, Mrs. Dykes—a tall, round, robust lady, old and wrinkled, in her 60's, spectacles, pleasant disposition—beheld me with jaw-opened wonder, amazed at how well I could read, and how well I could do arithmetic.

In contrast, the other first grade students were sweating it out, struggling to read, struggling to do their arithmetic, staring at me flabbergasted that I was having no trouble at all. I could even read better than most of the second grade students, and some of the third graders as well.

"Who is that puny kid?" Some third grader cracked.

"Some drunk sharecropper's brat," came an answer.

My face remained red. Socially I was no great hit, but academically I was. That's all I wanted, and I could feel flashes of deliverance dancing in my bones. But those flashes vanished at the end of the school day, and I agonized at the prospect of what now awaited me. While waiting for the school bus to take me to the shack, a tight pain began pounding within my head, the thought of going home brining on a sharp stab of despair.

That evening I had a triple-header nightmare. The murder of Uncle Gus; the murder of Colin Culpepper; and Daddy buried in feces and roasting in hell. Then the odd dream, the young man sitting behind his impressive table laughing at me. I had no sooner awakened from the dream, confused and frightened, suffocating with asthma, urine and feces underneath me and all over the bed, when I was further stunned by Mama's shouting, forcing the family out to the storm pit.

CHAPTER 8

SCHOOL WAS A Godsend. A promising escape of permanence. It wasn't just that the work and learning of the first grade came easy to me that made it so stimulating and uplifting—my only other comparable experience at being so elated was when I was at Pea River or Pea River Swamp. It was also that I had a constructive impact on the other students, becoming a kind of emblematic presence. During recess, lunch, and while the teacher was with the other grades, I helped to teach the other first graders how to read and do arithmetic. And in doing so my eyes beamed like the sapphirine glaze on a sword, leaving me with the thrill of a warrior winning his first major fray.

One of the students I helped was Donald Singleton, not knowing at the time he was the son of Hubert Singleton, Mama's lover. He was the dumbest kid in the first grade. Hard core dumb. And, uneasily, he reminded me of my brother, Red. Not only did he behave like Red with his indifferent, aloof attitude, but his physical resemblance to Red was uncanny—stocky, red headed, oval freckled face, his hair stacked on top of his head like a woodpecker gone to seed.

Later, I would dwell on this resemblance more disturbingly.

In addition to its uplifting stimulation and allowing me to be helpful, school introduced me to a new entertainment. Baseball. I fell in love with it, even though I had to borrow a glove, bat or ball from someone whenever I played. But this didn't diminish my enthusiasm for the game. I played baseball at every opportunity, during recess and after school while waiting for the bus to take me home, becoming good at it, my rock throwing and hitting rocks with sticks already having honed my skills for the game.

In contrast to home, school made me feel I was someone special. And important. I was involved there, making a contribution, providing some relief from the pain and agony at the shack, alleviating a little of the siege of my torment at home. Yet, sometimes this torment carried over into school, no matter how I fought to leave it at home. Many a day, because of the previous night's forced trip to the storm pit, I would leave for school in the morning with little or no sleep, on some occasions racing straight from the pit to the school bus. Then at the end of the day I'd sadly have to return home, the excitement of school yanked from me, replaced by the torment awaiting me.

And that torment summarized itself at night in my nightmares, my only interruptions unpleasant—either waking up terrorized, soaked in urine and feces; or being awakened and forced out to the storm pit. The young man from my odd dream again began making fleeting appearances in my nightmares, his enigmatical face popping in and out. Then for a time the only nightmare I had was the one of Daddy in hell, and in this dream the young man was there for its duration, watching me, vivaciously laughing at me, and laughing at Daddy, speaking not a word.

My horror in the dream with Daddy suddenly shifted from his agonizing screams and merciless burning in fire to the pile of feces surrounding him; packed up against him, smothering him. Reacting to his cries of help, I ran to where he was chained at a stake and grabbed frantically at the feces entombing him, pulling them away from him with my hands.

"Help me Donald! Help me!!"

"I am Daddy! I am! I'll get this shit off of you!"

But no sooner would I remove feces than they'd be replaced by others, the amount of feces encircling Daddy remaining constant.

One night during this dream the young man's laughter became so infuriating that I turned to him and shouted, "You bastard—get Daddy out of this shit! . . . Get him out! . . . Get him out! . . ."

The young man's reply was his incessant laughter, now becoming hideous and increasing in volume until it was deafening. I picked up a lump of feces and hurled it at him like a baseball, hitting him smack in the ambiguity of his face. He instantly disappeared and I awoke from the dream, soaking in my urine. But there wasn't the queasy, squishy-squashy feeling of feces under me. I hadn't defecated in bed! Nor did I the next night. Or the following night. Or any night after that.

My defecation in bed ceased altogether, and the celebration taking place in me was so magnificent that I felt close to explosion.

Mama wasn't too displeased herself. "Thank the Lord! Ya got over yer laziness!"

In my subsequent dreams of Daddy in hell, he was no longer buried in feces. There were no faces. And there was no laughing. The young man no longer appeared in that dream. For a while he appeared in none of my dreams.

But my other nightmares were back in all their horror.

CHAPTER 9

THOUGH MY DEFECATION in bed ceased, my bed-wetting and asthma attacks didn't. Both would intensify.

In April of 1952, as I approached the end of the first grade, after living nine months in Shack 5, Daddy obtained a sharecropping job with my uncle, John Stuart, and we moved into Shack 6, owned by my uncle. Located three quarters of a mile from Shack 5, Shack 6 was near a dirt road with a wooden bridge over the Conecuh Creek and close to a house owned by Billy Green, thus came to be known as the Above The Billy Green place.

John Stuart was a distant relative of William Stuart and the husband of Mama's sister, Pearl—giving me two Aunt Pearls, Pearl Stuart and Pearl Dease. As was the case with William Stuart, I never called John uncle. I didn't like him. Whereas I wouldn't call William Stuart uncle because he was mean and a killer, I wouldn't call John uncle because he was a downright scoundrel. Corrupt. A crook. A snake-in-the-grass who would cheat anyone. Being the high volume moonshiner in the Corinth community, John Stuart was in and out of jail for moonshining, serving one hitch in prison for it. Still, he continued to moonshine, hiring other people to make the moonshine for him, making an excellent living from selling it, buying a new car each year from the profits. A man with a sharp nose for fishy undertakings, the vote selling kingpin in the Corinth community and Bullock County, John Stuart was always hobnobbing with politicians, acting as their middleman, buying many votes for them at five and ten dollars each, and handsomely rewarded for his efforts. He bought anything he wanted. Cash.

Not liking John Stuart, I didn't like living in his shack—beyond the usual reasons. But an incident occurred in Shack 6, involving Mama, escalating my dislike to hate.

A beautiful woman when younger, attracting men like bears to honey, this didn't change as Mama became older. Hubert was an ongoing thing in her life, just another of her several constants disturbing me. But I suspected she was involved with other men besides Hubert but never witnessed this for myself— until we moved into Shack 6.

One Sunday Daddy was away, as was Red and Inez. Leaving Marilyn and me at home, Mama walked the mile to Bud Youngblood's honky-tonk place, which doubled as a store during the day. While she was away I became engulfed in my usual tense, apprehensive Hubert syndrome of anger, thinking that was who Mama was gallivanting off to meet.

It wasn't. In about an hour I saw her returning to the shack, walking on the dirt road with two men, their sight prompting a new restlessness; something a touch stronger than foreboding. One of the men was Ralph Riley, Franklin's brother, one of the infamous "three musketeers," a rowdy tough who thought nothing of cutting people with his knife, his quick two hundred pound bulk enabling him to do this with the efficiency of a shark. The other was Pete Singleton, a distant relative of Hubert, bulky, over six foot, his tiny nose out of proportion to a huge face.

As Mama walked into the shack with the two men, sneaky looks on their faces, I was there with Marilyn and our five-year-old cousin, Robert—Aunt Chellie's son, who had come over to play. Upon seeing us, Mama immediately squawked:

"Ya youngins git outside and play—or I'll take the switch to y'all!"

Ralph, with a surreptitious glance at me, let out an involuntary grunt of approval, causing my throat to become thick and breathless. I didn't want to go out and play. I knew what was going to happen. But I didn't fancy one of Mama's switch lashings either.

"And don't hang around outside the house," Mama emphasized. "Go way off and play."

Mama scooted us out of the house and we moseyed down the road a ways. But growing more anxious, unable to dam a swelling flood of emotion, I turned around and galloped back toward the shack. Pete Singleton was standing at the front door on the porch, a lookout for Mama and Ralph. He and Ralph were taking turns with her, Ralph first.

But Pete, nervous, looking glassily about, was a lousy lookout. Quicker than he, before he could alert anyone I was past him and into the shack, darting for the back room, there finding Ralph and Mama naked in bed. Mama's thighs hugged around him, legs extended in the air, her pelvis gyrating in furious motion, a salacious racket of grunting, groaning, erotic abandon.

Because I suspected what I'd find, I was more disappointed than shocked. Still, a sick, sinking sensation took hold of me, stiffening my eyes. Then my face blanched, my mouth gaped open, outrage pulsating through me. Hubert was bad enough, but for her to be doing it with Ralph? A dirty, lowdown, scumbag?

I couldn't believe it. But it was true. And as the revelation settled within me a strange disquieting stiffness came over me, an odd type of alarming resistance, and what little respect or trust I had left for Mama was gone. Permanently.

Then Mama saw me. Abruptly she pushed Ralph off of her, her face suddenly ashen, casting desperately about in her mind for something appropriate to say, the idiocy of her eyes caught in the futility of her search. "Donald, I was bathin' myself and Ralph here jest barged right in on me!" She managed to squeak.

My face sank, incredulity raking my face as Ralph cursed at my interruption then slid awkwardly off the bed to his feet, rubbing his stiff, greasy-looking dark hair, slimy sweat on his brow and stomach and legs. Taking his time, he began pulling his trousers on beside the bed, grinning scornfully at me as he did so.

"How's the runt?" He rasped, his voice thick, the tone unkind, mocking.

I tried to speak but couldn't, my throat tight, feeling hoarse, my tongue like iron. Seeing my contemptuous look of hurt Ralph then let out a bitter laugh, loud and throaty. I hated him. Hated Mama. Hated Pete for being their lookout.

"Git out of h'ar and let me git some clothes on!" Mama screeched with an apoplectic jab of the finger, her voice cracking across the room, her eyes jittery and maniacal, her breasts swollen, her hair hanging on strings about her face.

Disoriented, feeling mindless, I hastily turned on my heel and shuffled out to the porch, joining Marilyn and Robert there, so ashamed and confused and hurt and anxious and angry and lost that I didn't know what to do. Ralph came out behind me, shaking his penis at us, his face set in a mask of defiance. Marilyn let out a bewildered whimper. I stared at him stunned.

Ralph enjoyed our reactions, shaking his penis more maliciously, finding his exhibition pleasing. Then he laughed at me, a sarcastic, sadistic, cocky laugh, piercing and shattering—like the laugh of the young man in the odd dream, twisting his fat face into the sleazy epitome of low life arrogance and disrespect, a reminder to all and sundry that he did what he wanted to do.

I wanted to kill that hyena right there on the spot. But weak and chilled all I could do was just wilt, the guilt and shame crucifying me; the fury ravaging through me mercilessly, churning my insides, strangled screams having no release. I didn't dare tell Daddy. I didn't dare tell anyone.

My anger ate me alive until I couldn't stand it. Until I repressed it to the world beyond my consciousness. After this episode between Mama and Ralph, even before my nightmares arrived, or the storm pit, I couldn't sleep at night, tossing and turning, sleeping only in snatches, my bed-wetting intensifying, the asthma attacks becoming worse, my concentration becoming sporadic, even in school.

Nothing more was ever said about the incident with Ralph, by either Mama or myself. But the vibrations it set in motion between us were laced with acid, leaving the hate lying like a black knot in the center of my chest. I became cold and distant with Mama. After Ralph she could never do anything right for me.

Living with Mama after that was bad enough, but in addition I had to keep facing Ralph and Pete. They frequently dropped by the shack to buy moonshine from Daddy, and the sight of them precipitated my fury again, unleashing it, but with nowhere for it to go except to tear away at my insides, paining my guts as if a ravaging pack of rats had been turned loose down there, ripping away with jagged teeth. Each time they dropped by, Pete stared at Mama with a lusty look that said: "You owe me something, lady; and one day I'm going to get it." And Ralph would saturate me with that infuriating cocky, seamy, sleazy grin, arrogant and defiant, the jagged teeth tearing away more fiercely at my insides, consuming me with a murderous glow.

I wanted to kill him!

Later on, someone came close to doing it for me.

I overheard the story from Daddy while he was talking to his drinking buddies. Ralph and William Stuart had gathered one night at John Stuart's house and began drinking, triggering their short fuses. Then, drunk, each thinking they ruled the roost, they became entangled in one of their many fights and William Stuart busted Ralph's head open with a lead pipe. Nearly dead, Ralph was hauled off to a hospital in Troy, where the doctors had their hands full putting his head back together with stitches and saving his life. Very close call.

However mean and ornery William Stuart was, however the number of people he might have murdered, after that I became a secret admirer of his, in my heart thanking him for busting Ralph's head open for me. I felt so elated that I even considered calling him uncle.

The reminders of Ralph Riley were always with me, especially whenever his brother, Franklin, and Ruby Lee, visited us from Phenix City. They as a couple were also reminders of something else. By now Franklin and Ruby Lee had a one-year-old son, Roger Dale, a cute little bugger but in a hopeless situation. On their visits, Franklin was invariably drunk, and terrible fights erupted between he and Ruby Lee over his drinking, these fights going on at the same time Mama and Daddy were battling it out over Daddy's drinking. Double turmoil. And little Roger Dale looked on terrified, crying, like myself helpless to cope with that for which there was no coping.

Franklin and Ruby Lee were Daddy and Mama all over again, the new generation producing new victims to carry on the legacy.

For me, Shack 6 definitely wasn't accumulating fond memories. Not yet. And a shack wouldn't be a shack without its own nightmare to add to the list. One evening, when school had just let out for the summer, a battle raging between Mama and Daddy was abruptly halted by the alarming specter of leaping flames lighting up the night sky, flames glowing and mushrooming in the distance.

"Oh, Lord have mercy!" Mama screamed, startled. "Somebody's burning up! Lord protect them!"

Mama was deathly afraid of fire—particularly house fires—ever since one of her own shacks had burnt to the ground before I was born, the result of J.P., Red, Ruby Lee and Inez's carelessness while Mama and Daddy were away.

"Who is it?! . . . Who is it?!" Mama kept repeating fearfully, her panic intensifying.

She was determined to find out. The family scampered over to John Stuart's house, a short distance away, where Mama persuaded Aunt Pearl to take us to where the fire was raging. We all hopped into John Stuart's new car, Aunt Pearl driving, and headed in the direction of the flames, clearly visible from miles away.

There was this black couple, man and wife, no kids, Mama and Daddy's age, sharecroppers, who were much like Uncle Bill and Aunt Martha, spending several days holed up drunk in seclusion in their shack. And during this time of isolated drunkenness they would have terrible, screaming, knockdown, drag-out fights—the legacy's typical married living. Well, once we arrived at the fire's location we saw that the burning shack belonged to this black couple. A huge crowd had already gathered around outside but the heat was so overwhelming that it was impossible for anyone to get near the blazing remains of the shack. The black husband was outside, delirious, screaming, his wife still trapped in the shack, cremated alive.

The blazing shack, with the black woman burning horridly to death inside, became to me a graphic display of hell's inferno, terrifying me, reactivating the horror of Daddy burning in hell. A hell like this one.

"See what fire can do to ya!" Mama later emphasized to me. "That's how yore Daddy's gonna burn in hell!" But she wouldn't let it go at that. This became her new gore story. "That nigger killed his wife while they were drunk and started that fire to cover it up!" Then she went over the details of how he did it, adding, "Yore Daddy's gonna burn in a hell worse than that! Really burn—forever!"

A new nightmare. I'd dream of that black man butchering his wife and tying her up and setting fire to the shack. Then she was burning in flames and, though already dead, she'd scream in horrible agony, Daddy screaming and agonizing in flames right next to her, awakening me in the night in a shuddering sweat, cold and terrified, the bed wet beneath me. Then came the frightening, suffocating asthma attack.

The nightmares of that woman burning in fire were terrorizing enough, but the dreams of Daddy burning in hell, crying out for my help, were back in full force and unbearable. The real terror came before I went to sleep; came in not knowing what horror form my dreams would take, and not knowing how severe my resulting asthma attacks would be.

With the emotional pulverization of these nightmares, and the intensification of old ones, until I was back in the haven of school I was in desperate search of distracting escapes. Anything. At shack 6, one pounced on me, without me looking for it.

Within easy walking distance of our shack was John Stuart's house—a beautiful six room frame home of natural pine, with a high porch, lovely furnishings and plumbing inside, a luxurious castle compared to the small, cramped, dilapidated monstrosity we lived in.

John Stuart and Aunt Pearl had two daughters, Lola Mae and Helen, my first cousins. Lola Mae, nine years old, totally lacking in coyness, was outspoken, daring and didn't mince words or intentions. High strung, she had a tomboyish look, short brown hair, a pointed nose, beady brown eyes like her dad and, most pronounced, her dad's cocky disposition.

One early summer day, under the siege of my nightmares, I wandered over to the Stuart's house, grimacing over what was coming in my dreams when I slept that night. There, standing on the high porch, was Lola Mae, and out of the blue she said to me. "Bet I can pee further than you!"

"Ummmmmmm," I muttered under my breath, surprised at her challenge. "I don't believe you can."

"All right. Let's have a contest!"

With that, she walked spiritedly over to the edge of her porch, slipped down her panties, unceremoniously squatted down. And sprayed a stream of urine way out to the side of the porch, the longest stream of piss I'd ever seen, longer even than Daddy's.

Looking on amazed, I wondered where she got all of that power. Also I wondered what I had let myself in for.

"Beat that!" Lola Mae gloated.

Wishing this were a rock throwing contest instead, I strolled up onto the porch and none too confidently over to its edge where Lola Mae had squatted. Then, glancing warily about, nervous that someone would see us, I pulled out my penis, gave it a "don't fail me now," look, then strained out my best effort. No cigar. My spray of urine fell far short of the spot Lola Mae had reached with hers.

"I win!" She reminded. "You didn't even come close!"

Then my other cousin, Helen—five years old, pleasant, pretty round face, pug nose, dark brown hair, who had been watching us, insisted on joining in on the contest too. Her squatted effort fell the shortest.

We held these pissing contests every day for weeks, Lola Mae always winning. They ended up being a child's version of foreplay for, after every contest, Lola Mae said mischievously, "Let's go out to the barn and play!"

We'd then scurry off to the barn in back of her house, Helen, not wanting to be left out of anything, trotting after us.

On our first visit there, Lola Mae purred, "Let's do somethin' nasty!" Then without comment from me she wiggled out of her panties and raised her dress up, a sheepish look coming into my eyes as I stood there beholding the slight silky hairs of her pubis. "What you waitin' for?" She gritted at me. "Git it out! Let's see if yer better at this than peeing."

What the heck?, I thought. At her egging, I flipped out my penis and rubbed it against her crotch, acting as though I knew what I was doing, feeling light headed and dreamy. As I did, Lola Mae emitted little sighs and moans, and her beady brown eyes sparkled with beady pleasure.

Helen, watching us, threatened sulkily, "If ya don't do it to me too, I'm goin' to tell on ya."

"Okay." I said. "Just for a little bit."

And a little bit was all that Helen had, though she made the most of it by imitating and mimicking her older sister.

So each time we went to the barn, like some transfixed bull calf attempting to service two young cows, I rubbed my penis against the crotches of both my cousins, going through the motions of sex the best a seven-year-old could, the three of us feeling each other's bodies, snickering, giggling, saying ribald things to one another, our forbidden activity adding all the more to its appeal.

Each time we finished our "playing" in the barn, Lola Mae exclaimed adamantly. "Let's do it again tomorrow!"

"Yeah."

"Me too," Helen chirped.

After one of these crotch-rubbing sessions, Lola Mae, rather jovially, said to me. "Donald, ya won't believe what happened last night."

I gave her a "Well,-so-tell-me" look.

"While daddy was gone, Hubert Singleton came by and I overheard him and mama doin' it in the hall. And I remember Hubert sayin', 'Is it in yet?'" Then she giggled.

It was then that I realized that Hubert was more slimy than I thought. A damn screwing gigolo! Suddenly I was envisioning him hopping from one woman to another in the area, screwing each one, becoming so exhausted that he couldn't even tell when it was in.

That night, before my nightmares began, I had the only pleasant dream of my childhood; I was hopping from shack to shack, screwing every little girl living in each one.

As always, something goofed up my escape. In this case, my barn "playing" was severely curtailed when Daddy initiated me into the family's main business—sharecropping. I was none too happy. In fact, I almost literally had to be dragged out to the field. And once there it took me only one second to confirm what I already knew; I wasn't cut out for sharecropping. Daddy, Mama, Red and Inez worked hard in the field without complaint, taking it in stride as their inevitable lot. I took none of it in stride, bellowing with complaints. I hated sharecropping work.

Surely, doctor, you gave me to the wrong parents.

Picking cotton was the worse. I had to bend over so much that it hurt my back. And when I crawled through the field for relief, rocks and sand spurs stuck to my knees, digging in with pain. My fingers weren't spared either. Not paying much attention to what I was doing, sharp dried up cotton bowls jammed in them, causing my fingers to bleed. And the cotton picking started at the crack of dawn, before the morning due evaporated, leaving me soaked in shivering wetness from the dew on the tall bushes. Then, later on, when the sun birthed forth in full summer bloom, I found myself on the other end of the continuum, my face roasting in the open field sun, frying like an overcooked egg in the scorching heat, leaving me panting, "I'll never make it I... I'll never make it! Dang, where are those blasted rain clouds when you need them?"

The storm pit was heaven compared to this.

Mama, Daddy, and Red each picked several hundred pounds of cotton a day. With my tongue wagging from heat exhaustion I wasn't able to approach even a measly hundred. And in addition to the hell slaving toil of picking the cotton, I also had to hoe and chop the stuff. The idea—certainly not mine-was to clean out all the weeds and leave a single, well-spaced plant. Yeah. Sure. With my uninspired hoeing, my mind constantly wondering if there was a Foreign Legion for kids, I left gaps all over the place, chopping away needed, defenseless plants as though they were coiled rattlesnakes.

Cotton wasn't the only crop. I also had to dig and pick peanuts, a relief compared to working in the cotton fields. Still it was slave labor, with the same broiling sun. But there was one consolation; fresh dug peanuts were delicious to eat. During the digging process I wiped the peanuts clean on my pant legs and heartily ate them raw throughout the day. A big mistake! Raw peanuts cause stomach aches resulting in severe diarrhea, and this propelled me into the nearby woods—back and forth all day, where, hurriedly dropping my pants at the last second, I'd let the insistent stomach cramps blow out its relieving stream. Not exactly top sharecropping form.

"Git back to work, Donald!" Mama yelled. "What's all this runnin' to the woods?!"

After a few weeks, when the stacks of peanuts had been rained on and dried by the sun—looking like bundles of brown Christmas trees with their long vines, a farmer with all the equipment for harvesting the peanuts was hired to pick them.

Following a hard, wearisome day of slave work in the field, I'd stagger home exhausted, near collapse, burnt out, dried out, sunburned, in pain, my muscles aching all over, in no mood for Mama and Daddy's vitriolic fighting, the storm pit, the nightmares, the bed-wetting, the asthma attacks, or any of the remainder of Mama's chaos. But unable to break out of the silence in which I felt corralled, unable to strike back at Mama, I suffered through them anyway, and all the misery in the world seemed to start and end with the muffled fury of my body.

A madness began developing within me; a portion of it out of my awareness.

Matters weren't helped that summer when Hut Dease, a second cousin of mine, the son of Mama's uncle, was killed in a questionable auto accident. A pleasant, down-to-earth fellow in his early 20s, Hut loved his boozing and was one of the few people whose company I enjoyed during the times he came over to buy moonshine from Daddy. Plagued with a stuttering problem, Hut had difficulty speaking clearly, and when he heard a joke he liked he'd light up with, "Pu-pu-pump it. Lu-lu-ther."

Hut's shortcoming was that he was attracted to the wrong crowd, the wild bunch in the area with whom he didn't fit in. On the Saturday of the auto accident he was out drinking with a couple of the local rowdies; namely, Ralph Riley and Leon Golden. Earlier that day the three of them drove to our shack in Leon's car and bought some moonshine from Daddy, and I watched them as they noisily drove off, wasting no time guzzling it down. Later that day came the car accident. Hut was killed and, quite mysteriously, the other two suffered only minor scratches.

"They killed Hut and faked the wreck to cover it up!" Mama declared. Then came her gory details of how it happened, Ralph stabbing Hut with his knife while Leon beat him with his fists. Her images came horribly alive in my dreams. Another harrowing nightmare. More muffled gasps in the night. More silenced pleas of terror closing in.

How I needed school to start again. But that was nearly a month away. I had no escapes. My onerous schedule in the sharecropping fields precluded my barn "playing" with Lola Mae and Helen, as it did playing camera with Carolyn.

I wasn't going to make it!

CHAPTER 10

I WOULDN'T HAVE made it if one facet of my misery hadn't rescued me from all the other. Shortly before school started my asthma attacks became so bad that they laid me up in bed, keeping me from working in the field. Then I sort of had a reversal of my one and only pleasant dream, only instead of being a dream it was real. Rather than hopping from shack to shack seducing girls, the girls, as if under divine guidance, came to me, seeking me out while I was laid up in Shack 6, and suddenly I was saturated with escapes.

It began with Carolyn, wanting to play camera, and we played in erotic abandon, with me getting in my long awaited, much needed "clicks." Carolyn was truly a rescuing heaven. Sweet smells. Harmonious moans. The delicate touch again of taffy skin.

Then someone unexpected sought me out. Since I quit defecating in bed, I was back to sleeping with Red, Mama deciding he could survive my bed-wetting. Inez, as usual, slept with Marilyn. One night Marilyn stayed at Aunt Pearl Stuart's house and Inez came up to me, asking cryptically:

"Would ya sleep with me tonight?"

"No. I'll probably pee on the bed." Red complained enough.

"That's all right. That don't matter."

"Well… okay—if it won't bother you."

I welcomed sleeping with Inez, thinking she wouldn't hog the bed like Red. And sleeping with her aroused no concern from Mama or Daddy. Inez was fifteen and I was only seven—and what could a seven-year-old do?

Inez wanted to find out.

It was one of those rare nights when Mama and Daddy's fighting ended early and the evening sky was such a clear, calm peaceful softness of stars that the threat of the storm pit was nil. After everyone was asleep, including me—creeping into one of my nightmares, Inez nudged me awake. Without saying a word she then startled me by taking my hand and guiding it between her legs and to her pubic hairs, laying it on her slit, wetter than wet, a deep cavernous flood of flowing juices.

She wanted to be fondled sexually. Inez was hot and breathless, wanting to be felt and fondled, and I was it. But I didn't want to be it. I wanted no part of this. God only knows what Mama would do if she became alerted as to what Inez was up to. It wasn't worth the risk. I tried pulling my hand away but Inez wouldn't let me. Her grip was too firm, determined that I would use my hand in the way she wanted it used. But touching Inez's crotch, unlike touching Carolyn, or even Lola Mae's, didn't arouse me with that exciting stir. Rather than spark my senses, touching Inez dulled them, leaving me with an empty, almost nauseous feeling. And confused.

Inez was so persistent that finally I simply gave up on pulling my hand away, letting it lay where she wanted it—in the push of her pubic hairs. But my hand lay limp, without movement, irritating Inez, who wanted my finger thrust into the sticky wetness of her juices. After a few minutes of the limp treatment she yanked my hand away from her; yanked it hard, disgusted. During the whole ordeal not one word was exchanged between us. Inez never asked me to sleep with her again, and she never said a word to me about that night.

A few days later, on a Saturday, while Marilyn was away and the remainder of the family in the field, leaving me alone in bed to wrestle with my asthma, I was visited at the shack by an eager Lola Mae and Helen. To my pleasurable surprise, the two brought with them another cousin of mine, Marilee, Aunt Chellie's fifteen-year-old daughter, a beautiful girl—streaming black hair; the shapely build of a young woman; a fantastic set of buttocks. Enough to make me forget my asthma.

I hopped out of bed to greet the trio, becoming as bad as Hubert. A gigolo in the making. It took no time for the four of us to become silly and giddy, and quickly Marilee, a most willing participant, was initiated into our "barn" playing, me teaming up with Lola Mae, Marilee with Helen.

Now there was a group of soldiers who for several months had been on training exercises on top of a nearby big hill not unlike a mountain. One of the soldiers had acquired a local reputation for being a great lover, causing a 'buzz among the women in the neighborhood. All they could talk about was how good-looking and sexy he was.

Quickly becoming sexually aroused and embolden, Marilee said to Helen, "I'll be that good-looking, sexy soldier, so you're in for the treat of your life."

"Goodie!" Helen beamed.

Not wanting to be outdone, I said to Lola Mae, "I'm that soldier too."

Lola Mae gave my asthma face a quick glance of appraisal. "That'll take some doin'."

For her "play" with Helen, Marilee stripped butt naked, revealing a firm, curvaceous peachy tan body that would stop a parade. It stopped me, and noticing that I was noticing her, Marilee turned away from Helen and shot me a captivating smile as she fingered the hairs of her pubis, jet black. Then in a *coup de theatre,* making certain I got an ample view of her crotch, she piped silkily to me. "Turn your head and don't look this way, Donald. It may be too much for you."

It was too much. But it was just as obvious that Marilee wanted me to play with her. It was obvious to Lola Mae as well, and before I had a chance to pursue any of the escape of Marilee's delights, Lola Mae, fixing me with a minatory glare, interjected ponderously, "Don't ya go messin' with her! Yer for me!"

With that, the most I could do was to just gawk at the splendor of Marilee's nakedness, a frustrated glee, drooling over her natural sleek beauty, voluptuous and inviting. And Marilee made it no easier for me, teasingly making certain that I saw the dazzling, writhing sexual acrobatics of her body in movement with

Helen's. Every now and then she paused to glance at me, grinning softly, displaying her long curving neck, her eyes dark and arresting.

"Quit starin' at her ass!" Lola Mae objected. "Take care of mine!"

Shack 6 had suddenly turned into a sex shack for kids. Within a week there I had "had" my sister and two cousins, and a third in my frustrated fantasies. Then just as suddenly these sex escapes abruptly ended. The family moved to Shack 7, out of range of Carolyn, Lola Mae and Helen, and out of range of the most luscious one of them all—Marilee.

My escapes lost again. My only solace; school was about to begin.

One and a half miles from Shack 6, and closer to Corinth School, we moved to Shack 7 in September. Located across a creek from Thad Green's home—a man who owned an old country store, Shack 7 was known as Across The Creek from Thad Green's place. The move to Shack 7 was necessitated when Daddy obtained a new sharecropping job with Olin Riley, uncle to Franklin and Ralph. A big, rotund, grizzly like fellow, gentle yet outspoken, Olin was unlike most of the other Riley's in that he didn't moonshine or drink that much.

On my first day back at school I was in for an unexpected surprise. Sitting at my desk in the second grade section, Mrs. Dykes walked toward me, her arms full of books which she placed on a nearby empty desk next to Lola Mae, who was in the third grade—in fact, the only third grader. Then, coming over to me, Mrs. Dykes said. "Follow me. I want you to be in the third grade with Lola Mae. You did so well in the first grade I think you can handle it."

With a burst of glee, happier than a frog on a lily pad, I rose from my desk and followed Mrs. Dykes over to the desk next to Lola Mae. But Lola Mae wasn't happy about the move, letting out a disgusting grunt, not thinking it fair that I was allowed to skip the second grade. Not too bright, having a tough time with her school work, this was just another reminder to her of that. And it humiliated her. Lola Mae wasn't asked to skip to the fourth grade. A student skipping a grade was unheard of, especially with the motley crew attending Corinth School.

So being the only one to have ever skipped a grade, I felt honored, and for the first time a bit cocky, slipping Lola Mae a sly, sideways glance, as if to say, "Now you're in my domain, where I win all the contests."

But Lola Mae wasn't the only one perturbed at my promotion. The entire student body erupted into a jealous uproar over it, and I had an uprising on my hands.

"That smart alec punk Donald Oakes skippin' the second grade—don't that beat all! What's this place comin' to?"

But I ate it up. Finally it was me who was gloating for a change; shining in all the glory of my big escape. And I played it to the hilt.

Glory, though, comes at a price. And that price was that the other male students were out to get me. One of them, Donald Singleton, the school's redheaded slob and insatiable scapegrace—his mean freckled face an amalgam of unchecked rowdiness, beat up on or hassled most of the kids at Corinth School.

Well, he didn't like my promotion—he was left in the second grade and not promoted, so one day, expressing his ire over it, he ripped my brand new wool jacket off it's hanger and tossed it down one of the school outhouse's dark stinking holes. This made the other teacher at the school—Mrs. Annie Mae Brabham—so furious that she yanked Donald Singleton by the knap of the neck, pulled him to the outhouse, there picking him up by the heels and holding him that way while he slithered down the hole and retrieved my jacket. Then he was ordered to take it home, clean it up, and bring it back to me as good as new. And that he did.

That's when I discovered why Donald Singleton disliked me so intensely—aside from the fact that I was allowed to skip the second grade. I finally found out that Mama's lover, Hubert Singleton, was his daddy, making the Oakes' name pure manure in his home. Hubert's wife, Josie—on the ugly side, knew all about Mama and Hubert, and never let anyone in her household forget it.

Next, Gaither Williams, a tall, skinny sixth grader, big for his age of twelve, big ears, big nose, white-haired, a buddy of Donald Singleton, came after me. During recess, he muscled up to me, snarling officiously:

"I think yer too big fer yer britches skippin' the second grade. They shouldn't allow the son of a *slut* to do that!"

Hearing him call Mama a slut, all I could see was bellicose red. I was extremely frail and skinny, maybe weighing 40 pounds, and standing next to Gaither I was dwarfed by him. But still I tore into him with a slashing, combative style, as frisky as any scrawny kid could be, swinging my fists at whatever part of his body I could hit, at the same time kicking wildly at his shins.

My spunk taking him by surprise, Gaither, with his long spider arms all over me, tried to grab me with a firm hold to keep me from landing my blows, but he couldn't. I was too agile and slippery for him.

The skirmish was broken up by the teachers, but after that neither Gaither nor Donald Singleton bothered me again. Donald's behavior even turned more cordial toward me. After my fight with Gaither, he invited me, during recess, to the woods near school to join in the activities of the other boys—a sign that I was finally being accepted, especially after the courage I displayed in my battle with Gaither. Several students, including Gaither, were gathered there in the woods at a smoking hut made out of tree limbs. All chummy, they passed lighted cigarettes among themselves, offering me a couple of drags on one, sort of an initiation into the group. After that, I belonged, and when not at the smoking hut, we'd gather in the woods during recess and play cowboys and Indians, many of the boys wanting to be on my side.

Finally I came to be held in high prestige at school, academically and socially. And the third grade, with its basic three R's—reading, writing and arithmetic, proved to be as easy for me as the first grade had been. But at home I was back to zero. And because of all the chaos and commotion going on there at night, it was impossible to concentrate on homework, especially when you're sitting in the blackness of a storm pit listening to Mama and Daddy verbally going for one another's throats. Nevertheless, I continued breezing along in school, my ups there at least managing to checkmate my downs at home, never changing, remaining chronic and permanent.

During the off-season Daddy devoted his time fully to moonshining, refusing, since his auto accident, to return to working in the Josie sawmill. By the time spring arrived I was eight years old, feeling eighty, and the start of a new sharecropping season began, meaning I had to hit the fields again after school and on Saturdays.

Sharecropping for Daddy was actually a partnership between he and the man he worked for, Daddy—and the family providing the labor to raise the crops, the man he worked for providing the land and the supplies, with the money they earned from their joint effort split fifty-fifty between them. And in this family partnership I now was old enough to take on more sharecropping duties, the main one of which was plowing with mules. Very slow mules. As with picking and hoeing cotton, I hated it.

Plowing with mules was the ultimate in aggravation. A continuous struggle of conflict and frustration. On the one hand I attempted to push these lazy, tired critters to their limit so I could finish my work and get in some reading. On the other hand the mules were stubborn and ornery and refused to be pushed, no matter how much I yelled at them, at times becoming totally intractable. Making matters worse, the mules had a filthy, distasteful habit of flatulence, coming in two speeds. When a mule raised its tail fast-like, the fart blew on past quickly, with little lingering. But when the tail raised very slowly, you were really in for it, especially when you were in a dead corner where no breeze was stirring. Then the fart did nothing but linger, grabbing your full attention, lingering full force in your face, changing it to a choking grimace of repugnance, the fart blending in as part of your dust and sweat-soaked body, hanging there forever. Usually this type of flatus was unloaded on me when I was screaming at the animals, pushing them—nonverbal communication at its best.

Daddy knew how much I hated sharecropping work. He also knew of my quest to seek knowledge and my keen interest in school. But to Daddy, as with most sharecroppers, school had a low priority. The high priority was working in the fields. And working as much as possible. Thus Daddy's problem with me was getting me to leave that which I loved, to do that which I hated.

Though I was a lousy sharecropper, my heart never in it, to Daddy I was better than nothing, at times even adequate, and he set out on a campaign to ease me into sharecropping full time, beginning by trying to coax me to work during the school day.

"Stay home from school today and help me in the field," Daddy would say to me in his halting grovelish style, essaying a trusting smile as his tongue switched his cigarette from one side of his mouth to the other in a bubbly wad of spit.

"I can't. I have to go to school."

He'd take his cigarette from his mouth and raise it, as though he were going to tap the air with it. "Aw, good God Almighty, boy," he drawled, his voice coarse and guttural, "school ain't all that important. Believe me!" He'd give me a cryptic grin; that enigmatic expression insinuating he knew something no one else did. "Anyway, missin' one day won't hurt."

To me, Daddy was attempting to ease his foot in the door. I figured if he could persuade me to stay home and work one day, the next time it would be two days, then three, then I wouldn't be in school at all, as had happened to J.P., Ruby Lee, Red and Inez. But it wasn't going to happen to me. School was not only my escape from Mama, but my escape from the wearisome, tormenting, defeating legacy Mama and Daddy had ushered me into. There was no way I was giving up school to be irreversibly trapped as a tortured slave picking cotton, peanuts or corn, and to be farted at all day behind some frustrating mule leaving me bilious and out of sorts.

NO WAY!

"Yes it would." I'd answer. "I have a test today. Extremely important. No way I can miss school."

Daddy would grunt and shrug his shoulders. "Okay." He'd sigh, a disappointing edge to his voice. He gave up for then, waiting for another day. But the outcome was always the same. I never missed one day of school to work in the fields.

In contrast to Daddy, Mama did see how important going to school was to me—though she never understood why, and this was the one aspect of my life she somehow sensed she shouldn't discourage. And she didn't. At times she even went without so that I could have a few things for school—pencils, paper, every now and then a new jacket, shirt or blue jeans. But it was too little too late. They could in no way obviate my anger and rage toward her; or the shame and despair and chaos and torment and torture and horror she had created for me, and continued to create.

This pathos kept our relationship in a state of conflict. And since the sexual incident with Ralph Riley, Mama could never do anything right for me. After the fuss Mama made about my poor dress and appearance at the hospital following Daddy's accident, I became obsessed with my appearance, making certain I appeared neat and my clothes were clean. In fact, I became extremely picky about my clothes. They had to be pressed perfectly. If there was even one small wrinkle in my shirt I'd throw it back at Mama, exclaiming:

"Press it right!"

Or if the biscuits weren't cooked to my satisfaction—and after Ralph they never were, I'd demand that they be cooked better. Or if she cooked cornbread instead of biscuits, I'd yell, "I want biscuits, not cornbread!" Any minor complaint about anything to get back at her.

"Ya damn youngins—thar's nothin' I can do for ya right. Yer drivin' me crazy!"

The lines had been drawn and would never change. Mama, and most of my home life, I had written off as a total loss. My saving grace for this loss was school, supplemented by whatever other escapes presented themselves.

School and home presented existences so opposite from one another it was like living on two different planets. On one planet things went miraculously; on the other, horribly. And in the spring of 1952 things couldn't be going better on my miraculous planet at school—everything positive, creative, uplifting, inspiring, ebullient. With such wonderful feelings spring turned my fancy to girls. Having tasted their delights, I missed their escapes. I needed replacements for Carolyn, Lola Mae, and Helen, no longer available.

Corinth School was in walking distance of Shack 7, so I had my choice of walking to school or taking the bus. Sometimes I'd walk, sometimes I'd ride the bus, depending upon my mood and the weather, and whether or not I had spent the previous night in the storm pit. Now the high school for seventh-graders and up was just down the road past Corinth School, and those students attending the high school from my area rode the same bus as I did, the bus continuing on to the high school after its stop at Corinth School. And often, after school let out for the day, on the bus's return trip, high school students living near Shack 7 would leave the bus at the Corinth School stop and walk the rest of the short distance home.

One of the students who did this was Shirley Jean Culpepper, a thirteen-year-old seventh grader and one gorgeous plum—a leggy ingenue with the smoothest creamy skin and the nicest, roundest, cutest swinging swaying ass I'd ever seen, rattling my eyes in their sockets. It took only one rattle at her swishy derriere for me to fall hopelessly in love with it, bringing on feelings of deja vu, reminding me of Marilee, causing a lusty, bug-eyed, "Awwriiight!" To whistle under my breath. The perfect sexual escape. Camera. Barn playing. Asthma alleviation. You name it.

Energetic, outgoing, friendly, Shirley Jean's girlish demeanor matched her figure. Not believing my luck, she also lived close to me, so on some days she and I walked home together from Corinth School rather than take the bus—invigorating new life walks of spring; gentle sweet glances between us; exchanges of giggles in a floating dream.

And with each walk with her I became more helpless; reduced more down to the life of the senses until my urge to grapple with her mesmerizing tush became an all-out obsession, those swaying buttocks simply too potent for my crumbling restraints. I was so far gone that already I could hear her purring; see her body quivering, panting gasps, yielding totally to the cunning of my fingers nestling in between those sweet, swivel cheeks.

Carolyn, Lola Mae, and even Marilee—not to mention Inez, all craved my fingers. Why shouldn't Shirley Jean? So all that was needed was for me to let her know I was willing. But how to approach her? Before, the girls, quite boldly, had always approached me. I had acquired no experience or know how in approaching them, leaving me lacking the courage and daring to just come out and say. "Shirley Jean. I'd love to feel your ass! How about it?"

I wanted to—oh, how I wanted to, but I couldn't. So, instead of saying it, I wrote it.

One day, while I was alone on the route we walked home. I took a piece of notebook paper and, without subtlety, scribbled on it:

> Dear Shirley Jean,
>   I want you to know that I think you're a pretty girl and your butt is pretty too and I'd sure like to play with it.
>   Donald Oakes

I left the note on the Thad Green bridge, flapping in the breeze to one side, a rock on top of it to keep it from blowing away. I was absolutely confident that Shirley Jean would be the one to find it because the note was meant for her, never for a second thinking that someone besides Shirley Jean might pick it up instead; never for a moment feeling that leaving the note on the bridge like that might turn out to be an outrageous blunder.

It was a blunder. The most damaging of my young life. There's a point of no return unheeded at the time in many lives and for me that point came when I left that note on the bridge. Someone other than Shirley Jean found the note and in no time its contents spread like wildfire all over the school and the community. But most devastating, what I wrote in that note got back to Mama and she brought the wrath of God down on me in a rabid *coup de grace*.

"Are ya crazy?!" Mama expostulated, beginning a tizzy of all tizzies. "To think that I raised somebody who would do something like that! . . . Ya think ya'd have more sense… anybody as smart as ya are!... But no—ya gotta be a *pervert*!.... A sex fiend! Now everybody *knows!* Lord have mercy! How can I face 'em all?!"

Mama's lamenting raced into raging, pacing, and screaming, her voice ripping from her throat like gritty chalk on a blackboard, juggling the eyebrows in time with her sanctimonious outrage. "I do without—not as much as a co-coler, and jest look at what ya done! It looks ya could be a decent somebody instead of a…"

Her eyes inflamed venomously, hot daggers of fire, the fire daggers of hell!

"…oh. What's the *use!* I'm gonna git me a stick of dynamite and blow myself to Kingdom Come! Donald …how could ya do such a …a … a shameful … awful … disgustin' thing?! To *yer* Mama? Yer gonna kill me! I work my fingers to the bone like a nigger and jest look what I git for it—*disgrace!* I'd ruther be dead and buried over yonder at Ramer Church graveyard than facin' yer disgrace! Lord have mercy! The day's gonna come when ya'll look back on this terrible, disgustin' deed and regret it. I had ruther be in Diddy Wah Diddy—or tied to a tree in Pea River Swamp… than put up with ya!

"Yer worse than a slimy, low down whoremonger!"

Over the next several weeks, Mama, every chance she got exploded into this deranged, invective, uncontrollable, black-visaged, high-decibel diatribe with me, as if cursing Satan himself, reiterating it, expounding at interminable length on the unforgivable sin I had committed, shattering me with it until I became senseless, never letting me forget, crucifying me much too much, her rancor clawing at me until it seemed the meat on my bones had been torn away and set on fire. I got to the point where I wasn't even breathing. Didn't want to breathe. What I wanted was to slither under a rock like some low life worm and die, my shame with myself beyond the edge of endurance, my self-loathing beyond belief, a blackness inside destroying me, encompassing my emotional ruin, leaving me feeling that what I had done was so filthy, so deviate, so unspeakable, so unconscionable, so inhuman, that I had to be some hideous, despicable creature not deserving to live. A vile disgraceful scamp causing people not to like Mama or the Oakes family.

Already I regarded Mama as a rock bottom character. But now I turned the full import of all my negative, chaotic feelings in toward myself, making me a rock bottom character as well, some desolate thing consubstantial with Mama's madness. A thing not even fit for the rock bottom, austere, ne're-do-well society of the sharecropping lot.

At school, my miracle of life ended. I became a loner, refusing to mingle with anyone, feeling unworthy of friendship. I couldn't face Shirley Jean anymore. I quit having anything to do with girls. I quit playing cowboys and Indians with the other students. I declined to go to the smoking hut. I became morose, unreachable, isolating myself from all social contact, feeling castrated and out of sync with my environment, my perceptions soured, my emotions frozen, the spirit choked out of me.

When the note scandal first broke, the kids at school teased me mercilessly with combers of laughter. And that laughter carried over into my dreams. The young man was back. A nightmare of laughter. The vagueness of his face and the deep penetrating shining black eyes the total of all creation laughing at me.

CHAPTER 11

MY DREAMS WERE not only in turmoil but they went haywire, becoming crazy, so much so that I preferred my nightmares to the young man. Then he began appearing in all of my nightmares as well, introducing them, ushering them in with bristling, deafening laughter, converting my dreams into a hotchpotch of laughable terror.

Then there were dreams centering on the young man alone, senseless dreams, as vague as his face, no logic, shifting, obscure settings, but with one constant; the loud, tormenting, mocking laughter.

"Who *are* you?!" I'd challenge. "What do you *want* from me?! Why are you *laughing* at me?"

I'd keep asking, he'd keep laughing, never answering. Then his face took on different identities—Daddy, Mama, Hubert, Ralph. And they were always laughing. Laughing at me. In some of the dreams the young man's face even became my face. I was laughing at myself. It made no sense.

In my awakened world there was little sense either. With Mama's incensed reaction to the bridge note incident continuing after school let out, my inner chaos became unbearable. My mind began dividing against itself. Under these circumstances, with the escape of school gone for the summer, this should have been it; a gigantic nervous breakdown or suicide; or something as equally disastrous.

Only one thread kept me with the world; kept me functioning with any semblance of sanity. The remembrance. The ghostlike figures. Their vague promise of deliverance. But to survive even with this I had to shut out Mama's rancor; exile the devastation of her madness to the phantom regions of my mind, out of my awareness, there joining the most vicious elements of my wishes against Mama. But in my dreams I was witness to the severity of that rage.

During a nightmare of Daddy in hell, with me struggling frantically and unsuccessfully to rescue him, enraged by the monstrous roar of the young man's laughter, I was suddenly out of hell and with Mama, a knife in my hand, stabbing her repeatedly, then strangulating her bloody corpse with my hands. Then just as suddenly I was awake, suffocating, unable to breathe, my eyes rigid, horrified, suffering the most frightening asthma attack imaginable.

That began a series of bitter, dreadful asthma attacks that summer of 1952; attacks so severe that I was bedridden with them all summer, feeling like a hapless fish marooned on a beach, helpless and immobile except for last ditch flapping about, gasping for oxygen that wasn't there, waiting for the last gasp, the end, the most terrorizing subjugated physical feeling—not being able to breathe in air. Not knowing from breath to breath whether or not during the next gasp you're going to be able to take in the oxygen needed to sustain life.

This was the terror of my summer. Wheezing and gasping for air; making all kinds of "flapping about" noises trying to breathe. Noises of convulsive gasps sounding like huge death rattles. The asthma attacks were the worst at night, when the air became thin. And since I could faintly breathe better sitting up than lying down, during the attacks I slept very little. Most of the time I was sitting up in bed, shuddering, trying not to awaken Red in my panicked struggles to breathe, my precious thin breath dry and harsh in the throat, what composure I had being spent praying for the sun to hurry and rise, bringing daylight, when breathing became slightly easier. But then, as dawn broke the horizon, and I fell under the bombardment of Mama's attacks over my note to Shirley Lee, I didn't want to breathe.

At times, when not burdened by trips to the storm pit, to avoid disturbing Red in his sleep, I'd arise from bed in the middle of the night and, in the dark, sit by the fireplace, my eyes wide and starry as I rummaged through the burnt coals searching for Daddy's discarded cigarette stubs. I'd find one, light it, then with a tremendous sucking gasp I'd take a drag from the end of the stub, hoping that inhaling the smoke would help my breathing. Such was my desperation.

The family couldn't afford a doctor or a trip to the hospital for me. No member felt it necessary anyway, seeing no urgency in my asthma attacks. Red, Inez, and Marilyn were confident that I was faking the attacks to keep from working in the fields, and Mama and Daddy shared this sentiment too. Subsequently, they ignored me during my attacks, offering me no aid, no help, no comfort, no encouragement, leaving me suffering alone, stranded with my fears, waiting to expire in my own loneliness.

During these summer fears, while retreated unto myself, while wheezing with awful noises, while gasping for my next breath, while left alone, without escapes, without the ability to pursue them if there were, my eyes remained far away and cloudy as I thought of school approaching. Unpleasant thoughts. Even if I survived my asthma attacks, school no longer offered the lure of the great escape, so convinced was I that all the kids there would regard me as the same low life, worthless, shameless, monster deviate that Mama claimed me to be.

I survived. School began. But my mind and emotions had been so warped by Mama that there was no way I could enjoy it. The old eager enthusiasm and exuberance for school were gone, replaced by a sense of gloomy dark unworthiness. Though my heart wasn't in it, I still went to school, fighting off Daddy's pleas for me to stay home and work instead, seeing school as the lesser of two evils, humiliation there better than disaster at home. But I was a depressed robot, vulnerable and wary, prone to sullen self-pity, a slack empty expression on my face. Regardless, all of my friends at Corinth School greeted me as warmly as ever, the note incident forgotten. But it made no difference. Mama wouldn't let me forget. And so, though my friends at school displayed no evidence of it, I was convinced they held me in low contempt, as Mama did, and this feeling—a profound sickness weakening me, I couldn't extinguish.

And other factors kept school from being pleasant. Often I'd be up all night with my asthma attacks—surprisingly, my asthma didn't act up at school—and, with no sleep, drawn and tired, I'd go to school the next day sick and worn out. And there were pressures coming from others besides Daddy for me to stay home from school and work in the fields. Red and Inez, and even Ruby Lee, expressed the opinion that I was lazy, attending school only for the purpose of getting out of sharecropping work.

Red was particularly vehement—and jealous—in his protests that I wasn't helping in the fields.

"Looks like ya'd stay here and *help!*" He'd complain to me just before I left for school.

"I want to go to school and learn something," I'd counter glumly.

"Oh, *God dang*, Donald. Don't give me *that!* Yer goin' so ya won't have to work!"

Wallowing in the legacy, helplessly and hopelessly chained to it, Red, along with Ruby Lee and Inez, and later, Marilyn, all viewed me as the skeleton in the family, the black sheep, thinking not only that I was odd, lazy and a malingerer, but thinking also that I saw myself as better than they. Because of this, it was rather pointless for me to reveal my real feelings to them, to talk to them of my nightmares, my inner distress, how really low I regarded myself. Daddy, I thought, was an even less likely candidate to talk to. He viewed anyone who worried over anything to the point of emotional disharmony as being an utter fool. And Mama, the major culprit behind my disharmony, was no candidate at all. Even if there were people I could talk to, they couldn't understand my agonizing. It was beyond words. And much of it was related to matters I dared not discuss anyway. Better to keep a lid on it. Deal with it myself.

At least my humiliation in school was lifted when, in February, 1953, after I had just turned nine years of age, we moved from Shack 7 to Shack 8, located right outside of Josie. This move out of the Corinth community and away from Corinth School, away from the Shirley Jean scandal and those who knew about it, brought me tremendous relief—a fresh start, a new beginning and, most important, the much needed escapes again of Pea River and Pea River Swamp.

But Shack 8 still had Mama. And it was near Shack 3, where Daddy had slaughtered a pig, a crime as yet unsolved, and my worry about Daddy still being apprehended for it returned to haunt me, though now with stiff competition from newer hauntings.

Shack 8, the only place available at the time to Daddy for his new sharecropping job, was the most dilapidated of shacks in a long series of dilapidated shacks. Though it had five rooms instead of only three, it still didn't afford the family any more living space since two of the rooms were occupied by a boarder, Nat Mitchell, coming with the territory.

Not a sharecropper, living only on the meager proceeds of welfare, Nat Mitchell was the dirtiest, filthiest, most slothful and most terrible smelling human being on earth, making Shack 8 the cesspool shack. In his early 50's, unkempt and dusty-looking, dressed in ancient, grimy, filthy, smelly tattered clothes making Daddy's old garb look resplendent by comparison, Nat Mitchell was a frail skeleton of a man, short and skinny, about five-seven, weighing not an ounce over 100 pounds. His hair was thin, a disheveled brown, never combed, splattered on top of a chiseled, lugubrious face heavily shadowed with beard stubble; a face of high cheekbones, sunken rubbery jowls, a pointed hawk nose, rotten teeth and only one eye—small, flinty, deep-set, and slightly unfocused. His cheeks were hollow, his lips swollen and cracked, and his skin worn with an unhealthy sallow pallor, giving him a dismal, disheartening, pinched deathly look, like a broken down werewolf on its last legs.

Nat spoke very little, but when he did his speech was flat and unpleasant, slightly raspy, sometimes slurred, sometimes maundering, giving the impression that he was always somewhere between consciousness and unconsciousness, strung out and fried on hash oil, hearing his own questions somewhere in the remotest realm of his brain and trying to answer them, never successfully. And he had the most rotten sour odor, a cross between a mule's slowest tail-raising fart and a garbage dump, convincing me that he had never taken a bath in his life.

When we first moved into Shack 8 all the rooms were so squalid and filthy, in such a messy disarray from Nat's unbelievably slovenly living style, smelling like a raw sewage plant, that even Mama was lost for words. She spent several days of hard toil, using pot ash and lye soap, and a homemade scrub broom made out of corn shucks stuffed in the holes of a rectangular board attached to a wooden pole as a handle, scrubbing down the floors and walls of the family's three room living quarters.

This done, Daddy, to Mama's frowning displeasure, invited Nat to share a fried chicken meal with the family. When the pitiful man sat down at the table, covered in slimy filth and dust, fixed with a bleak stare, looking like a mugged corpse, smelling like a decaying carcass, all stomachs ceased growling, overtaken by unsettling nausea. The sight of Nat's bare eye socket with the missing eye, in and of itself, was enough to ruin any appetite, the socket one big, gooey, runny, dripping festered sore, with its own entourage of flies and gnats buzzing about it.

Without a word, or acknowledging anyone, as soon as Nat sat down he gruffly stuck his filthy hand into the plate of chicken and helped himself, the flies and gnats joining him. We all watched stunned, none of us able to eat after that.

"Lord have mercy!" Mama snorted dazedly, glaring at Nat with startled eyes.

We let Nat finish off the chicken. Afterwards, all of us realized that the only way we were going to survive sharing the shack with Nat was by keeping him isolated to his two small rooms in the back. And that Mama insisted upon. Nat never again set foot in our quarters.

I had little to do with Nat. He was the antithesis of any escape. But one time I did step inside his two back rooms. The nauseous odor hit me at once, a putrid smell hanging thick and heavy, overwhelming, the same smell entombing Nat. The order of the rooms matched the odor, looking like a condemned Turkish whorehouse, overflowing with rotting food, foul junk, unclean empty cans and empty boxes, other scattered debris, everything covered with thick dust and cobwebs, all of it making a complex assault on the senses. Situated in one of the rooms was an old wooden stove where Nat cooked bread on its bare top, paper and cardboard crammed in disarray all about the stove, making me wonder how he avoided setting the place on fire while cooking.

How could anyone live in such filth?

Since the chicken supper invitation, the only time I saw Nat was when he sauntered around aimlessly in the yard. Daddy and Red were the only members of the family who associated with him. Since Nat liked to drink, they got along with him fine, Daddy having his fun plying Ned with moonshine, talking to him with bearish good humor.

"Nat's the only one I know who can fart at will." Daddy exclaimed on one occasion, rich dark laughter bellowing from his chest. "Quiet or loud … dependin' on which way ya ask him to fart. Dangest thing I've ever seen!"

Word got around that Nat was hired by Unice Green to sweep his store. Before the job was finished, Nat helped himself to a brand new pair of overalls and made an attempt to slip away. He was caught red handed and stripped of his new outfit. Unice made him change back into his old clothes and sent him on his way.

Nat also had a widespread reputation of braying like a donkey. He would travel by foot throughout Pike and Bullock counties mostly at night choosing to do his braying in front of his chosen subject's house. After being warned to move on down the road on many occasions, he was often kicked and beaten by the offended party.

At Shack 8 I transferred into the fourth grade at Banks Junior High School, offering grades from the first through the ninth. I had no more desire to attend school there than I did at Corinth School, but at least at Banks I wasn't submerged in desolation. There were no aspects of the note scandal to humiliate me, so no students for me to face holding me in scorn or ridicule. No one at the school knew me. No one had any knowledge of my farcical, backfired quest to get my hands on Shirley Jean's tush. I wanted to keep it that way, maintaining a low profile, remaining unobtrusive, letting no one know of the "notorious" among them. All lovely buttocks in the area were safe. The urge had been taken out of me. Now I lost myself in the school library, reading everything I could lay my hands on, some of it weighty material, taking whatever books I could obtain home to read.

On the weekends J.P. began visiting us frequently from Phenix City, and aside from my reading he became my only link to sanity, the only one in the family who didn't share the view that I was faking my asthma attacks and attending school only to escape working in the fields. I dearly loved his visits. Each time he came my asthma seemed to be less bothersome.

During one of this visits, while we were alone, J.P., a kindhearted person who would give the shirt off of his back to help anyone, and well aware of the chaos Mama was creating and was capable of creating, said to me:

"I know what you're going through, Donald, but just hang in there. I regret never finishing school, so don't let that happen to you. Get your education then get away from here. And if it gets too bad, when you get older you can come live with me." A remote look of retrospect combed his eyes, then he added, "But that would be one heck of a battle with Mama!" His voice becoming soft again, a brightness to his eyes, he then said, "Now let's go fishing."

J.P. took me fishing at both Pea River and Pea River Swamp, and also took me hunting and for drives into town, either Union Springs or Troy. When not engaged in these activities we played baseball together, though J.P. was not as well coordinated at this as I. But just to be with him, doing things with him, talking with him about the outside world, was refreshing excitement, a most needed escape, and I savored every second of it.

At times Red came along with J.P. and me on our fishing excursions. Sometimes just Red and I went fishing. On rarer occasions, Daddy took me. And if Red was around he'd occasionally want to tag along, stating to Daddy, "Looka y'hea. I wanna go with ya." When speaking directly to Daddy, Red addressed him as "Looka y'hea." As if that were his name. He never called him "Daddy" to his face.

At other times, J.P., Red, Daddy and I all went fishing together, and when we did it was either hand fishing or seining, Daddy's favorite methods of fishing. Often Daddy went off to seine for fish with his drinking buddies, either in Pea River or at a nearby farmer's pond, and on such outings, in the grandest wild and wooly manner, he proceeded to get drunk on moonshine as they seined.

A couple of times, when I was in dire need of relief from Mama, Daddy took me along with him on these seining trips with his buddies. He stripped naked when he seined, and because he was ruptured he wore a special belt to keep his rupture harnessed, a pint of moonshine jammed under it, guzzling from it as he fished. On one of these fishing trips, feeling encumbered by the belt, Daddy took it off, leaving his testicles dangling, bulging to the size of small watermelons. I cringed at his exposure, fearing he would hurt himself since he seined with such vigor, exerting tremendous pressure on his lower body. He needed the support of his belt.

On this occasion, in his great vigor, Daddy hemmed up a large black fish between his legs. Then:

"AAAHHHHGGG!! Goddammit!" He screamed, jumping back in the water with rubbery agility.

"Daddy... wha... what's wrong?!"

"Sonofabitchin' fish bit me on the damn balls! ... If that don't beat all!"

Of all the places I was taken to, Pea River Swamp was my favorite, its soothing sounds of solitude a sweet rhapsody, a peaceful stillness caressing me like some magical cloak, this calm of Nature catalyzing a salutary peace within myself, enabling me to think clearly. Good thoughts. Thoughts that on one occasion prompted me to recall a passage I recently read in the school library, a passage from Voltaire's play, CANDIDE:

"... Cultivate your own garden rather than the spring of the
Universe."

Strangely, recalling that passage, I thought of Nat Mitchell. Then, swallowed
by the harmony of the swamp, I thought of the ghostlike figures and was overcome
by an eerie feeling, as if in their presence. At that moment, a passage I'd never read
before, uninvited and unadorned, simply popped into my mind:

Find the spring that controls your own Universe.

The passage kept repeating itself in my mind, invigorating me. And in that
invigoration my thirst for school was revitalized.

And something else, I could live with myself—at least in the swamp.

CHAPTER 12

I DEFINITELY FELT better, eager to make the most of school again.

Find the spring that controls your own Universe.

Since that passage came to me in Pea River Swamp, I repeated it to myself every day. Somehow it helped, seemingly warding off my nightmares. For a while they ceased, and with them the young man with the tormenting laughter. Mama even eased up crucifying me over the Shirley Jean note. But she didn't ease up about Nat Mitchell. Taking her only six weeks to get her fill of his filth and unsightly appearance, she then recoiled, demanding of Daddy that we move. We did, moving into Shack 9 in the latter part of March, 1953. Owned by S.E. Green—the landowner with whom Daddy had his next sharecropping job. Shack 9 was located a mile from Shack 8 and was known as the S.E. Green place.

At school I immediately came out of my social shell and began playing basketball and baseball. During P.E. I helped organize a fourth grade baseball team which played the teams of other grades. This inevitably lead to me being invited to join the school's "incrowd" club, an informal, rather select social society at Banks Junior High consisting primarily of the better-heeled class of kids, but also including the smart ones.

When we moved into Shack 9 my only friend was William Henry Austin, a short eight-year-old kid, snotty-nosed, pudgy, shabbily dressed and pathetic-looking. And dirt poor. Like me. We rode the bus together to school, sitting together and chatting, and from these chats we became friends. Now, before acceptance into this "incrowd" select group, I was asked to quit associating with William Henry Austin—I wasn't even suppose to talk to him on the school bus. Whereas I was poor but smart—acceptable to the club, William was poor and dumb—unacceptable.

I rejected the group's invitation, choosing to continue my friendship with William. But having firmly established that I was the smartest kid in the fourth grade, not having me as a member was too much for the "incrowd" and they dropped their demand that I quit hobnobbing with William. With that, I joined the club, acquiring the reputation of a person with convictions, though to me my behavior was more of human decency than conviction.

Banks Junior High was a large, U-shaped, somewhat sprawling brick building in which, unlike Corinth School, each grade had its own room. And since the school served a larger area than did Corinth School, there were more students to each grade, the fourth grade alone having 25 students. And I wasn't the only bright student in that class of 25. Three other fourth graders shared that superiority with me, one of them Lurlene, who took a fancy to me.

But girls as sexual escapes were no longer on my agenda. Not only because of Mama's castigation of me over the Shirley Jean note farce, and not wanting to repeat it, but more deeply, believing Mama, I now regarded myself as unworthy of any decent girl, even on a social basis, the significant ramifications of this buried out of my awareness, belonging to a world I dare not see.

And Lurlene was certainly a decent girl. The daughter of a churchgoing family, she lived in a nice home in a nice community, belonging to a life vastly above the sharecropper lot. Nine years old, rather tall, she leaned toward the skinny side but still had a nice figure; and nice hair, a long brown the color of an autumn leaf before it falls. And her face was pretty, touched with a sprinkling of freckles and a small gap between her front teeth, covered by an energetic mouth radiating into a wide captivating smile, caressing, flowing from her freely like a refreshing slice of springtime.

She began directing that smile at me. I'd have nothing to do with it. Then one day Lurlene passed me a note in school which read:

I like you. Do you like me?

Of course I liked her. But that wasn't the real question. Do I dare like her? No.

I read her note with mixed feelings. Why was she doing this to me? Aside from being a decent girl, she was out of my league in another critical way; she lived a normal life with a normal family. I couldn't expose her to my life, or even let her know of it, an abnormal life with an abnormal family, not only dreadful and outrageous, but totally unbelievable and impossible to explain.

It struck me that the best thing to do was tell Lurlene that I didn't like her. But I couldn't lie. So I returned the note to her without an answer, letting it go at that.

But Lurlene didn't, not in the least seeming discouraged. She began flirting with me, and the persistent sincerity of her springtime smiles began melting me down. Then boldly, Lurlene just finally came out and said to me, "I want to be your girlfriend," her voice rising and falling like miniature chimes.

Her declaration, softly chilling, caught me by surprise. I wish she hadn't made it. Still, I couldn't resist a sense of pleasure; a feeling of tenderness filling my heart.

"Okay." I found myself agreeing, complex feelings of regret and sadness slicing through me. "You can be—at school."

Springtime again. "Okay." She smiled, and my knees became rubbery.

From that point on Lurlene was my girlfriend at Banks Junior High School. Our association could be nothing more than a superficial social relationship limited to school, a simpler solution than explaining why she couldn't be my girlfriend. My *real* girlfriend. But it was a wonderful feeling being genuinely liked by Lurlene; a tenderness sustaining me in a way I'd never experienced.

Then the honeymoon was over. The honeymoon with my emotions. The nightmares returned!

One of the notorious "three musketeers" of the county, Leon Golden, a tough rowdy along with William Stuart and Ralph Riley, and the major moonshining outlaw in the county, also was its most reckless speed demon, with the fastest car. While working in the fields we often heard the loud engine of his automobile racing over the distant roads. And when you heard his fast car roaring nearby you immediately knew to stay clear of the road, or else Leon would run you over.

Loaded up with moonshine, caring for nothing or nobody, behind the wheel Leon was a driving maniac, and everyone knew it was just a matter of time before he killed somebody. And that time came in mid May, 1953.

My family had been chopping cotton in this field—me along with them, my asthma attacks having subsided—with several black workers. One day, while I was in school, these same black workers were waiting by the side of the road, next to the cotton field, to be picked up and taken to the local country store for their lunch of sardines and crackers. One of the young black male workers waiting to be picked up happened to be standing in the road when, like some monstrous phantom suddenly springing from the deep, Leon came roaring out of nowhere in his car at tremendous speed, jostling into the unfortunate worker and killing him instantly, then dragging his corpse several hundred feet under the car before Leon managed to bring it to a halt, meanwhile mutilating the body so badly that all that was left of it was the gruesome sight of a mangled bloody pulp.

Because of his contributions to the county sheriff's election campaign—made from selling moonshine, Leon had persuasive influence with the sheriff's office. As a result, in a shenanigan worked out with the sheriff, the black's death was unceremoniously dismissed as an accident.

The dolorous news of the black worker's death spread through the school immediately after the incident occurred, not only leaving me feeling horribly for the victim and his family—with whom I had worked, but prompting new and renewed terror within me. And Mama kept the terror going, for now she had a new gore story to fulfill her ongoing obsessive need to milk any horror tale to its limits, and beyond.

"That blame Leon," she began, "we all knowed that he'd do that sooner or later. Even if that young feller was black, he didn't deserve to die that way!" Then working herself into a frenzied tizzy, Mama proceeded on into the macabre details and agony of the black's death at Leon's hands.

A new nightmare, reactivating all the others. And with them my asthma attacks began to intensify. This, combined with another jolting incident, totally unraveled me.

Two days following the black man's death, while working with Red after school in a peanut field—I refused to set foot again in that cotton field near where the black worker was killed. Red, drinking moonshine, was weeding peanuts with a "weeder", a large metal gadget with teeth that yanked up weeds when pulled by a mule. I noticed that he had stopped oddly in the middle of the field, and for some reason appeared to be standing on top of the weeder in the soft, dry 80-degree air, his figure clearly outlined by the cooling sun lowering in the western sky. I approached closer to him then abruptly halted, jarred by the sight in front of me, stiffening my body as hard as a pine log.

Red was standing on top of the weeder and having sexual intercourse with the old female mule pulling it, grunting and screwing the mule like it was some bewitching whore he was falling in love with.

"Red, what are you *doing*?!" I yelled incredulously.

None too happy with my interruption, Red, in a petulant, drunken tone, yelled back. "Not a God dang thing, Donald! Go on! . . . Jist git out of here! . . . Mind yer own dang business!"

Startled, my face downcast, coloring with shame, I dropped the water jug I was carrying and ran all the way home, breathing heavily, confused somehow frightened, my emotions tumbling in debacle, incessantly worried about Red. Damn! Screwing a mule! What if someone else saw him? What if Mama had shown up?

That night I had a different type of nightmare. One in which Red was screwing every mule in the county, and getting caught by Mama. The dream startled me from my sleep, a harsh gasp escaping me, awakening me to the worst asthma attack yet, the precious air thinner than ever, contorting my face into the gasping wheezing of terrified panic, certain this was my end, I flung myself out of bed, unable to walk, becoming hysterical, desperately crawling over to the fireplace, poking around in it frantically for one of Daddy's cigarette butts. Finding one, I hastily lit it, instantly dragging the smoke into my wheezing lungs. It didn't help. Nothing did. I began quavering, fighting for my life, my body taut and glistening with perspiration, praying for the sun to come up. When it did my struggles to breathe weren't diminished, and staying alive with each breath became and immediate urgency, turning me into a gasping lunatic.

I missed the last two weeks of school, bedridden with the most severe, dehabilitating asthma attacks I had ever experienced, attacks carried over into and throughout summer—during which time Inez, at the age of 18, was married, moving out of the shack and leaving me envious that I couldn't go with her. It seemed impossible, but the attacks were more crippling and terrifying than the summer before, so disruptive that I was given Marilyn's bed and she was forced to sleep with Red or on the floor. I neither had the will nor the physical ability for even one fishing trip to Pea River or Pea River Swamp, so much did the asthma lay me out flat, though everyone was still convinced that I was faking my attacks, not realizing that I would have taken triple shifts in the fields any day if it would take away just one of my asthma attacks. Their severity was such that I had serious doubts as to whether I'd ever be able to set foot in school again.

When fall came, though, and school began, gasping and wheezing, I miraculously managed to make it back to Banks Junior High. But the first day in school I was all confused and upset. Because I had missed the last two weeks of the fourth grade, I didn't know whether or not I had been promoted on to the fifth. I didn't have my report card and it wasn't sent out in the mail. So unsure of which grade I was in, the fourth or the fifth, that first morning back to school I collapsed on a bench in the hallway, my inner perturbation breaking me down into wracking sobs.

Startled by seeing this, seeing my body convulsing uncontrollably, all my friends, including Lurlene, rushed over to where I was sitting, shaking in sobbing uncertainty.

"Donald—what's wrong?!" Lurlene frowned, her face ashen with alarm. "What's *wrong* with you?!"

"I don't know what grade I'm in!" I contemplated aloud, a sobbing, bewildered, frustrated, embarrassed whimper, my eyes brimming with tears.

Laying on me an amazed look of both relief and disbelief, Lurlene then began laughing, her laughter deep and honest. "Is that all that's *bothering* you?! You're in the fifth. As smart as you are, you know you're in the fifth."

I gazed up at her in question, my eyes a bit more eased. "Are you sure?" I sputtered, my voice shaking. Then my eyes misted over as I attempted to blink back the tears, encouraged by the warmth of her reassuring smile.

"Come on I'll show you." She soothed, taking me by the hand.

I drew in a deep breath, a wheezy gasping rattling sound as Lurlene led me to the fifth grade room and up to the teacher's desk, there asking the teacher to give me my report card. The teacher did. I gawked at it, my despair subtly shading into hope. Then my eyes became fixated on the notation indicating that I had been passed to the fifth grade. My first reaction was a smile. Quickly my smile went from winter to spring. Finally, unable to contain myself, I began laughing loudly, expressively, ecstatically, wanting to hug the teacher and caper about. The students in the room began laughing too, then began clapping their hands for me, vibrating the air with their merry sounds, knowing how upset I had been in the hallway and seeing how happy I was now.

Suddenly my wheezing and gasping disappeared.

From then on, in school, my asthma eased up. But at home it continued to be devastation.

On March 1, 1954, almost a month after I turned ten years old, Daddy obtained a sharecropping job for the coming season with Noah Williams, and we moved into the shack provided by him. Shack 10, the Noah Williams place, located one mile from Shack 9. Noah Williams was one of the few people with whom Daddy sharecropped that I liked. And he liked me. A tall lanky man in his early 40's, thick lips, long face full of life, he looked and acted like a clown, an animated cutup always joking and having fun, several times taking me with him to the cotton gin in Josie, on these trips noticing my gasping and wheezing. On one occasion, after my attacks became so sever I was unable to walk at home for about three weeks, Noah approached Daddy with an urgent reproach:

"If you don't take this boy to the doctor he's going to die!"

Put on the spot, this prompted Daddy to take me to a doctor in Brundidge. There I was given a shot providing me instant relief, and to breathe normally again felt absolutely wonderful. But the effects of the shot were only temporary, and soon my harsh breathing difficulties returned. I wanted to visit the doctor again for more shots but Daddy wouldn't hear of it. He couldn't afford it. Besides, he was still convinced that I was faking my attacks and didn't need the shots.

Thankfully, while at school, my asthma was much less severe. Along with Pea River and Pea River Swamp, school and reading were the only nurturing sources in my life. Those and Lurlene. Wonderful Lurlene. Her caring and peaceful softness added a new dimension to my life. We laughed together. We traded stories. We giggled at the same silly jokes. We wrote notes to one another and exchanged gifts. On Valentine's Day we buried one another in valentines, each of us giving the other 44 cards. In school we were together constantly, I longed and craved to be with her after school but that was an impossibility. The thought of her seeing where I lived, the miserable destitution of shack living, was unbearable, bringing a lump to my throat, the kind you can't swallow.

I attempted to keep home and school separate, but every now and then the two merged.

"Looks like your daddy would just farm instead of making that moonshine stuff!" I heard with embarrassment.

And there were snide comments from students about Mama running around with other men, and hearing these comments humiliated me. Everyone seemed to know about Mama. It finally dawned upon me that if everyone else knew, surely Daddy knew, causing my fears to deepen and darken. What I feared now was that during their fighting, while Mama was viciously attacking Daddy for his drinking, he would counter with Hubert. A time bomb waiting to go off, making me even more apprehensive than the fear of Daddy not knowing about Mama and Hubert but suddenly finding out about them. But during their fighting Daddy never threw Hubert up to Mama. He wasn't a jealous man and apparently he wasn't concerned about Mama's sexual indiscretions, taking them, like everything else, in easy stride.

To Daddy, life was too short to squander its joys with hassle. Too short to make an issue over something he could do little about anyway.

Daddy was never bothered with bed-wetting, asthma, or nightmares.

But I was, this torment increasing again as another summer approached. I hated to see summer come. Out of the haven of school, my major respite from all the hell at home, summer meant asthma attacks day and night, with no saving interruptions. And this summer was no exception, the attacks hitting me like the death plague, filling me again with fear and desperation, my gasping and wheezing making my facial skin feel dead and heavily waxed.

I'd resort to anything to diminish the attacks. I even tried repeating the Pea River Swamp passage aloud since from the day it popped into my mind things afterward seemed to go better for me for awhile. I needed things to go better now.

"Find the spring that controls your own Universe…Find the spring that controls your own Universe…"

While reiterating this sentence, for some reason I began concentrating on the swarm of houseflies that were always thick in the shacks, irritating pests worse than the mice running around over everything. To counter the flies, Fly Bait, pink pellets of poison, were sprinkled about the shack. The flies would eat it and die, dropping to the floor like rain drops, belly up, forming a massive, thick dark carpet of tiny black carcasses.

As usual, I was standing in the midst of these carcasses, sweating in the summer humidity, my eyes bulging as I gasped and wheezed while repeating the sentence, my breath rattling in what I was convinced was my throes of life, when I took my right bare toe and began squashing the dead flies on the floor. To my amazement, hearing each fly "pop" as I squashed it brought some small pleasure; a soothing, relaxing kind of sensation. Wanting the sensation to continue, I gleefully began squashing every dead fly on the floor until the bottom of my toe became one darkened glob of fly blood and guts. And more surprising, as I squashed the flies my breathing became easier.

I didn't know what was going on but I didn't care. What mattered was that squashing those dead flies lessened the strangulation of my asthma attacks, easing the attacks just enough so that my breathing wasn't such a frantic life and death desperation. From that point on I became the mad fly squasher, day and night squashing every dead fly I could lay my feet on, thus maintaining my sanity at home.

I wasn't the only one resorting to peculiar means to maintain sanity. Red was screwing mules; Mama was running around with Hubert—and others; and Daddy was a prankster of the first order.

One of Daddy's favorite practical jokes was betting a guest that he couldn't pick up an eating fork. The guest, certain that he could, would make the bet. Daddy would then leave the room for the kitchen where, grabbing a fork, he'd heat it burning hot out of sight of the guest, then pick the fork up with tongs and lay it on the kitchen table. Prancing back to the guest in the other room, a bounce to his steps indicating he was in good humor, Daddy would yell, "Okay, come in and pick it up!" His voice smiling with satisfaction.

The guest would come to the kitchen table, pick up the fork and, his eyes agonizing over the message of the hand nerves to his head, immediately drop it, shaking his hand and screaming in pain. This immediately broke Daddy up, the roar of his laughter seemingly making his eyes younger. "I told ya ya couldn't pick it up!"

But Daddy's most memorable practical joke, one I observed, was one he pulled that summer when we were living in Shack 10. He came across an old red cowhide, huge enough to cover his body, and early one evening, as dusk was falling, he took it and some moonshine with him to the bridge over a creek just below the shack. A dirt road crossed over the bridge, and the road was the route for about 15 black workers going to and from their work in the fields. As they were returning from work on this occasion, Daddy suddenly jumped out from under the bridge, looking frighteningly spooky covered in his red cowhide, and let out a long, terrifying, bloodcurdling scream:

"EeeeooooowwwwwAAAAARRRRGGGHHHAAWWWRRRR!"

Like cockroach vampires hit with the sudden death of light, the black workers immediately scattered in all directions, scrambling off the road and into the woods, horrified out of their wits. One heavyset woman, carrying a child on her hip, fled in such panic that she attempted leaping a barbed wire fence along the road, not making it, she and her child hitting flat on their faces, skinning themselves badly. But that didn't delay them for a second. Instantly picking herself and the child up off the ground, the woman scooted off into the woods as fast as the terrorized motion of her legs would move her, screaming in fractured syntax, certain that the bogeyman was after her.

Drunk, still cloaked by the cowhide, his spooky shape silhouetted against the brightness of the moon. Daddy was laughing so hard that it brought tears to his eyes, seizures of laughter shot through with an unhinged quality, drowning out the chorusing sounds of frogs and crickets, causing him to sway to and fro, barely managing to keep his balance.

"There's somethin' *real bad* down at the creek!" was the story that rumbled throughout the community. The black workers never again used that route over the bridge to come and go from the fields.

Fall came bringing the long summer of asthma attacks and fly squashing to a partial end. I was back in the haven of school, entering the sixth grade, happy again to be in an uplifting, sane environment. And especially happy to be around the soothing presence of Lurlene. Then came winter, rolling into spring, and in March of 1955, after had turned 11 years of age, we moved to Shack 11, the Garrett place, located two miles from Shack 10. By then I was excelling in the sixth grade, and school was improving in other respects. I was developing into a versatile baseball player, playing the positions of pitcher, shortstop, and outfielder all equally well, becoming a better hitter, all in spite of my puny, sickly physical frame. I was quick. Excellent eyes. And determined. What some may call true grit. And my relationship with Lurlene developed deeper, with much fond interaction and sharing between us. We became a noted and devoted couple at school, an ongoing mythology, her smiles warming the cockles of my heart. Still there was no touching and kissing between us. This Lurlene didn't understand. Many times the subtle stimulus of her eyes would gaze at me in a way saying she wanted to reach out and touch me and bring me close to her. And I certainly wanted to return such affection, but I didn't dare allow it. And each day at school's end it became tougher leaving Lurlene. I needed her warmth. There was none at home.

But one good thing at home during the spring was that my asthma attacks eased up every now and then, enough to occasionally allow me to go hunting or fishing on Sunday at Pea River Swamp—Saturdays and after school I spent in the fields, my asthma permitting. My favorite person to go hunting with at Shack 11 was Uncle Gussie, Daddy's youngest brother. Like Daddy, Uncle Gussie was a sharecropper. But unlike Daddy, he always seemed to have more material things, including a nicer place to live in and an automobile.

Shorter than Daddy at six foot, solid physique, oval face, black hair, Uncle Gussie had a nervous habit of sucking in spit through his teeth and making sucking clicking sounds out of the corners of his mouth. Fixated with his teeth, he constantly had a twig or blade of grass in his mouth picking at them. But this in no way diminished his skills as a hunter. Quite the contrary. Uncle Gus was a superb shot. He hunted with a single barrel twelve-gauge shotgun that looked so old and dilapidated that I was certain it would fall apart in his hands the very next time he fired it. But it never did. And when he flushed a quail and it took flight, it was the quail's last. Uncle Gussie never missed. No one could shoot quail like he.

When summer came my hunting trips with Uncle Gussie abruptly ended. I was now under the siege again of around-the-clock asthma attacks, becoming more crippling and frightening with each new summer. I was back to fly squashing. But now it didn't help. Wait! I forgot the sentence. The passage. Gads. I was becoming as superstitious and as ritualistic as Mama.

"Find the spring that controls your own Universe... Find the spring that controls your own Universe ..."

Expectantly, I began squashing other dead flies. Nothing! Not the slightest relief for my breathing. Quickly, in panic, I repeated the sentence again, then squashed more flies. Still nothing. But something happened that night.

While everyone in the family, with the exception of J.P., believed I was faking my asthma attacks, many outside the family knew I wasn't, and this began to garner a groundswell of sympathy for me. That evening, following my earlier foiled fly squashing effort, a man, Mr. Thompson, oddly dropped by our shack, bringing with him a strange-looking gadget having a rubber bulb attached to a clear plastic apparatus with a hole in it.

"I heard of your terrible asthma attacks." Mr. Thompson said to me benignly. "I had asthma myself and am only too willing to help anyone suffering from it." Then casting a disbelieving sideways glance at Mama and Daddy, he continued, "Only an asthma sufferer knows the awful desperation another sufferer goes through. To help you, you can have this apparatus and I'll see that you're supplied with its medication."

Mr. Thompson's little gadget was a Godsend. When I sprayed the medication into my mouth during an asthma attack, its extraordinary potency brought instant relief, and I let out a jubilant shriek, euphoric, my eyes sparkling and dancing. Miraculously, I could breathe normally and easily for long periods of time. I didn't know what the medication was, or whether it had any short or long term effects, but I didn't care. It was like a saving antidote to an impending coronary occlusion.

I couldn't believe it. My asthma attacks *were over*! As long as I had the medication. The magic. No more creeping around the shack at night struggling despondently to stay alive. No more frightening existence laid up in bed doubtful I could breathe my next breath. I was ecstatic, thankful, as though some new, serene, joyous celestial region had just been opened up to me, casting out the morbid darkness within.

That night I could sleep again. I dreamt of Mr. Thompson, his visit to me at the shack. But instead of his naturally saturnine appearance and the mirth of his craggy, gargoyle face, in the dream these features were transformed, first to skeletal cheeks and black-circled eyes, then to a coarse, humorless, brutal face; chalky, mean dark eyes in deep sockets. Then he only had one eye, and suddenly the face became a pinched deathly look, a lugubrious face with sunken jowls, a pointed hawk nose and rotten teeth, flies and gnats buzzing about the eye.

It was the face of Nat Mitchell. And he began laughing at me. And as he laughed the face transformed again, becoming that of the young man, his black marble eyes seeming to possess me. But unlike the other dreams, his features now were not as vague, suggesting an ageless face, seemingly eager and earnest, at other times not as noble, a majestic sweep of flesh on either side of an aquiline nose. Then the face wasn't that of the young man. It became the face of Daddy. Then Mama. Then Red. Hubert. Ralph. Then Nat Mitchell again. Then back to the face of the young man. He looked down at Mr. Thompson's breathing apparatus beside my bed and burst into that thundering, tormenting, mocking laughter.

I awakened in a suffocating sweat, gasping and wheezing, gulping at thin air. Frantically I reached for the rubber bulb of Mr. Thompson's gadget, immediately spraying the medication into my mouth. Instantly I felt relief, the gasping and wheezing gone, my breathing easy, normal.

The medication, as before, eliminated my suffocation. What was the young man laughing at? The dream didn't make sense. I sighed, unable to go back to sleep.

CHAPTER 13

M Y FLY SQUASHING didn't cease after control of my asthma attacks through use of Mr. Thompson's breathing gadget and medication. It simply brought me too much pleasure stomping to pieces those little black buggers to stop doing it, the sound of the "pop" each time I squashed a fly carcass becoming music to my ears. Music that soothed the savage beast within me, a beast mostly out of my awareness I knew not was growing, my only glimpse of it in my dreams.

I discovered that each time I smashed one of these dead flies with my bare toe it served as a release of my anger toward Mama. With each fly I squashed, I was squashing Mama. And with the conscious anger built up inside of me against her—the unconscious anger more terrifying, thus repressed I required plenty of squashing.

In March, 1956, after I had turned 12 years old, we moved into Shack 12, just below my Uncle Shell's house and three miles from Shack 11. One aspect I didn't like about Shack 12 was that, again, it was out of walking range of Pea River and Pea River Swamp, cutting off my treasured escapes there. Another was that unlike any of the other shacks we had lived in, Shack 12 looked weird and silly. Besides being the usual rundown, dilapidated shack eyesore, it had a pronounced round curvature to it rather than being rectangular shaped, a funny appearance, looking as odd as the fairy tale residence of the old woman who lived in the shoe. On the plus side, Shack 12 was the first shack where we had electricity.

In addition to dislike, Shack 12 became associated with more traumatic feelings. Grandma Oakes, who had brought me into this world, lived with Uncle Shell and, shortly after we moved into Shack 12, she died. At her funeral Daddy cried, the first time I had ever seen him sad and tearful. Seeing that, and seeing Grandma laid out stiff, a lifeless dead body, frightened me, exacerbating my fears, Daddy calmed me.

"No need frettin' over this, Donald. If she ain't in a dang better place than we are!"

Daddy's next sharecropping job was with his brother, Uncle Shell. A pleasant, mild-mannered, easygoing man with a square face and a little nook in the side of his nose. I wasn't as close to Uncle Shell as Uncle Gussie. But I was close to his wife, Aunt Lisa. A short round person, wearing her grayish-brown hair in a tight ball on the back of her head, Aunt Lisa, with her sad, droopy, round face, wasn't attractive physically, but she was attentive and kindhearted, a spirited person, her large brown eyes caring and wise-looking.

Unlike Mama, Aunt Lisa was positive and bubbly with life, bringing good cheer. I could talk easily with her and often we'd discuss Lurlene.

"I want to marry her badly," I confided in her, naked in my pain. I would never dare say that to Mama.

"Donald, sweetheart, I wish to the good Lord I could help you do that for I know deep in my heart what she means to you," Aunt Lisa said kindheartedly. "Maybe some day things will work out. I surely hope so."

Lurlene was the happiest, most miserable time of my young life. I daydreamed of marrying her, savoring how wonderful life would be with her, just the two of us. I was well aware that this was pure fantasy, with no chance of becoming reality. Lurlene was not only a decent girl, but one of the most decent. I didn't deserve her. Not even close. Besides that, it would be unconscionable to expose her to my family, my way of life; expose her to all its crazy idiocy and hell. Not a marvelous normal girl like Lurlene.

Marrying her would be the cruelest thing I could do to her.

But the specter of her finding out about my family and its way of living couldn't be hidden. During one of our discussions, Lurlene, to my horror, informed me that she was planning on spending the night at a girlfriend's house, which was located on my school bus route, and to get there she had to pass directly by Shack 12. The apprehension and worry drained my face, literally turning me sick at the idea of her seeing the weird-looking, dilapidated shambles that I lived in, that image becoming more disconcerting than the dread of my nightmares.

The night that Lurlene spent with her girlfriend, I had an appalling dream. The young man, his nose curving like an eagle's beak, darkly gleaming, matching the intense blackness of his eyes, had Lurlene and I trapped in Shack 12. She was filthy-looking, clothed in dirty rags and held in leg irons chained to the wall so she couldn't escape. And I was forcing her to squash dead flies with me. As she squashed, she began whimpering, then crying, then her big toe turned to blood and she screamed:

"Donald, you're a monster!… A monster! … A monster!"

The young man chuckled, then he was bellowing, a deep, unhinged, fiendish laughter. And I joined in his laughter, our roar becoming one. Then the young man's face became mine, and I had his eyes, two glaring discs of glistening ebony knifing at Lurlene. "Now *eat* those squashed flies! Lick them up with your tongue!"

I woke up terrified, drenched in sweat, becoming so sick with nausea and stomach cramps that I couldn't attend school. I couldn't face Lurlene. I couldn't face myself. By now, Lurlene finally knew of my horrid life-style. I could no longer look her in the eye, so mortified that she had seen the shack in which I lived.

Overnight I withdrew from her, becoming detached.

Lurlene couldn't understand it. "What's wrong with you?" She quizzed, cornering me in the school hallway. "What's bothering you?"

Feeling squalid, I forced a smile. "Nothing really, I'll be all right."

But I never was. Our interaction after that was never the same. She had seen where I lived—the home life that I had kept from her, though she never mentioned it. But she knew that I hadn't been honest with her. There was nothing left but to ease out of her life; ease away from her smiles and warmth, never giving that horrible dream a chance to come true.

I joined the gods of winter, and their cold froze me to the bone.

All I could think of after that was the wretched dream, forcing Lurlene to squash flies, her calling me a monster, the young man laughing at it all. Why was he in my dreams? Who was he? Where did he come from? He'd never say. He never said a word. He only laughed at me. And those black, shining, piercing eyes. Possessing me.

I retreated to my reading, some of it Shakespeare. In his 53rd sonnet, a passage jumped out at me:

> "What is your substance, where of are you made,
> That millions of strange shadows on you tend?
> Since every one hath, everyone, one shade,
> And you, but one, can every shadow lend."

The young man. A shadow. The Shadow. I gave him an identity. A name. The Shadow. My shadow. Always following me in my dreams.

CHAPTER 14

THE SUMMER OF 1956 was the first summer since I was four years old that I was spared the suffering of asthma attacks, meaning that my fly squashing was replaced by spending most of the summer in the fields, wearing myself out with cotton, corn and peanuts, and frustrating myself behind slow, obstinate farting mules, then returning exhausted to the weird-looking dump of Shack 12, my evenings there entertained by fighting, nightmares, bed-wetting, and the storm pit. Then when fall came and I entered the eighth grade, I had to write an essay on how I spent the summer. I lied.

School was both heaven and hell. The heaven was that I was back to my passion for reading. The hell was that I had to keep Lurlene at a distance. Then on my thirteenth birthday in February, 1957, calamity of the first magnitude struck. Daddy announced; "We're moving back to Bullock County."

My world was shattered. We were moving back to the Corinth School area. I would no longer be attending Banks Junior High. But Banks was my whole life. All my friends were there. I was doing excellent in my school work. I was established in basketball and baseball. And there was Lurlene. Even relating to her at a distance was better than relating to any other girl close up.

I was in shock. I didn't want to move to Bullock County. I didn't want to leave Banks Junior High. With a stricken expression, I pleaded with Daddy.

"Let me live with Uncle Shell and Aunt Lisa so I won't have to change schools."

Scratching his scrotum, Daddy said evenly. "No. We're movin' and yer comin' with us. That's it."

My heart froze, quietly allowing the anguish of Daddy's words to settle within me. There was nothing I could do to change his mind. Really, Mama's mind. To both, my school situation was insignificant, the two feeling I was fortunate to be attending any school.

My last day at Banks Junior High was nothing but sadness. All of my friends wanted me to keep in touch by letter, making certain I had their addresses. I couldn't leave without saying good-bye to Lurlene, and when I approached her we both had tears in our eyes, gazing at one another with wistful expressions.

"I'm going to miss you." Lurlene said in a quiet softness. She broke into a sob, losing her composure, grabbing me on the arm. I felt her tenseness, her moistened hand, and a sunken feeling hit in the pit of my stomach. I wanted to cry.

I choked, backing away, breaking her grasp. "I'm going to miss you too."

She drew in a deep breath. "At least write." Her voice came back thin and faint, shaking, only a shade beyond a whisper. "Keep in touch."

"I will."

My voice was dreary, and at that moment a dusky feeling of remembrance and gratitude swept over me; gratitude for her years of laughter, her smiles, her warmth, her caring, her touch of spring, her soft childlike innocence. Now all lost.

We fell silent, the stillness of the moment tightening its hold upon us. There were no further words that could pass through the tightness of our throats. For a long moment we contemplated each other, then we parted.

And then it hit me. The pain. A hurting, agonizing stab of pain. Then part of me inside died.

That evening the Shadow was back. In the dream we were at the bottom of a huge cavernous pit filled with rattle snakes. But instead of snake heads the snakes all had the heads of Mama. The Shadow handed me a sword and I began swinging it, slashing Mama's head off all the snakes. But with each head I severed, another replaced it. Then the heads became that of Lurlene and I dropped the sword.

"Get me out of here! Get me out of here!"

The Shadow began his horrid laughter. I awakened, bolting upright in bed, still screaming. "Get me out of here! Get me out of here!"

At the beginning of March we moved to Shack 13 in the Corinth community, located five miles from Shack 12. Daddy's new sharecropping job was with a landowner by the name of Pete Culpepper, and since he owned the shack it was known as the Pete Culpepper place.

My new school was Inverness High School. Withdrawn there, I never did fit in socially as I had at Banks, lacking the will to do so. And I never wrote Lurlene as I told her I would, sparing her further cruelty. But one thing remained the same at Inverness High. My eagerness to learn. I excelled in my school work. Also, I made the basketball team, though later I had to leave it. I had no transportation to facilitate being on the team and I wouldn't let anyone go out of their way to haul me around.

I didn't want anyone to see where I lived.

Summer came, and with my medication keeping me breathing, I was back working in the drudgery of the fields again—with only Sundays off, then returning home at night to be further clobbered by chaos. Also, living again in the Corinth community, with its easy availability of moonshine, I was back in the land of real drunks. There were simply too many of them for any one to be designated the "town" drunk. They were all town drunks. The question was: who was the champion town drunk? Even here there was no clear choice. But one, Em Kilpatrick, was clearly in line for a shot at the title.

A sharecropper, Em Kilpatrick had at one time worked in a sawmill until he caught his hand in a saw and nearly lost it, leaving him carrying around a "nub" for a hand. Aside from this, and aside from his little round pudgy nose, and the old brown khaki baseball type hat he always wore, and the fact that he was totally lost as a moonshine alcoholic, there was little to distinguish Em. At five-nine, medium build, 41 years old, his face was rather plain, one easily lost in a crowd.

But Em shied away from crowds, preferring instead to drink and drive, forever driving into some ditch while intoxicated on moonshine, hitting and grazing anything in his path. And while inebriated out of his senses, he'd frequently stop by the shack to see if Daddy had any moonshine. With the haggard look of a veteran alcoholic, a sloven in old tattered clothes, Em would stumble out of his car and stagger toward the shack with an unsteady motion, sometimes moving stiff and languid, as though he were walking on ice and unable to make it, many times falling.

On many Sundays, as I walked down the dirt road that passed Shack 13, Em would drive by me in his '46 Chevy Coupe, swerving in and out of the road's ditch to either side. While walking on the road this one Sunday, Em drove by me; then suddenly stopped his car in a series of jerks, so drunk in his habitual sorrowful state that his head was stooped over the steering wheel, long webs of slobber dripping from his mouth. Barely conscious, his chin visibly sagging, eyes puffy, he rolled his head slowly to one side, belched indignantly, and shot me an unfocused, bleary-eyed, red-faced stare, slurring unevenly in a whiskey voice, hoarse and raspy.

"Donaaaaaalld, I'm in… in real baaaaad shape." He belched again. "Co… could ya drive me over to… to Char… arrrrlieee Haaaaarrrdy's for me to git more whi… isky?"

More whisky was the last thing he needed. But I was more impressed by the exciting prospect of driving his car. "Yeah!" I said eagerly, my eyes a dilation of joy.

I ambled up and hopped into the Chevy, Em slouching over onto the passenger side in an alcoholic spasm. All excited, I sat behind the wheel, my first time at driving a car. I pressed on the gas pedal and the car jerked and lunged forward a few times. I knew nothing about using a clutch. But I learned quickly. Finally, getting the hang of it, the car's motion became smoother. Because it was my first time driving, I kept the car's speed down to a crawl. This didn't suit Em.

"Damn, Donaaald," he slurred from out of the vague air of his delirium, "give it some *gaaaaasssss!*"

I goosed the pedal and the car took off, the feel of its fast motion a new, exhilarating thrill—as free as the wind, where no one can touch you. I managed to make it to Charlie Hardy's house and waited in the car while Em bought some moonshine from Charlie, the two of them taking swigs of the shine as they talked outside. Then, more stunned, more disoriented, looking glassily about, Em staggered back to the car with a pint bottle stashed in his rear pocket.

By now, though, he had had it, lapsing into a deep drunken slumber once slouched back in the car. After more lunging and jerking, I controlled the car well enough to drive Em to his house, each foot of the way an euphoria of motion, the speed of the car ecstatic. Once to Em's house I exited the Chevy, leaving Em in it, passed out and gone to the world. Shaking from the excitement of driving, I walked the few miles back to our shack. But the nearer I came to home, the more my excitement waned, replaced by apprehension that Mama might find out what I had done.

Mama did find out. Two days later, shortly after I dragged myself exhausted in from working in the fields. Em staggered by the shack and rather idiotically bragged to Mama about my driving.

"Y'all should have seen Donald drivin' that car." Em blinked inanely, looking stupid and wishy-washy. "He did good."

Mama's eyes almost jumped from their sockets. "*What*?!" Her face was startled. Twisting it, she snapped. "Donald *drove* yer car?"

Em smiled vainly, I grimaced. "Yep. Good driver. Use him again. Ya folks should be proudful."

"Lord have mercy!" Mama looked on the edge of a faint. But recovering, she steadied her eyes on me, her face a rage of purple. Then she let loose at me with the painful cacophony of a conniption fit, screaming at the top of her lungs as she whisked me away and clobbered me severely with a switch.

Mama ordered Em never to come to the shack again, or anywhere close. My car racing days were over. For a while, anyway. But the feel of its thrill was embedded in me.

Fall came and I entered the ninth grade at Inverness High, excelling in my schoolwork but still detached in my school social activity, hanging around with only a few male friends. Then in February, 1958, just after I turned 14, Mama's daddy, Popper, died of cancer and his death sent Mama into a barrage of outpouring grief—awful screams, raspy and shrill, unhinged and uncontrollable, elevating my fear of death to outright terror. Less than a month later we moved into Shack 14, one mile from Shack 13, the Ezra Black place. Ezra Black, Daddy's new sharecropping partner for the upcoming season.

For several years something that had been nagging at me subliminally at first, then in conscious patches of haziness, then becoming more unsettling in its clarity, finally crystallized into certainty at Shack 14; Daddy wasn't the biological father of all his children; namely, Red and Inez.

J.P., Ruby Lee, Marilyn and I all had facial features resembling, in varying degrees, those of Mama and Daddy. J.P. looked just like Daddy. My features tended to be more like Mama's. Ruby Lee and Marilyn's were a recognizable mixture of the two. But Red and Inez? Neither one resembled Daddy in the slightest way. But more telling were the features they possessed rather than lacked. Both had red hair and deep freckles, and no one in our family, on either side, dating way back, had those features.

It had long bothered me that Red and Inez looked so different from the rest of us kids, and now I strongly suspected—really, I was convinced, that they were fathered by Hubert Singleton, the roving community gigolo. There were a lot of red-haired, freckle-faced kids running around, most of them probably Hubert's, and Mama was one of his breeders.

It was at Shack 14 that I fully recognized Mama for what she was. With all of her dervish, sanctimonious blustering dispensing fears as positive truths, devastating me for seeking to play with Shirley Jean's buttocks while passing hers around, what I recognized was that Mama was the biggest hypocrite of all, and I wanted away from her. I wanted out!

At the age of 14, at Shack 14, this resolve caused the complete division of my conscious mind against itself. One part of that mind was still the fixated small kid chained to his roots, still frightened and fearful of Mama, still quietly submissive to her mental brutality. The other part was the growing young man in me seeking liberation from that brutality, now ready to fight Mama. This division of my mind was a tugging in different directions. A tug of war between roots and horizons.

CHAPTER 15

J.P. HELPED FOSTER the growing young man in me more than anyone. At Shack 14, on his weekend visits, he helped me to organize a scrub baseball team playing other teams on Sunday. The players on the team ranged from ages 8 through 16, and we traveled up to 30 miles to play opponents, J.P. helping with the transportation. And J.P. continued to take me hunting and fishing at Pea River and Pea River Swamp, sometimes just the two of us, sometimes with Uncle Gussie along.

It was while with J.P. that the seeds of mutiny against Mama were laid. Helping to get me out of working in the fields one Saturday, J.P. and I journeyed to Union Springs to purchase shotgun shells. He was dressed in new clothes and so was I—a new shirt and a new pair of blue jeans Mama had just bought me. Driving back to the shack, J.P. said;

"I heard of a place near here that's loaded with fish. Let's check it out."

The place turned out to be a hole of water along Conecuh Creek, where a large concentration of fish had been stranded when the creek abruptly lowered its water level after a heavy rain. The fish were so crowded together, so hapless and helpless to escape, that we couldn't resist jumping in the water after them, new clothes and all.

When Mama saw how I had ruined my new jeans and shirt grappling after those fish, she exploded into one of her patented tizzies, her wrath far more than warranted by the deed. And I displayed resistance; an odd type of resistance protesting being one of her captive victims.

"Mama, I'm fourteen years old. Treat me as such."

"I'm yer Mama and I'll treat ya as I see fit. Now…"

I stomped out of the shack, the first time I had walked away from her while she was blistering me verbally.

Except for the time I spent hunting and fishing with J.P., and playing ball on our scrub baseball team—mostly on Sundays, my other time was spoken for; school during the day; work in the fields after school and on Saturdays; and work in the fields six days a week during the summer. Then the nights were spent captive in Mama's turmoil. The set pattern. The pattern the growing man wanted to get away from. The pattern the small fixated kid didn't know how to get away from.

Our stay in Shack 14 didn't last out the regular sharecropping season. Ezra Black, Daddy's sharecropping partner, hated moonshining, and when he caught Daddy plying this trade he terminated the partnership, asking Daddy to move out of his shack immediately. Being three quarters into the season, it wasn't easy for Daddy to find a new sharecropping job. But he did. With John Stuart, that cheating scoundrel uncle of mine—he even attempted to cheat Daddy the last time he sharecropped with him, but was caught in the act, intensifying my dislike for him.

So, to my chagrin, in the fall of 1959, when I was 15, we moved into one of John Stuart's terrible shacks. Shack 15, located one mile from Shack 14, below Mommer and Popper's old house. Also that fall I entered the tenth grade at Inverness. Though I was trying to keep my social activity there detached and low key, concentrating primarily on my school work, an event occurred throwing me into an unwanted limelight.

Red was caught having sex with a mule.

The news of his perversion spread like a tidal wave throughout the Corinth community, becoming a laughing tale at school. There I was ribbed mercilessly about it.

"Red in the weeder, dippin' his peter."

"I bet your brother would dip his peter in anything!" a male student chuckled at me with sarcasm. "Mule…cow … an old bitch in heat." he paused and laughed, making an odd face. "They should put Red in a circus. Darn. Donald, can you imagine fucking a mule?! How does Red hold one still long enough?" He laughed harder. "If we see any redheaded mules running around, we'll sure know who the daddy is!"

For a while I had to put up with this every day at Inverness High, over and over, the gossip concerning Red's unnatural sexual inclinations thick and heavy, me being the focal attention for the stinging barbs of students, always in my ears, a noise of mocking laughter in my head; a noise of giggling and maniacal sounds; a noise of wagging tongues invading the air with thunder.

Each time a student drew me out about Red and the mule, I smiled wanly, acting as though it didn't bother me, nonchalantly brushing it off, belying the fact that I wanted to punch the person in the nose. The gossip on Red ate me alive, churning my guts with agonizing embarrassment and humiliation, leaving me feeling the laughing stock of Inverness High. Leaving me with sleepless nights. And when I slept, nightmares, all introduced by the Shadow's laughter.

Our stay in Shack 16 lasted only six months. In March of 1960, when I was 16, the family moved to Shack 16, Mommer and Popper's old house, right up the road from Shack 15. Since Popper had died, Mommer had moved to Phenix City to live with one of Mama's sisters, Aunt Vernie, and the house was vacant.

Of all the shacks we lived in. Shack 16 was by far the best one. Aging with gray color, it was bigger, more spacious and built better than any of the other shacks that had been our home. With no cracks in the walls or floors, it was imbued with a certain warmth noticeably lacking in the other shacks. And Shack 16 had four rooms rather than three—two bedrooms, a family room and a kitchen, and a large hallway. Outside there was a big porch with a swing, an outside well nearby, and the house was surrounded by the shade of several large oak and fruit trees. Compared to the other shacks we had lived in, Shack 16 was paradise.

But the paradise ended with the shack's appearance and surroundings, for it was in Shack 16 that terror accelerated to a new, frightening dimension.

We had moved there shortly after Red was caught screwing the mule, and my social life at Inverness High was still a disaster because of it. The embarrassment and humiliation wouldn't go away. Red's perverted *faux pas* still making my nights at home a string of sleepless fits, nightmares and sick thudding headaches.

On a day in late March, after an arduous time in the field following school, I returned home unusually exhausted. After a quick supper I went straight to bed. Then it hit me, overcoming every nerve and fiber in my body, the strangest and most petrifying feeling I had ever experienced. My ears began ringing and I sensed the room closing in on me, jumping my heart into my throat, clamping my jaws together, my mouth suddenly dry and sour. Then I couldn't move. My body was totally paralyzed. A spark of fear, like the hissing of water when it meets its boiling point, pierced through me, claiming every ounce of my being.

This *is it*! I thought. I'm *dying!* This time really dying. But I wanted no part of dying. No part of Daddy's burning in hell! Death and hell were more terrifying than the horror of living. But now death was overtaking me, the imminence of fire and hell, and the rush of panic invaded me, pushing through every inch of my body.

Literally paralyzed with fear, my ears ringing louder, the room closing in tighter, strangling on the acid-etched screams that couldn't get out, my panic mustered every ounce of adrenaline to break out of my paralysis. But it was like breaking out of mummification in a cement block. I struggled and struggled, and kept on struggling, but still I couldn't move.

Oh. God! *I'm dead!*

But as long as I had living consciousness, as long as I wasn't yet consumed by fire, I kept on struggling. Then miraculously, slowly, in muted grunts of terror beyond terror, I could move my fingertips. Then my fingers and toes. Then my hands and feet. Then my legs.

Finally I had enough movement to stumble out of bed. I staggered into the family room, pinched and wan and shadowed a look of deathbed shock.

"Mama!... Mama!... *Help me*!... I think I'm *dying!*"

"Lord have mercy! What next with ya youngins?"

Mama quickly dispatched Red to get Aunt Pearl Stuart, who rushed me to the emergency room at the hospital in Troy. After an extensive medical examination, the doctor informed Mama; "There's not a thing physically wrong with him. It's nerves!"

"*Nerves?*" Mama's mouth dropped. "Lord have mercy! That's all we need fer people to know about!"

I had undergone a severe anxiety attack. There would be more. But the ensuing attacks I suffered out, toughed out, in silence, not wanting to admit that I had "bad nerves." That was as bad as Red screwing mules. In those days, in the shack communities, people frowned upon anyone having "nerve" problems. It was expected of you to be strong, overcoming your nerves on your own, so there was no way I, or the family, was going to acknowledge such a disgraceful malady.

Strangely, when my anxiety attacks began, my bed-wetting stopped, as though one replaced the other. I much preferred the bed-wetting.

That night of my first anxiety attack, my great uncle, Charlie Dease, died, and following that, each time I had another attack, fear encased me like a tomb of iron, terrifying me with the dread that someone else in the family had died, fueling my anxiety more. For days after every anxiety attack I became apprehensive, tense and frightened, dreading to hear of the horrible news as to who in our family had died.

Summer came and I was back to the toil of the fields full time, my "closet" anxiety attacks continuing, adding to the other turmoil and torment at home. And summer brought with it another painful agony of a physical kind. I began having monstrous toothaches, but Mama couldn't afford to take me to a dentist. On two summer occasions these toothaches became so horribly painful that, out of desperation, I hastened into our barn, found some rusty nails, and used them to pry and gouge the decayed tooth out of my gums—piece by piece. The pain was excruciating, blood gushing out of my mouth, tears gushing from my eyes, but I was determined to rid myself of the decayed tooth. Afterwards, my jaw became badly swollen, protruding out to the size of a baseball; and my gums became infected with painful abscesses.

Then, when school began in the fall, once more a small measure of hell was brought on by Red. This time he was caught peeping in a window at several scantily clad young females at a party and that news spread all over school as if it had been delivered special delivery.

"Hey, Donald, what's your brother up to? Trying to make the mules jealous?! Or can't he make up his mind what he wants to screw? Hey. I got this horny horse…"

More humiliation. More shame. More disgrace.

Going to school now became anxious, tense and discouraging. I no longer had the grit to face the other students; to hear their teasing and jokes and stinging sarcasm and snide remarks regarding Red; to act nonchalantly in the face of their snickering bombardment. I shut out all social contact at school.

And at home I had to hear Mama verbally massacre Red, yelling and screaming at him about his "peeping" in much the same way as she had massacred me over the Shirley Jean note. It only deepened my shame for myself and for the entire family. And it intensified my anxiety attacks. My sleepless nights. My poor concentration at school.

It ripped my nerves apart, emotionally tearing me asunder. Shakespeare's 24th sonnet came to haunt me, describing me perfectly:

> "When in disgrace with fortune and men's eyes,
> I all alone be weep my outcast state,
> And trouble deaf heaven with my bootless cries,
> And look upon myself and curse my fate."

But cursing my fate with family members didn't stop. After I turned 17, disgrace of another variety developed. With six kids, Franklin and Ruby Lee ended their marriage in divorce, Ruby Lee pushed over the limit by Franklin's increasing boozing and womanizing.

After placing her three oldest children with J.P. to live, Ruby Lee obtained a job in the cotton mill in Phenix City, then went on a lascivious tear of her own, bringing her in bad odor with the welfare department which threatened to take her three youngest kids away from her. This was prevented only when Ruby Lee agreed to leave Phenix City and move herself and three youngest children in with us. We didn't have the food nor the space at the shack to accommodate them, but Mama and Daddy had no choice but to take them in, compounding the shack misery with overly cramped quarters and severe food rationing. And our forced trips to the storm pit became even more complicated with all of those additional bodies. In the pit, Glenda, Ruby Lee's youngest daughter, was forever bawling and constantly messing her pants, adding more havoc to an already chaotic situation.

One night while we were all in the storm pit, feeling an anxiety attack coming on, I could no longer abide Glenda's hysterical screaming and messy stink and became so uncorked that I shoved her head into a five-gallon bucket to shut her up. The top of her nose caught the edge of the bucket and began to bleed profusely. But the angered reaction warded off my anxiety attack.

"Mama. Glenda fell and hurt herself!" I yelled in the dark dampness. "Badly! Her nose is bleeding!"

"Lord have mercy!" Mama screeched, momentarily diverted from her ranting and raving at Daddy.

My hurtful reaction toward Glenda was totally out of character for me, an unheeded hint, as were some of my dreams, of a monster brewing outside of my awareness; taking firm root in my unconsciousness.

For a while after she moved in, Ruby Lee, at Mama's insistence, refrained from pursuing her Phenix City habit of going out and carousing at night, seeking rowdy fun. But then she became just too restless and itchy for romantic action.

"Mama, I jest gotta git outta here! Go dancin'. Or somethin'!"

"Yer on probation." Mama reminded. "Them folks at the welfare place are still watchin' ya. This is no time for foolishness. Lord have mercy! Ya youngins are gonna be the death of me!"

After weeks of this Ruby Lee could take it no longer, her urge for renewed plucking just too great. Totally ignoring Mama's raving opposition, men began picking Ruby Lee up at the shack and keeping her out to all hours. Word of her promiscuity got around and the welfare department took her three youngsters away from her and put them up for adoption.

More disgrace. More humiliation. More shame. More nightmares. More anxiety attacks. More sleepless nights.

Just before completing the eleventh grade at Inverness, word was announced that Inverness High School would not be operational the following year but instead would be consolidated with the high school in Union Springs. That fall of 1961 Daddy's difficulties with moonshining forced the family to move back to the Josie area, into Shack 17—a more familiar rundown, dilapidated place, situated four miles from Shack 16. Because of the location of Shack 17, I had my choice of beginning my senior year either at Union Springs—thus being with the students I had attended school with at Inverness—or at Brundidge High School, where I'd rejoin my old Banks Junior High classmates.

My humiliation, shame, embarrassment and disgrace associated with my classmates at Inverness caused me to decide against going to school in Union Springs. Brundidge was my choice. But once enrolled in that school I immediately discovered that attending Brundidge was a colossal mistake. All of my old friends had changed. Everyone had their own cars and were dating. I was the oddball. I neither had a car, nor was I dating. The social gap between me and my friends existing now, compared to when I had attended Banks, had expanded unbelievably. More so than when I left, I felt unworthy to be with them.

And seeing Lurlene again made matters no better. She had developed into a fine young woman—her breasts more full, her hair more shiny, her lithe figure mesmerizing. Upon first seeing me again her eyes danced and sparkled, and I was still touched by her underlying goodness. She wanted to become friends again but there was no way I'd bring such cruelty upon her. So I ignored her. Ignored her when I desperately craved her warmth and caring. And it tore me apart all over again.

At Shack 17 everything was going bad that could go bad-exhaustion in the fields, fighting at home, nightmares, anxiety attacks, the storm pit, sleepless nights. The agony of my unhappiness seemed endless, particularly at school, my once great haven now collapsed into a prison of pain by my own tormenting reality— and my prohibitive desires for Lurlene.

One day at school, after only three weeks in the twelfth grade at Brundidge, I simply reached my limit of misery. The growing man in me finally took charge. I realized that I didn't fit in at Brundidge. I didn't fit in at the shack with Mama. I had to get out of both places or I'd be totally and irreversibly destroyed.

That evening, a cool night in September, was finally the showdown with Mama. The decisive moment of reckoning. Her or me. The string had run out. The one thing I had learned from Ruby Lee staying with us in Shack 16 was that Mama could be backed down when confronted with determination and forcefulness of will, as Ruby Lee had backed her down in getting her way to carouse.

Taking my cue from Ruby Lee, I approached Mama determined and forceful. "Rumor has it that Brundidge might close before school is out," I lied to Mama, a tight voice, "and I don't want to chance not graduating. I think it best if I live with J.P. and finish school in Phenix City."

Mama quickly drew her brows together and looked at me in question. A scorching look. Then she recoiled. "Ya can't *leave home* like that!" Her voice growled in querulous objection, embedded in crackles and beeps. "Ya know better. Quit *talking* nonsense!" Her resolve was as determined and as forceful as mine.

For an instant her force battered me back down to the small, fixated child afraid of her. I knew that in the next instant if I didn't recover all would be lost.

"Find the spring that controls your own Universe."

"Huh?" Mama looked at me flabbergasted. "What kind of fool nonsense talk is that?"

Her dictatorial tone failed in its effect on me. Instead a spring was released that neither Mama nor I anticipated. Before she could say another word I countered with the force of a bow suddenly released. "Mama, I'm *going*! This is something I've got *to do*! No matter *what* you say!"

In that moment a strange, instinctual savvy beyond definition jarred Mama, then altered her. Suddenly her face became pale and drawn, uncharacteristically subdued, startled by my formidable demeanor, looking at me coolly and appraisingly, perceiving in me something she had never seen before; a man. A determined, forceful man not to be denied.

"Ya know if ya do that I'll worry myself sick about ya," she said, more a whimper, dim shadows dulling her eyes as control was yanked from her. She was no longer Captain Bligh. No longer the abusive tyrant. She was more confused, more hurt than angry.

"I can't help that. *I'm going*!"

Mama acquiesced.

Later that evening I had difficulty falling asleep. When I did I had an unnerving dream. I was in the dining room of a spectacular palace, sitting at a long elegant table with silver trays bursting with drink and food. I was at one end of the table and across from me was Lurlene; and in all of the other chairs were my acquaintances from Brundidge High. At the head of the table was the Shadow, in a festive mood, splendidly attired in majestic robes of bright colors, his face appearing serene and noble, his ebony eyes subdued.

It was a going away party. For me.

Lifting a goblet of drink, the Shadow nodded at me in salute, as if to say. "Touché." The others around the table saluted in kind.

The festivity suddenly ended, the Shadow's eyes becoming that intense, shining, black, jeering glare. Then his face changed to that of Nat Mitchell, and Nat began laughing loudly at me in contemptuous, fried-in-hash-oil mimicry. Lurlene was no longer there, but replaced in her chair by Mama. And all my other Brundidge acquaintances were gone, replaced by Red, Inez, Ruby Lee, William Stuart, John Stuart and other relatives. We were now in the shack, sitting on the creaky floor full of holes, everyone dressed in ragged clothes, laughing at me mockingly, shouting:

"You'll be back! You'll be back!"

I woke up from the dream screaming. "I won't be back! I can't be back!"

CHAPTER 16

THREE DAYS LATER, on a Sunday, I left Shack 17 with J.P. heading for Phenix City, about as prepared to venture out into the larger world as an earthworm was prepared to survive in the Sahara Desert. Daddy, well aware of this, said to me in parting, "Donald, ya know nothin' 'bout the life yer goin' to outside. Shouldn't be in such a dern hurry to git thar. Don't make no difference, anyway. Here or thar."

He was standing on the porch, seeing me off with the rest of the family. Red expressionless and indifferent. Mama resigned. Marilyn was the only one who cried, her long brown hair stringy about her face, round and pudgy, her flat nose sniffing gently at first, then breaking into wracking sobs. She was unhappy and fat, her belly protruding out as if she were pregnant. But the family's reaction didn't matter. I was so excited to be leaving, in such a hurry to get away, that I absently took only a few of my belongings.

The next day I was in my new school in Phenix City, Central High School, a large, sprawling red brick complex with endless windows, twice as large as Brundidge and about five times the size of Inverness High, its students a mixture of offspring from cotton mill workers and the well-to-do. I was neither, and when classes began that day I was in the principal's office thinking about it while waiting for my class assignments. Overly self-conscious about my puny size and my inappropriate clothes—an old pair of jeans and a tattered shirt, I was actually thinking about much more. What was going to happen to me? Did I really belong here? Was I ever going to be at ease? Was I ever going to be normal? The truth be known, I was an emotional wreck!

While sitting there in this emotional daze, into the office walked this short student, my age, about 130 lbs., his face a funny oblong shape with a long nose, his hair combed straight out over his forehead like a bill on a cap, his overall appearance that of some goofy-looking creature straight out of a freak sideshow.

Catching me staring in disbelief at his hair, a mischievous grin now raking his face, the student said to me in sort of a lackadaisical, punky attitude, "What kind of trouble are you in?"

"None. I'm new here. I'm getting my room assignment."

"New, uh. What's your name?"

"Donald Oakes."

"I'm Floyd Lester. Where are you from?"

"South of here. Down around Troy. What are you doing here?"

"Trouble again."

Finally receiving my room assignment, along with a heavy load of books, I headed for my first class. Upon entering my assigned room I found it already filled with students, seemingly a sea of stoic faces, uptight faces, all eyes upon me. Apprehensive and on edge, definitely feeling out of my element in a big city school, I could almost read the codicil in their minds; What a weirdo the way he's dressed. What's he doing here? What God forsaken place did he come from?

The only empty desk was in the first row at the front of the room. I moseyed over to the desk, my movements stiff and self-conscious, betraying my inner perturbation, and set my heap of books on the very front edge of the desk top, intending to walk around and sit. But as I began that motion, the weight of the books tipped the desk over, the desk hitting the floor with a loud shattering crash, hurling the books in every which direction across the floor.

God, what am I doing here?

Immediately the uptight demeanor on the sea of faces disappeared, breaking the stoic ice, and several of the students rose from their seats and helped me pick up my books. Then setting my desk upright I sat down and my first day of big city, big world school began.

J.P. and his wife Doris—a pleasant woman, pretty face, dark brown hair, big bosom—were childhood sweethearts and had married young. They were a pleasure to be around and lived in a modern, well built, comfortable eight room single-story white house in the southwest part of Phenix City. Compared to the shacks I had lived in, living there was living in that spectacular palace in my last dream with the Shadow. With stylish modern furniture, indoor plumbing, electricity, a TV set, my own room and a maid, I felt I was the Sultan of Baghdad. But it took some getting use to, as much as required of a tribesman from the bush suddenly thrust for the first time into the glitter and complexity of modern life. But I was thrilled, especially being around J.P. and Doris, talking with them in normal conversation, going with them to the movies, going fishing with J.P., playing baseball with him.

What required getting use to the most, though, was that J.P.'s home was such a peaceful, relaxed, quiet environment. No moonshine. No exhaustion in the fields. No Hubert. No fighting. No storm pit. No nightmares. No Shadow. No anxiety attacks. No chaos. No torture. No torment. No embarrassment. No humiliation. No disgrace. And amazingly, no more asthmatic problems—even without the use of Mr. Thompson's medicine and gadget breathing machine.

Ultimate paradise!

But one aspect of J.P.'s living did present me with an awkward problem. He and Doris both worked the third shift at the cotton mill, leaving me alone in the evenings. Alone except for the black maid, Gloria. A single woman in her 20s, attractive, good figure, she had an eye for me that couldn't be mistaken. She made it a point to pull her dress up above her knees whenever we were alone in the house together, reinforcing this flirtation with a grin, inviting and seductive, an almost fixed expression of lust. Then her crooked grin would widen, asking me to make my move on her. But I ignored her sexual advances, keeping my distance.

J.P.'s peaceful environment gave me new thrust in school. Not only did I establish myself as a superior student in the classroom, but most of the students became friendly with me, accepting me with the warmth and reassuring jostle of comradeship. Then once I was settled in school, I returned to Shack 17 to pick up the remainder of my clothes, hitching a ride there with an acquaintance visiting his family in my area and returning to Phenix City after a short stay.

When I arrived at the shack I was surprised to find Daddy there alone and the place brimming with cigarette stubs.

"Where is everyone?" I asked.

Daddy took a deep breath, rather reluctant to answer. For a moment I saw lines edging his eyes that had never been there before. "Thar down at Troy in the hospital," he said in a colorless voice. "Marilyn jest had a baby."

Marilyn wasn't married. "Who's is it?" I grimaced.

"That Andrews boy."

He was quite older than Marilyn, another Hubert on the loose, the cycle of the legacy continuing. "That beats it all!"

More shame. Wouldn't it ever end? I was so upset that I couldn't continue the conversation, too emotionally ravaged, retreating into the woods to collect myself, wanting to return to Phenix City as quickly as possible. I wasn't able to endure any more disgrace within the family. And after that I couldn't bring myself to speak to Marilyn.

One of the senior students at Central High with whom I became friends was a tall, handsome, dark complexioned kid by the name of David Grissett. We had that natural affinity of the same mischievous spirit, as did I and his tenth grade brother, Ricky. The two lived with their mother and had access to her car, often our transportation to pool rooms and the drive-in theater. The excitement of the drive-in theater was to sneak into it. Ricky and I hid in the trunk of the car, then David drove in, paying only admission for himself. But then, becoming suspicious, the drive-in attendant searched the trunk one night, nabbed us, and that gig was up. But undaunted, we switched tactics, sneaking into the theater by crawling under the fence to the far side of the screen. We would have been much better off trying the trunk again for on our very first attempt we were practically pounced on by two fierce-looking German Shepherd guard dogs, putting to full use our adrenalin and forcing us into a blind running retreat taking us over a ten foot drop off we didn't see except for the hard way—after we fell to its bottom with bone jarring impact.

That ended our sneaking in, but not our other mischievous adventures together.

Floyd Lester, the freaky-looking kid I met in the principal's office my first day at Central High, lived not too far from J.P.'s house, and we also became friends, sharing adventures of another kind. Though Floyd seemed constantly in trouble at school, and with the police—he stole hubcaps and anything else not nailed down, around me he was restrained and mellow, never getting out of line, never stealing anything, never the bad-boy prankster.

Except with women.

One evening, early, before J.P. and Doris left for work, I invited Floyd over to the house. We wandered into the kitchen where the maid, Gloria, was bustling about and Floyd sized her up quickly. A blunt person coming to the point with the animated style of a car salesman, Floyd said to Gloria:

"If I come back after they go to work tonight, will you give us some?"

As if she thought he'd never ask, she smiled happily, exclaiming, "Yeah, I sure will!" Floyd's goofy rebellious edge, seemed to give him an androgynous appeal to women.

Floyd left and returned later after J.P. and Doris had gone to work, and we took Gloria to my bedroom. Since Floyd set this up, I went along, having no problem with this since, by my standards, Gloria was far from a decent girl. Floyd had the first stab at her while I waited in the living room, watching TV. When he had finished with Gloria, and it was my turn, Floyd tossed me a condom, grinning, "Here, use this."

Taking the condom, I felt nervous and scared. This was my first adult sexual encounter, one I wouldn't have initiated on my own. Walking into my bedroom, I found Gloria waiting for me on my bed, naked, smiling, motioning for me to come over to her.

"Floyd warmed me up for ya," she purred.

A bit startled, I moved over to the bed, my penis becoming incipiently erect at seeing her smooth firm body, a dark sleek nakedness of flat stomach and strong breasts aimed perkily at me. Taking the condom from my hand, Gloria eagerly slid it over my phallus, then laid back and spread her legs, revealing the inviting wetness of her crotch. Immediately I was in her, warm and exciting as she moaned and writhed to the squishy-squashy noises of our motion. But I ejaculated quickly, my enjoyment bushwhacked, instantly transforming to a sordid shame. The feeling was beyond my control. I jumped up off of Gloria, wanting to flee the room. But Gloria yanked me back down on top of her.

"No, don'tcha go just yet," she whined sulkily, dull confusion in her face. "Stay with me!"

I laid there limply, feeling her body pressed hard against mine, positioning my mouth into the deep ebony cleavage between her breasts as she emitted loud sighing groans, her hand adroitly fingering my flaccid penis. I grew taut, my face becoming like stone, expecting Mama to scream at me at any moment. Suddenly I felt closed in and claustrophobic.

"I've got to go!" I cried, raising up off of her, clench-jawed, my words tumbling out quickly. "I've got to!"

"You're one strange boy!" Gloria frowned as I sprung up from her, then stood by the bed, hastily rolling the condom off my penis, my knees about to buckle.

Once the rubber was off, I gawked at its content of sperm and my face hung slack, and I felt weak, chilled, a dreadful feeling overtaking me. Ignoring Gloria's complaining, I scuttled out of the room, my face becoming more drawn and pale as a more pressing worry assaulted me:

What if J.P. and Doris find out what we've done?

Then later, after Floyd had left, when I returned to my room, I couldn't find the used condom.

Where's the rubber? Where's the damn rubber? I couldn't find it. It had disappeared. My thoughts took a brooding turn. My God, what if J.P. or Doris find it?

For months I searched for that used condom, never finding it, all the while tense and fearful that J.P. or Doris would. Each time J.P. spoke to me, I jumped, thinking; This is it! The rubber! Seeing me looking a bit green, J.P. would ask, "Why are you so dang edgy?!"

"No… nothing!… Nothing!… No, nothing!"

"Relax, Mama can't get you here."

But she could.

Gloria wanted a repeat performance from me each time we were alone in the house, but I steadfastly refused. And I never invited Floyd back.

But away from the house Floyd and I still ran thick together. Floyd seemed to be loaded with girlfriends, particularly in the 35 to 40 range, and sometimes he'd let me meet them. One quiet evening the two of us were out joy riding in his father's '58 Mercury when Floyd said to me:

"I'm going to stop by and see if Cynthia wants to go for a ride."

Shortly Floyd parked the car in front of a nice two-story house. Going in, he soon returned with an attractive brown-haired woman in her late 30s with a slim figure and big bosom. She slid in the front seat between Floyd and me, and as Floyd put the car in motion the woman looked at me very bubbly and said, "Hey, you're kinda cute. Where'd you come from? What's your name?"

"Donald Oakes," I said, embarrassed. I thought she was kidding about the "cute," making fun of me.

"I'm Cynthia. Glad to meet you."

Floyd eventually parked the car at the end of a dead end street. Then surprisingly, he said to me. "I'm going to be first, so take a short walk while I thrill her!"

I exited the car and walked a few feet away, marking time in the air's stillness and feeling my heart thump like a tom-tom. About ten minutes later Floyd was out of the car, zipping up his pants, a mischievous grin on his face. "Okay, Donald, it's your turn now." He giggled in that silly way of his, as goofy sounding as he looked—swarthy and cherubic, suggesting a baby sunk in dissipation.

"Are you sure that…" I hesitated, flustered and red-faced. And a bit scared.

"C'mon. C'mon. It's okay with Cynthia. She likes you!

You shared Gloria, I'm sharing her. What are friends for if they can't pass around a piece of ass?" He let out a loud snigger.

Cynthia was far from a decent girl. "Okay."

I climbed in the back seat of the Mercury where Cynthia was waiting, lying on her back, her dress pulled up above her waist, her panties on the floor, her hair mussed up, looking as though it had been beaten by a pastry chef, the hairs of her pubic triangle clearly visible in the still light of the night.

"Come here, you cute thing, you!" Cynthia emoted, excited, lively, ready, reaching her hands up to me, her eyes dark and glowing wildly in the moonlight caressing through the car windows. Excited, frightened, I was on her, then in her, into the juiciness of her warm squirming moistness. She pressed inward, harder. "Ooooohhhhh!...OOOOOOHHHHHH!! You're so big! Soooooo *big*!... OOOOOOOOOOHHHHHHHHHHHH!"

As soon as I ejaculated I was overpowered again by that vile feeling of shame. I tried to dispel it but it was no use. But this time I had better control of my anxiety. I didn't get up and run, though I wanted to. Instead I trembled, sighing in self-reproach.

"Cutie, you can come see me *any* time!" Cynthia sing--songed, sighing deeply.

But I never did. I was through with sex for a while, fearful lest the shame suffocate me again. Its aftereffects were too devastating. Too anxiety producing. Even with indecent girls. Escaping Mama was far more complex and far less tangible than I imagined, involving something much deeper and more undefined than distance.

In June of 1962, at the age of 18, I graduated, the only member of my family to graduate from high school, or even come close to it. A time of pride and excitement. Celebrated accomplishment. But I could only share this celebration with my classmates—and with J.P. and Doris. No one else in the family cared, already regarding me as overly educated.

Once the celebration died down, I began looking for a job. The cotton mill had no openings, and because I was a prime candidate to be drafted for the Vietnam war, no other employer would hire me. Then, after two months of fruitless job searching, J.P. informed me that there was finally an opening at the cotton mill and, through his efforts, I was as good as hired. I obtained the job, but to my dismay it was worse than working in the fields. The cotton mill was a slave camp.

My work task there was to haul spools of thread, in a huge buggy, to the weavers, who in turn put them in their looms. My job required that I service several dozen looms, and it was a hectic, tiring pace keeping up with them, the timing hectic, unloading the spools of thread from the buggy into the weavers boxes fast enough to keep on schedule. This never left me with a relaxing breath. I was continually hauling, running, unloading. And inside, the cotton mill was filthy, hot, noisy and muggy.

For such pressurized slavery I cleared $39.75 a week.

That wasn't for me. It wasn't the horizon I had strived so hard toward in school.

After three months at the cotton mill, I quit. Time for the boy from the sticks to set out on his real rite of passage.

CHAPTER 17

I WAS RIPER than ever for the draft, so seeking a decent job was pointless. Among the fellows of my age, the major topic of conversation was not jobs but the likely prospect of being drafted into the Army.

"Joining the Air Force beats being drafted into the Army," was the word on everyone's lips. "At least there you have a choice in your area of training."

I agreed. I wasn't going to sit around and wait for the Army to come and drag me off, even though I had mixed feelings about joining the Air Force. What's it like? Did I have what it takes? Could I survive? Whatever my questions, I assured myself, the Air Force should be happy to get me.

There was no Air Force recruiting office in Phenix City, but there was one across the Chattahoochee River in Columbus, Georgia. On December 23. 1962, I traveled over there. Before joining, I was required to take a series of tests, returning on December 29 for the results.

"You did excellent on your tests," the Air Force recruiter advised me, a clear-eyed, spit-polished airman in his 30s, one who would look good on posters. His eyes darted back and forth between the documents in front of him. "The results show you fit best in the General category."

I was pleased. "I'd like to wait until after the holidays to join."

The recruiter furrowed his brows. Then clearing his throat, he said curtly, "Look, can I give you a tip?"

"Sure."

"To beat the Army draft, everyone will be joining after the first of the year, and when that happens it will be tough getting a choice assignment." Pausing, the recruiter clicked his tongue sympathetically, then continued, as if launching into a speech he'd been rehearsing. "On the other hand, if you join before January first, you'll have your pick of the choice assignments. There'll be far less competition for them from only a handful of recruits. So why wait and lose the assignment you want?"

"Okay, I'll join now," I said without hesitation. "I want a good assignment."

The recruiter smiled unctuously. "Good! "We're sending you tomorrow to Atlanta for your physical. Pack your bag."

Not a grand rite of passage, but it beat the Army.

With no asthmatic problems showing up, I passed my physical in Atlanta, and on December 31, New Year's Eve, I landed at the San Antonio Airport around 10 o'clock P.M. aboard a chartered Braniff Airlines jet crammed with Air Force recruits, pondering; This is a handful? At about the same time several other chartered jets, equally as crammed with recruits, were landing at the airport, a long line of buses waiting to take them to the Lackland Air Force Base about thirty miles away.

Instead of only a handful of recruits, there were close to two thousand of them. Grimacing at the unloading mass of bodies, a horde of confusion, I was reminded of a swarm of bees forcing its way into the wrong hive, and reminded too of my choice assignment going out the window. That lying recruiter. He conned me.

Welcome to the Air Force and the big world.

We were packed into the buses and herded off like cattle to Lackland Air Force Base. As soon as the recruits piled out of the buses, we were introduced to a Sergeant McDonald, a large, burly man in his 40s, rugged-looking, thick neck, dressed in a long sleeved khaki uniform.

"*Move it out!*" He barked in manly baritone, a gruff, abrasive, domineering voice invading the cool air, loud and booming, stretched to a peremptory scream from beneath eyes black and steely, fixed with a minatory glare. "Head for that building! Single file!"

We complied, packing into a long, domelike tin building nearby. There, McDonald snarled gutturally on:

"You wet-behind-the-ears rookies don't have the sense God Almighty promised a flea for being talked into signing up on a New Year's Eve! You bunch of stupid shits for brains kept me from going to Mexico tonight and partying with some hot senoritas. Instead, here I am baby-sitting with you ass-holes who your mamas don't even want. Well, you're going to *pay* for it!" He tacked on sinisterly, tone intensifying, his weather-beaten face now pugnacious, turning his black eyes rabid. "For your stupidity I'm going to drive you harder than any recruits have *ever* been driven! I'm going to *drive* you shits into the ground! Literally," he added unnecessarily, as though finding the idea pleasing.

I let out a muted screech in a tango of screeches. Shit, what have I let myself in for? Then I wondered if McDonald had ever been in a recruiting office.

From there matters slid down hill. The next day we were informed that because inventory was being taken—it was taken each year at this time—it would be two weeks before we could be issued supplies. Nevertheless, boot camp training had to proceed, meaning we trained in our civilian clothes.

The day before I joined the Air Force I bought new slacks, a new shirt and a new pair of shoes with my last $39.75 paycheck from the cotton mill, and I had them on now. My training uniform. Scrutinized every second by Sergeant McDonald's unceasing railing, I marched in those clothes and those shoes. After one day of marching, my heels felt like fresh hot-roasted peanuts. After one week of marching, my feet were literally a bloody pulp, mangled so badly that an ugly infection set in and I was shuttled off to the crowded dispensary for medical care and ordered not to march for several days.

While my feet were healing, a dread set in over returning to McDonald once they were. Fortunately, I never had to resume boot camp. What saved me was my exceptionally high scores on the tests I took before joining the Air Force. Because of those scores I was singled out from my flight—about 40 men equivalent to a platoon in the Army—to take more tests, dozens and dozens of them, some lasting a few hours, others lasting from one to two days. A few of the tests were rather weird, their contents pertaining to matters I had never heard about and couldn't begin to understand, some of the material even presented in foreign languages. It took me six weeks to complete all of these tests, and by then boot camp was over.

Not a few of the fellows in my flight, especially those from New York, sneered at me, complaining adamantly about me spending all of my time taking tests rather than suffering it out with them in training and being pulverized to exhaustion each day by Sergeant McDonald. It reminded me of home, where I was accused of going to school to escape working in the fields. Here I was accused of taking tests to escape the demanding rigors of boot camp.

At the end of the eighth week, everyone in my flight, except for me, had received their post boot camp orders. Most of those who enlisted in the "General" category, as I had, were being shipped off to cook school; the remainder to military police school.

But why hadn't I received my orders?

While waiting for them I was assigned temporary duty in the orderly room, mostly an idle and boring pastime. There I met James Orand, also assigned to the orderly room, and immediately recognized him as one of the group who had taken all of those tests with me. James, a 20-year-old bald headed man from Chicago, heavy face, thick lips, was in the same boat as me. He had enlisted under the "General" category and as yet hadn't received his orders either.

"We'll either end up flipping flap jacks or knocking someone over the head," he grunted with sarcasm, none too happy about doing either.

For three weeks James and I did little but wait on our orders and by now I was worried as to whether we'd ever receive them. Then we heard the blast over the squawk box:

"Oakes and Orand report to the commander's office for orders!"

"Oh, shit!"

"It's either flap jacks or knocking someone over the head."

It was neither. Our orders read: Report to Radio Intercept Analysis School at Kelly AFB on March 23, 1963.

Before reporting I had time to return to Phenix City for a week, and visited J.P. and my friends, all of whom were amazed as to how much weight I had gained during my eleven weeks in the Air Force from eating nourishing food on a regular basis. I had even grown a few inches, putting me now at five, five and a limber 130 pounds. And the Air Force had taken care of my dental neglect.

My assignment at Kelly Air Force Base in San Antonio was for two months, part one of an eight-month course. If I survived Kelly, the last six months, part two, would be completed at Goodfellow Air Force Base in San Angelo, Texas. The course was nothing but grueling, a constant reminder of the high rate of trainees who washed out, both in part one and part two. I was determined not to wash out. Washouts ended up as cooks or policemen. Survivors ended up with choice assignments.

Then crushing news. Heretofore unknown to me, before trainees could begin the course at Kelly, each one underwent a preliminary check scrutinizing his background before being issued a temporary security clearance, this clearance a must requirement to begin the course.

I'd had it! There goes the course! My family background would most certainly get me rejected. Christ, all those times Daddy had been arrested for making moonshine. And Red having sex with mules. And Mama and her extramarital affairs. All that fussing and fighting and carrying on. The craziness of the storm pits. Fly squashing. A murderer in the family, not to mention Ruby Lee's known promiscuity and Marilyn having a baby out of wedlock. I even had knowledge of corruption and vote buying that I never reported. Hell, my family's outrageous history would embarrass Attila the Hun, giving him a better chance at security clearance than me.

But someone with poor investigative ability must have carried out the preliminary check on me for, amazingly, I was cleared and allowed to begin the course at Kelly. My celebration, though, was short-lived. The trainees making it into part one were informed that during the two month course each of their backgrounds would now be more vigorously investigated, "raked over with a fine tooth comb," as it was put, before any trainee would be granted a permanent security clearance, another must requirement to continue part two of the course at Goodfellow.

That more-in-depth investigation was the one that would certainly finish me. Then the investigators sobered up and went for the nitty-gritty. My family background could never stand up under such a vigorous check.

I was geared and resolved to survive and pass the course on my own wits, no matter what they threw at me, but I was absolutely helpless against my family's screwed up, unbalanced, chaotic, perverted, criminal, immoral and disgraceful chronicle. Absolutely helpless against the resulting denial coming.

Under an anxious air of resignation, I expected the axe of rejection to fall any day. The stress and strain of this "any moment" expectation resurfaced my nightmares and anxiety attacks, though of lesser intensity than in the shacks. Up to this point these nightmares and attacks had been nil during my time in the Air Force, but now they were bringing on sleepless nights, particularly the dreams of Daddy burning in hell, though without the presence of the Shadow and his tormenting laughter. In spite of the nightmares, mini anxiety attacks and sleepless nights, I plugged away at my course work to the end, conditioned to perform well under severe stress from my earlier days of applying myself at school under the chaotic bombardment of torment at home.

"Find the spring that controls your own Universe… Find the spring that controls your own Universe … Find …"

There were 40 airman trainees in my class at Kelly, essentially a cryptographic training course breaking codes from classroom instruction and printed handouts prohibited from being taken out of the classroom. When not being used for training these handouts were kept under lock and key. The course started off with simple basics, then progressively became more complex and difficult, one purpose to weed out those unfit for this type of intricate, concentrated training. Of the 40 trainees, ten failed the course work by part ones end, and two more were dropped because of failure to pass final security clearance.

I not only passed part one, more miraculously I was granted permanent security clearance. I couldn't understand it. Something was screwy. But I made no complaints. It was heaven to be able to sleep again.

Part two of the course began in June and a few of we survivors of part one drove the few hundred miles together to Goodfellow Air Force Base in San Angelo, Texas. Compared to what was in store for us in part two, part one was kindergarten. The instruction and class work of part two was not only far advanced and much more complicated and demanding, but it was faster paced, difficult to grasp and all consuming, both mentally and emotionally.

But I was passing and surviving, doing well in class, mastering manifold and copious material, overcoming difficult obstacles in training, these exacting achievements fostering a new found confidence, one giving me a new sense of identity; a new psychic and emotional independence—enough, I thought, to finally wrest away Mama's emotional shackles keeping me from normalcy.

I seized upon an opportunity to prove it.

A part two Air Force training buddy, by the name of Crockett, and I were scouting downtown San Angelo one evening when my eyes suddenly focused on this woman departing from a swank clothing store. Slim, well figured, an eye-catching pretty blonde, about my height, around 115 lbs., her hair piled like a smoky cloud on an elegantly shaped head. I was instantly attracted to her, studying the smooth, crystal clear complexion of her face with a growing sense of pleasure.

Hastening into the clothing store, I asked the clerk if she knew anything about the woman. The clerk happened to know the woman quite well and, surprisingly, upon my request, provided me with her name, Patsy, and her phone number.

I phoned the young woman. "Hi, Patsy. I know you don't know me. And I don't know you—yet. But I'm going to." I was polite but determined, and very confident.

I could hear the sharp intake of breath over the line. "Who are you?… How'd you get my number?… My name?"

"I've got my ways. But that's not important. When can I see you?"

"See me? I … I know nothing about you!"

"Believe me, Patsy, I can be trusted. I won't harm you. I just want to get to know you."

"I…I really … I don't know." Her voice, very feminine, was mellowing. "You sound sincere, but I—Look, my girlfriend and I will be in front of Walgreen's tomorrow at five-thirty. You can meet me there."

Hanging up, a smile of freedom flickered across my lips, an inane Floyd Lester grin.

The next day, Crockett accompanying me, I met Patsy and her girlfriend at Walgreen's drug store, the four of us engaging in polite conversation revealing that Patsy was 17, two years younger than I, and a senior in high school. Then the four of us took a leisurely stroll, continuing our chatting, laughing, ending up at a place for a soda, Patsy's soft blue-eyed smile reminding me of Lurlene. The same innocence.

I never felt more in control, nor more confident that Patsy, at last, was a female I could have a normal relationship with. Have normal feelings for. A normal outcome.

It was evident that Patsy liked me as much as I liked her. After phoning her a few more times, she invited me over to the house where she regularly baby-sat a feisty, unruly little ten-year-old twerp by the name of Sammy. I began visiting her there regularly in the evenings while she worked, never attempting to touch or kiss her, relating to her much the same way as I had to Lurlene. But without the limitations. With Patsy I was looking forward to touching and kissing her, and making love to her, but at the right time, the right moment. I wasn't going to rush that moment, or push it. I wasn't going to goof this up. I wanted our relationship to evolve naturally, the romancing coming when it should. I was patient. Too much was at stake.

But apparently I was too patient. On one visit to Patsy while she was baby-sitting, Sammy said to me, "Patsy and I were laying on the bed before you came. Wanna know what we were doing?"

"What?" I asked, remembering what I'd probably be doing at ten years old.

"She took my penis out and touched herself with it."

Immediately I recalled that night in bed with Inez, when she took sexual liberties with me. Patsy was feeling sexual arousal. Ready to be plucked.

Listening nearby, Patsy's face went from light pink to dark red in solid blush. "*Shut up*, Sammy! Take your little butt to bed! *Right now!*"

"Aw, Patsy, I *don't wanna* go to bed! It's too early!"

"*Get out of here!*"

Sammy retreated to bed. Then Patsy and I chatted, popped some corn and watched TV, with no reference made to Sammy's "penis touching" comment. But I knew Patsy was ready, and our moment wasn't too far off.

It came a few nights later. An Air Force training buddy of mine, Wells, and I dropped by to visit with Patsy. Sammy was already in bed and while the three of us sat on the sofa, Patsy, with that sparkling look of intimacy, turned to me and said, "Don, if your friend will wash the dishes, I have a surprise for you."

With my eyes, I signaled to Wells to go into the kitchen, a look saying, "and don't return until I tell you." Wells immediately departed the room, then Patsy disappeared. Soon she returned, looking stunning in a pretty pink nightgown, the nipples of her breasts pushing out against the fabric. She sat down beside me, her blue eyes like china, her evenly shaped mouth touched with pale amber. Quickly she warmed up to me, putting her arms around my neck, the light aroma of some delicate perfume titillating my nostrils. Then, biting me on the ear, a delicious wet warm sensation. Patsy whispered softly:

"I should be ashamed of myself, I know, but I can't help it. I want you."

Wanting her, I was about to respond when the anxiety struck, uncontrollable, transforming my passion into disabling fright.

This is a *decent* girl!

It was Lurlene all over again. I choked, my mind foggy, my heart running in different directions. "Patsy, I… I like you very much, and I'm very much attracted to you, but not now, Patsy." I said nervously, cryptically, an adolescent rasp, feeling the control of my anxiety, a sexual straitjacket. "Maybe later. Not now."

Patsy gawked at me, startled, as one might look at a war hero suddenly turned traitor. I couldn't deal with it. My tongue seemed cemented to my jaw. I had to get out of there. Abruptly pulling myself away from Patsy. I hastily stood up and walked out of the house, yelling as I did so, "Wells, we got to go!"

One thing was clear; Mama's emotional shackles were still with me, my new found confidence no match for them. The old was the new. The same.

Patsy wasn't my only crisis. Back at Goodfellow Air Force Base the course work was becoming so brutal that some fellows went to any length to be dropped from the class, despite knowing that they couldn't quit. They were under orders and any attempt to quit the class brought unbearable stress and humiliation from Air Force instructors and sergeants.

A trainee with whom I had become close friends, a Southerner from Nashville by the name of Peyton, was one of those who couldn't take the brutal strain of the course any longer and wanted out of it at any cost.

"Peyton, hang in there, buddy!" I pleaded with him. "You can *make it*!"

Nervous and desperate, Peyton phoned me one day at the barracks, crying, "I'm doing it, Don. I'm overdosing!"

"Wait … wait! Good God! Don't …"

He hung up. I phoned the Air Force police and they rushed to Peyton's motel with an ambulance, luckily in time to save his life. He recovered in a few days and was discharged from the Air Force.

I saw Patsy a few more times but our relationship was never the same. I remained clear of any romantic entanglement with her. It simplified matters, obviating the need for an impossible explanation.

In October of 1963, the training class took its final test. Of the twenty-eight trainees beginning part two at Goodfellow, fourteen ended up passing the completed course. I was one of the fourteen. Those surviving part two were sent as a group to receive their overseas orders, being told from the start that each one in the passing group would be sent to either Turkey or Crete.

A trainee by the name of Dennis, from Minnesota, having received the highest class average, was the only one given his choice of assignment. He chose Crete, leaving eleven slots open for Turkey and two more for Crete, these assignments handed out in alphabetical order. Following alphabetically by the trainee's last names, the eleven slots for Turkey were assigned first. Thank God my last name began with an "O".   I was assigned Crete.

CHAPTER 18

I RECEIVED MY second stripe, a promotion from Airman Third Class to Airman Second Class, and a fourteen day leave. Then shortly before Thanksgiving I flew to New York and from there took the long flight to Athens, Greece, with stopovers in Rome and Paris. I didn't sleep a wink during the 16 hour journey, too keyed up about traveling to a foreign country.

My flight arrived in Athens on November 22, 1963, from where I was scheduled to board an Olympia Airlines flight to Iraklion, Crete. Deplaning in Athens I scurried to the terminal from where that flight would depart and, as it was announced, and the door to the corridor leading to the aircraft opened, I was startled to see the horde of people stampeding to get to the aircraft—pushing, shoving, running; a free-for-all riot. The problem was Olympia Airlines overbooked their flights, really overbooked, and to get a seat you had to be aggressively quick on your feet, pushing and shoving and fighting for it. Greek style.

When the dust cleared, the losers without seats, instead of having to make arrangements for another flight, were allowed to crowd in the aisle of the aircraft and fly standing up. I was one of the standing losers, huddled in the aisle with the others, a press of elbows and torsos. From my standing position I was finally relieved when I spotted Crete below from the aircraft, a Greek island in the Mediterranean Sea, about 81 miles southeast of the southern tip of the mainland, 7 to 35 miles in width and about 186 miles long, mountain ranges running from one end to the other.

When the flight landed, I was thankful to deplane from the sardine packed aircraft and set foot on the soil of Iraklion, the third largest city on Crete, near the middle of the island on its northern shoreline, presenting a beautiful Venetian port and distinguished by a medieval fort at its harbor, a constant reminder of the numerous tyrants in the past who had invaded Crete.

I was picked up at the airport by an Air Force bus and taken to the air base about ten miles away, traveling over a narrow, winding road along the coastline of the Mediterranean, awed by the spectacular natural surroundings—the smooth dark majesty of the ocean, the craggy plains and fertile valleys, the rugged mountains dropping down to the sea, forming dazzling stretches of sandy beaches and secluded coves. And there were donkey drawn carts all over the road, driven by weather beaten Greeks of impoverished simplicity, a reminder of home.

My awe continued at the base, setting on top of a jagged rocky cliff overlooking the ocean, a breathless panoramic view of the Mediterranean Sea and the magnificence of a long stretch of beach coastline 75 feet below. The splendor of Pea River and Pea River swamp magnified a million times.

Reporting in, I received my barracks assignment and met my two roommates. Marshal Elzy and Tom Conigerro. Marshal--short, redheaded, freckles all over his face—was a pleasant down-to-earth person. Tom was not. Tall, skinny, long protruding nose, he was as grumpy as the classical "horse's ass."

Worn out from my exhausting flight from New York, especially the jammed standing leg on Olympia Airlines, after meeting my roommates I excused myself and collapsed into bed. Later I was abruptly shaken awake by Marshal.

"Wake up, Don!" He said, grim and resolute. "Wake up! President Kennedy has been shot and killed!"

The news tore through me like one of my nightmares. The base was put on alert for several days, during which time I was unable to sleep, tossing in fits and night sweats.

The building housing my work site was not what I expected. A single story, lackluster cinder block, looking like a cross between a fortified prison and a languishing warehouse, large antennae sticking up everywhere, the block surrounded by an eight foot chain link security fence, a couple of feet of barbwire on top of that, sharply pointed glistening strands sinisterly on guard, the whole place was a dreary monument to perceptual distaste.

At the entrance to the building was an armed security guard and I was required to show my Air Force I. D. to pass. Inside were dozens of airmen sitting in several rows with headsets on their heads; a few others, with drawn faces, walking around and looking over their shoulders. My assignment was to be one of those walkers. Quickly adopting a serious look, I walked around searching for certain types of information that could pose a threat to the security of our country. The men with the headsets typed incoming information in code and I reviewed these incoming codes for patterns that had security implications. The work was demanding, but stimulating, requiring keen concentration and observation, and consistent alertness.

The next few weeks were a gradual adjustment to this type of work, and adjustment to the social environment. I was in a strange land with strangers doing strange work-drastically different from plowing behind mules. After work, to relax, Marshal and I occasionally wandered over to the NCO Club on the base for a few beers. But more often we caught a local Crete bus—always an old, decrepit clunker, its original paint barely showing through the rust and dirt—and went into Iraklion for Minos, a Greek wine, and shish-ka-bob. The bus was usually packed with dirty, smelly peasants, shabbily dressed in old, dark, worn out clothes, some of whom carried live chickens—or any other livestock they could cuddle in their arms. As with Olympia Airlines, the buses overbooked too, frequently leaving Marshal and I standing in the aisle staring down chickens.

But the scenery enroute more than made up for the standing and chickens. The pure rugged serenity of the countryside was enthralling, the jagged rocks, the cliffs, the gnarled olive trees, the slopes. And all the sheer beauty was entrancing— the colorful contrasts of the vineyards, the sea, the snow capped mountains in the background, the fertile valleys lying between—a keen appreciation of Nature spawned in Pea River and Pea River Swamp, now expanding. And again, I never ceased to be amazed by all the donkeys en route to the city—carrying loads, pulling carts, people riding them.

I soon discovered from Marshal that Crete had this strange custom when it came to their women. He told me of this airman who took a Greek woman on a date, just the two of them alone, without a chaperone.

"They were automatically engaged because of it," he emphasized. "The Crete custom protecting the virtue and honor of their women. Crete women are just not allowed to go out with men alone. If they do, they marry them. Period."

This made it hard on the men, and apparently the women as well. I received a firsthand glimpse of this, up close and personal. I was in downtown Iraklion one afternoon, dressed in my skivvies—civilian clothes, enjoying the sights on an overcrowded street packed with Greek humanity, as usual pushing and shoving and fighting for daily existence, when suddenly, from out of this shoving mob, there appeared a beautiful Greek teenage girl with silky black hair and the most alluring brown eyes. And those eyes were fixated on me. She darted straight for me, speaking to me in very clear, very crisp, unbroken perfect English, further amazing me.

"I don't like our custom! I want to have a good time and enjoy myself! Would you please help me? Take me out? Show me a good time?"

Before I could say a word, her father, a rather undersized, snuffy man, popped out of the crowd, shot me a Sergeant McDonald glare, yanked the young woman by the arm and shouted disapprovingly to her in Greek as the two quickly disappeared into the flowing masses of the street mob.

Though the Cretans had this strange custom with their women, the powers-to-be did have enough sense to allow for whorehouses, places where the local men could at least vent their urges. And the men of the U.S. Air Force.

Oddly, all of the Crete whorehouses were one girl propriertorships, usually packed more with horny airmen than with the locals. Between each trick the lady of the house doused herself with a little water from her wash pan, swiped herself, then went on to her next customer.

It was Marshal who introduced me to the Crete brothels. And it was the U.S. Air Force that kept them thriving, particularly during the winter months. Because no other type of Greek women were available to the servicemen, the Air Force expected them to frequent the Greek prostitutes. It was socially acceptable, sort of an airman's duty to patronize the whores, thereby keeping himself in a state of good emotional balance.

I did my duty. Sex with Crete prostitutes was never anxiety producing for me. For one thing, not only were they not decent girls, sexually they were the most indecent, and officially stamped as so. For another, I could always walk away from them. There was no personal involvement. Still, at times, I did experience some twinge of shame, but nothing compared to the shame pouncing on me after sex with Gloria and Cynthia. And certainly no overpowering crippling feelings preventing sex altogether, as with Patsy.

Whores were whores. So indecent that they could be used. Then forgotten. No emotions involved. Or very little.

After Marshal introduced me to Crete prostitutes, I went on a binge. Visiting them all. During this binge, on a winter night of rain, fifteen other airmen and myself were packed into this brothel, one of the best in Iraklion, waiting our turn downstairs in a modest room filled with a heady fragrance. The brothel was run by a 25-year-old prostitute, typically Greek in looks—black-headed, brown eyes, square jaw, this one attractive but not pretty, her body firm and curvaceous and bosomy, enough to satisfy any man's lust and fantasies.

This lady of the house screwed—or whatever—her customers upstairs, and when she finished with one, and was ready for another, she stood at the top of the stairs and yelled down in broken English; "Come on up!"

My turn was next, and while waiting for the "Come on Up!", upstairs with the prostitute was a radio operator by the name of Ramey. A heavy boozer, this night he was dead drunk, too plastered with liquor to have sex but stubborn enough not to come downstairs until he did, holding up my turn. And the prostitute was becoming impatient with him as well.

"Hurry up and finish!" We heard her yell at him. "You've been here too long! Get the fuck off me! I've got other customers waiting."

But Ramey held fast. Lapsing in and out of his drunken stupor, pitifully going through his flaccid motions, he slurred petulantly, "I'm not going anywhere til I'm finished! I paid you… so *shaddap*! Your rotten, filthy, mushy *cunt* belongs to me!"

"Why you—you *stupid* drunk … you *sonnabitch….* get *off* of me!"

"Shaddap and fuck!"

The next sound we heard was a loud KA-PLUNK as Ramey hit the floor. The prostitute, now raging out of control, then pushed Ramey, naked, down the stairs, his clothes and shoes under his arms, the prostitute chasing after him, infuriated and screaming, no longer speaking English but Greek, the intensity and tempo of her expletives picking up fiercely in her native tongue. We couldn't understand a word she was saying, but from the flashes of her eyes we got the gist of her message; *Everyone get out!*

Being next up, I was standing on the staircase when Ramey came hurtling by me, the prostitute right behind, swinging at Ramey with a vengeance. Ramey was the first to hit the door, the rest of us quickly behind him, all of us fleeing out into the pouring rain as if escaping from a police raid. In no time we all passed by Ramey who, with bewildered intoxicated effort, was attempting to get into his clothes, the rain drenching down upon him in stinging sheets unusually cool rain, making the late wintry evening damper and colder than usual.

We never returned to that prostitute's house.

Another thing I discovered about Crete was its lure to vacationers. With its mild climate, and its very dry season during the summer, Crete was a natural hot spot for tourists. But there were few tourists during the winter months, that being the rainy season, keeping them away. Beginning in October of each year, it rained constantly, a never ending downpour, the rain not stopping until spring.

But the rain notwithstanding, my first winter in Crete wasn't that bad, mainly because I was wrapped up in my work. And after work, rain or no rain, my pattern became one of going into Iraklion, either with Marshal or going there alone. With its jammed narrow streets, and small restaurants and shops—rather dark inside, the lighting not good—I found part of the city to possess a certain quaint charm. But around the edges of the city were the residential sections, multilevel homes all jammed together like crammed bee hives, with balconies protruding out everywhere, and here there was little charm. And there were the smells, always with you, the strange pungent aromas of all the food being cooked, rafting through the air, mesmerizing your nostrils with potent intoxication. But one smell knocked you over. The mordant smell of the wineries, a deep gagging odor, more sickening than a mule's fart.

I found novelty in visiting the bustling little shops and markets in the city because of the merchandise—bizarre items, mostly heavy and dark, and seemingly having no sensible function. But the flies swarming all over were certainly no novelty, especially around the markets with hanging whole chickens. The chickens, beginning to discolor, appeared as though they had been hanging out for days—too many days, taking on an odious, nauseating odor, as if beginning to rot. But the Greeks bought them anyway.

I never ate Greek chicken.

As spring approached I became friends with Sergeant Harris Parkell from Salem, New Jersey, 21 years old, puffy jowls like a chipmunk, receding dark brown hair, about five eleven, 190 lbs., a code breaker like myself. Harris had just completed his assignment in Turkey and was now beginning his second assignment in Crete. The Air Force was implementing a pilot program whereby any airman who agreed to serve back-to-back overseas duty assignments—one overseas assignment immediately following another—was promoted to Staff Sergeant. Harris had agreed to this, thus had been promoted to sergeant.

But this new Air Force pilot program had its drawbacks, the major one being that it resulted in the promotion of airmen unfit for the rank of sergeant. One such airman so promoted was Sergeant Simmons. A radio operator, overweight, wearing thick glasses, his face oval and fatty, distinguished by small eyes close together and a small pointed nose, thin sandy hair sticking up in the back like a cowlick, hands limp and damp, Simmons clearly wasn't a leader and he certainly didn't fit the mold of a sergeant. Rather than commanding respect from those of lower rank, he elicited their pity.

Immature emotionally, Simmons became so excited over matters that he'd slobber and spit on you while he was talking, quickly earning him the nickname. "Mad Dog."

Mad Dog became emotionally attached to this 26-year-old Crete prostitute—a petite, very pretty and very flashy and ostentatious lady with dyed blonde hair, spending all of his pay on her and buying her anything she wanted. He even asked the prostitute to marry him but she refused his offer, even though the one thing she truly prized was an opportunity to go live in America. That's how much of a loser Mad Dog was.

Harris and I frequently visited Mad Dog's prostitute girlfriend at her place of business, and every time we showed up Mad Dog was usually sitting on her sofa, alone, waiting for his girlfriend to finish screwing her customers, and Harris needled him mercilessly about it.

On one such occasion, Harris, making fun of Mad Dog's peculiar choice of masochism, got nose to nose with him and screeched. "I'm going to go back there and *screw* the eyeballs out of your girlfriend! Does that *bother* you, Mad Dog?"

Forcing his babyish features into an inordinately fatuous smile, Mad Dog sputtered excitedly, a thin piping voice, "No… nooo. Not at all." He now was slobbering and spitting, his eyes sort of popping out of his head, his sand cowlick suddenly whipping up in back. "She's… she's doing it only for the money. Love is not a factor here. No. Nosireee!" He then gave Harris a frowny, somewhat sanctimonous, so-there look.

"You dumb prick!"

The first time I visited Mad Dog's girlfriend for sex, she instructed me on how to properly make love to a woman.

"This is how women like it," she said matter-of-factly. "Put your cock right here"—with cunning fingers, she deftly positioned my penis to the upper end of her vaginal opening-"and make sure you move it up and down in this general area. Women just love a cock doing that to them."

"Whores wouldn't care." I commented.

"With one as big as yours they would."

Every time I visited Mad Dog's girlfriend she asked me to spend the night with her. I always declined.

Besides the prostitutes and the quaint charms of the city, I went into Iraklion also for the night clubs, several of them scattered about the town. My first visit, to a club was a surprising education. I was sitting, having a beer, listening to the music—loud blasting sounds, but enjoyable, when all of a sudden this Greek man next to me picks up a plate and throws it to the hard floor at his feet, smashing it to smithereens.

Startled, I jumped up from my seat, cringing, ready for anything, musing: What the hell is he so mad about?

I gazed about for the bouncers, expecting the man to be tossed out on his ear. Instead, several other Greeks began smashing plates on the floor as well, all of them laughing, having a great time. They weren't mad at all, but having fun, Greek style, that lively spirited manner of the spontaneous Greek nature.

Then a man, a smile and tobacco-sour breath plastered on his face, brought a plate over to me, gesturing toward the floor for me to break it. At first I looked at him reluctantly, then with a what-the-hell expression I took the plate and slammed it to the floor in a great crashing sound, pieces scattering everywhere. Everyone laughed and clapped, and surprisingly, breaking the plate gave me a kind of exhilarating, uplifting feeling, as when I squashed flies back home. So I smashed another one on the floor. Soon I was laughing with the Greeks, joining in on their hardy fun, smashing plate after plate in rhythm to the loud blasting music and gusty singing.

The arrival of spring in 1964, when I was twenty years old, brought an end to the ceaseless torrents of rain, ushering in the dry season, mild sunny weather without a sign of a rain cloud. In the early spring a bus load of airmen, me among them, taking advantage of this weather, made an organized Air Force trip to one of the Greek monasteries high up in the mountains. The monastery was a drab place; still it was an enjoyable experience talking with the old monks, those who spoke broken English. But it was on our return to the base that our trip took on its unforgettable moments.

The Greeks and Turks being natural enemies, feuding fiercely for years, they pass on no opportunity to cut each other's throats. On the way back to the base from the monastery the bus pulled into a quiet Greek village and stopped. Sitting in the back seat of the bus was a big, muscular Air Force radio operator by the nickname of "Boo." Six, one, 195 lbs., big head, square face, he had a large, scary-looking scar on his face, thus the name, Boo.

Well, Boo had a Turkish fez—like a beanie cap but taller, maroon in color, with a gold tassel on top of it—stashed in his pocket, and when the bus stopped in the Greek village he did the damndest thing ever. He took the fez out of his pocket and put it on top of his head, proving to be as much of a nerd as Mad Dog.

When Boo put on that Turkish fez it was the equivalent of war suddenly breaking out.

One of the Greek villagers, spotting the fez on Boo's head, thinking he was a Turk, quickly spread the news, and immediately that quiet Greek village was transformed into a noisy uprising. Highly offended, perturbed and aroused, every Greek in the area swarmed around the bus, hollering angrily, demanding that Boo be handed over to them, their malevolent clamoring scary and alarming, bringing stunned, hard looks to the airmen, including me, in the bus.

Those Greeks wanted to string Boo up. They were going to hang him!

The bus driver, an Air Force sergeant, not believing his eyes and ears, frantically beseeched the angry mob to calm down, but the Greeks would have no part of being calmed, becoming even more menacing. Boo's fez was like blood to sharks and they wanted his body.

It was only the quick arrival of two local policemen to the bus door that prevented the Greeks from breaking into the bus, dragging Boo out and hanging him. But the two policemen were little match against this raging mob and the best protection they could provide was a delaying action at best. The policemen screamed at the mob to disperse but, indomitable, the Greeks refused. They wouldn't leave the bus, still shouting at Boo inside, waving clenched fists murderously at him.

While Boo remained within the questionable safety of the bus—helpless, petrified, his eyebrows going up like sprigs of heather caught in a breeze, guarded oh so tenuously by the policemen, the bus driver, swearing angrily, was escorted to a phone where he dutifully put in a quick call to the base, apprising the commander there of the riotous Greeks holding our bus under siege, wanting Boo's neck. The commander, in turn, contacted the American Embassy in Athens, concluding our ticklish situation came under their bailiwick.

While waiting out the entrenched diplomatic procedures to take their course, we sat frazzled and numb for several hours in the stuffy bus, uneasily watching the inimical mob outside. Then the Greeks began rocking the bus, heightening our fear that they were going to tip it over and hang more than just Boo. Not a few of the airmen were as white as a ghost, raked by tension, teeth and jaws aching from gnashing and clenching, uniforms all askew, soaked with the smell of heavy sweat. The smell of fear.

Eventually three Crete officials arrived, proving to the mob that Boo was not a Turk, though he had to hand over his Turkish fez, which the Greeks noisily burned in the street. Then, reluctantly, they let our bus leave. I was never so glad to leave a place, with maybe the exception of Shack 17.

CHAPTER 19

IT WAS MAY. The splendor of spring. Crete's dry season. Beach weather. To the backdrop of white-capped waves, I relaxed, thankful to be alive; thankful for the ocean, its peace, an inspiring piece of Nature. And thankful for the apparent peace within me. No anxiety attacks. No nightmares. No fitful sleepless nights. No humiliation. No shame. No disgrace. The shacks of southern Alabama far away. Mama not existing.

I was appeased, even if my head was in the sand. Horror was still with me, but content for the moment to lay dormant, waiting for a trigger.

With the beach weather the tourists were now beginning to show up in droves, among them a lot of shapely young women. Harris and I, along with a more sobered Boo and a few other airmen, practically lived on this one stretch of Iraklion beach—fondly named "Florida," drinking beer, eating karpuzi and plotting our strategy for meeting the young shapely women.

Their arrival in numbers was ominous for the Crete prostitutes. By now the men were fed up with the brothels. Sick of whoremongering. Tired of the perfunctory, worn out bodies of the same ol' prostitutes. They wanted fresh meat. New faces. Bodies more lively, less used. They wanted the non-Greek, European females now descending upon the beaches like flies into a gourmet's garbage pit.

With the fiasco of Patsy still in the back of my mind, I had been overly reluctant to approach girls who weren't whores. But after the Greek village incident, figuring life could end any day, maybe tomorrow, I now wanted my share before it did. I'd just pretend they were all whores.

That sinuous reasoning, though, made approaching girls no easier for me. Harris, even with his seamed rugged face, was better at approaching women, possessing that glibness of speech and spontaneous savvy of saying things appealing to females right off.

I didn't. So I needed an edge. Some kind of gimmick to get me started. The gimmick I chose was to approach women with an unlit cigarette and ask them for a light, then take it from there.

So armed with an unlit Lucky cigarette, going forth in my spiffy green bathing suit as if some defrocked knight in quest of the Queen's jewels, I ventured out on the beach, eagerly scanning all of the near naked female bodies. Right away I spotted two gorgeous plums nearby. Chic swimsuits. Young. Pretty. Shapely. Swelling silicone breasts. They were lying on the sand, supine, kind of close together. Perfect.

Prancing up to them with the steps of a stalker assured of his quarry, trying to appear cool and suave, very European, I essayed an unctuous smile and purred to them in my most nonchalant, manly, rehearsed voice, "One of you lovely ladies have a light?" Since I had no idea whether they spoke or understood English, I pointed to the end of my cigarette as I asked the question.

Annoyed at my intrusion, one of the women—her sun lotion smelling a tad spicy, jumped to her feet, shot me a venomous drop-dead look, then began cursing at me vehemently in some foreign language. Then yanking the other girl to her feet, one gawking at me with an almost insufferable look of snootiness, the two hastily gathered their belongings up from the sand and scurried from my presence, leaving me looking rather silly.

On my first attempt I had entered a nest of lesbians. I asked for no more lights that day.

The next afternoon, after my shift at the base, recovered, undaunted, a pep talk from Harris, I was back on the beach with my unlit cigarette, ready to venture forth again, beckoned on by a fading brilliant sun lowering in the clear western sky, its rays of pink and gold skipping mellow over the stillness of a calm sea.

I was standing a few feet back from the water's edge when I saw her, walking with two other attractive girls. She was heading in my direction from 40 feet or so up the beach, one-piece ebony swimsuit, fawnlike movement, skin a smooth gleam in the mellowing sun, hair black and swaying, throwing off little points of light. Then her gaze caught mine, locking our eyes in discovery, and she smiled, sensuous, questioning, a special look. And seeing that look my heart sank. I forgot about the cigarette, dropping it.

Veering off from the other two girls she began walking directly toward me, her smile broadening, wide and inviting. "Hi, how are you?" She spoke with a little shake of the head, a perky, modulated English accent. About one inch shorter than me, her eyes glowed with a warm vividness, enhancing the loveliness of her smile, melting me immediately into the Crete sand.

"Fine. How are you?" I couldn't believe I was exchanging words with her. I'd never laid eyes on anyone so beautiful. Tall and slender, her hair was a lustrous spill to just below her shoulders, the face slightly long, angular, the features well defined, eyes a limpid-eyed hazel green, small pug nose, mouth full and evenly shaped, teeth white and perfectly straight, her complexion that clear translucent quality considered an asset in film.

"What part of America are you from?"

Suddenly I was embarrassed. I didn't need the reminder. "Alabama. Why?"

"Ohm… just wondered," she smiled through a curl of lashes. "Long way from home aren't you?"

"I'm in the Air Force. Are you on vacation?"

"Yes. School holiday."

At this point her two female companions joined us, as did Harris, who had been standing nearby, and we all began chatting and introducing ourselves. Her name was Pat, her girlfriends Hillary and Anne.

"Say, why don't we all go to the beach house for karpuzi?" Harris grinned mischievously, his oval face lighting up with a glitter.

"Karpuzi?" Hillary frowned. She was a short pudgy blonde, caked with more than her share of makeup. "What's that?"

Harris gave her a sheepish look. "Oh, you don't know what karpuzi is? You're in for a real treat. Come on!"

The five of us proceeded to the beach house, a long, weather beaten gray structure close to the water's edge, nestled at the foot of a small jagged mountain dropping down to the sea. Finding a table, Harris went for the karpuzi and when he returned with it Hillary frowned. "Hey, that's watermelon!"

"Right," Harris snickered, pursing his lips as though offering a kiss should one be wanted. "Karpuzi!"

Everyone laughed. As we were eating the watermelon, two more of Pat's girlfriends joined us, followed by two more of my Air Force buddies, Stu and Jim. The chatting became lively, during which Hillary looked at me and said gaily, "We have a flat downtown. Why don't you come over tonight?"

I glanced at Pat. I couldn't resist. "Sure."

Harris couldn't make it that night, but Stu and Jim could. Hillary gave me their address; Hotel Iraklion, fourth floor. Harris drove me back to the base in a jeep he owned, where I showered and dressed in skivvies, then joined Stu and Jim at the front of the base. From there we caught a local bus for downtown Iraklion.

At the girls' flat, Pat opened the door, giving me that delicious wide smile. "Boy, you look dapper tonight!" She enthused, a jolly mood, her thick English accent matching the elegance of her eyes, glowing and sparkling. And her lips, a moistly soft dark shade of pink, matched her pink dress, clinging exquisitely to her bodice, her hair tied in a bow on top of her head with a pink hair rope. She was more stunning than on the beach, and I felt I had died and gone to heaven, now in the presence of its most gorgeous angel.

"You look *wonderful!*" I managed.

Pat, Hillary, Anne and the other two girlfriends from the beach house—all staying in the flat together, along with Stu, Jim and I, walked to a Greek restaurant, Nikki's, a few blocks from the hotel. En route I suddenly became anxious, southern Alabama suddenly not so far away, its cloak now clinging to me, weighing me down, reminding me how far out of my element I was being so attracted to Pat.

God, man, this is a *decent* girl! The queen of decency! For Christ sakes, what am I doing?

I had to stop this from going any further. But not just this moment. This moment was too good.

At the restaurant we drank Minos—a Greek wine, listened to the loud, lively Greek music and ate shish-ka-bob with rice. Then I decided the moment had come. I asked Pat to take a walk with me and we excused ourselves from the others, leaving Nikki's and strolling around downtown in the mild night air, me desperately thinking of how to gracefully bow out of this. Gracefully quit seeing her.

"How long are you going to be here?" I asked.

"Couple of weeks."

Two weeks is not that long, I mused. Maybe I can just let this thing ride until then. Then she's gone anyway. "What are you planning on doing for two weeks?"

"Ohhh… you know, enjoy the beach. Sight-seeing. The ruins. Those sort of things." She gave me a quick, dazzling smile, softly glowing, her limpid eyes so lovely, so very, very vivid, so compelling and conquering and irresistible that my mind was gouged of all reality save her.

"I can get a jeep," I found myself saying, the words just popping from my mouth on a mission of their own. "Maybe we can sightsee together."

"*Really*! Oh. I'd love that!… I'd *love* that!"

For the next two hours we walked and chatted, and I learned that Pat was from England, 23 years of age, a school teacher and touring Crete with her other four British girlfriends. The more we strolled and talked, the more she pounded me with those dazzling, vivid, smiling hazel green eyes. And the more I was magnetized to her willowy grace and spunk, vibrant and fun loving. Yet she had depth. A solid classy maturity, reaching out, inexorably drawing me into her soul, caressing me, causing my whole being to become suffused with a decidedly emotion, and I didn't want the concealed horror within me to rise up and squash it. The spark of something wonderful wanted to happen, and who I suddenly wanted to be began putting up an all out struggle with who I had suddenly been reminded I was.

Stu, Jim and the other four girls were at the flat when Pat and I returned. A mass of white, the flat had one large sleeping room—three beds, two cots, and a small living room and kitchen. We drank beer and listened to records, with Stu and Jim dancing with a couple of the girls. As the evening wore on, Stu—a short, pointed-faced veteran sergeant of 12 years, early 30s—ended up drinking too many beers and, on top of the earlier Minos, rapidly disintegrated into drunkenness.

"I sure as hell don't want to go back to the base tonight!" He snarled peevishly.

Hillary, in her loud, non-subtle manner made more gracious by her distinct English accent, bellowed, "Then don't! Spend the night here! With me!"

"Yeeaaahh," he gloated. Then, throwing a half glance at Jim and I. "And my two goof ball buddies?"

"Fine by me. What do you think, Pat… Anne?"

Anne had no misgivings. Nor did the other two girls. But Pat did. But also outvoted, she kept them to herself. She glanced at me, an anxious smile. "Fine."

That settled, the matter reduced to who would sleep with whom. Here, things took a natural course. Stu and Hillary slept in one bed, Jim and one of the other girls in another, Pat and I in the third, with Anne sleeping on one of the cots—she liked Harris, the fifth girl on the other.

The anxiety of lying in bed next to Pat was overwhelming, reducing me to tense stiffness. She, too, was anxious and uncomfortable. Neither one of us anticipated or wanted this quick turn of events. Too quick. Suddenly I was scared. My peace shattered.

"It's okay to hold me," Pat offered.

I did, all night, but frightened to the bone, reiterating to myself the same questions. What am I doing here? In bed with her? Precious her? God, she feels so soft.

The morning couldn't come soon enough. When it arrived I rose early, sleepless, and disappeared quickly back to the base, my duty shift there beginning at 7 A.M. and lasting until 3 P.M. After work, Harris drove me to the beach in his jeep, and there we picked up Pat and Anne and drove around sight-seeing. Then dropping the girls off at the Iraklion Hotel, we drove back to the base, where I cleaned up, borrowed Harris' jeep, and returned to Pat at her flat.

Holding hands, Pat and I walked to a Greek nightclub, sat at a table inside and ordered a beer. Listening to the loud music, watching the Greek men dance with one another, I introduced Pat to a Greek style of fun—plate smashing. When everyone in the club began smashing plates at their feet, I showed Pat the trick of picking up a plate and throwing it hard to the floor, smashing it into countless pieces. She loved it, letting out jubilant shrieks, laughing with the Greeks, gung ho on plate smashing, its fun lighting up her eyes with special merriment.

From then on, when I wasn't working, Pat and I were together day and night. We swam together. We walked the beaches. We traveled all over Crete in Harris' jeep. We visited the Knossis ruins, took in the rugged majesty of the snowcapped mountains, the serenity of the dark blue ocean, the dazzling stretches of sandy beaches and secluded coves. We roamed the countryside, enthralled at the jagged rocks, the cliffs, the olive trees, the slopes, the colorful contrasts of the vineyards and the fertile valleys.

At the end of two weeks, Pat announced, "Don, we're having so much fun together that I'm extending my stay here for another two weeks! Does that make you happy?"

"Sure." Who I wanted to be was happy. Who I was was horrified.

We went night clubbing, our favorite place the Bamboo Club. They played American music. There, some airmen recognized me and invited Pat and I to join them and their dates. We did, though barely cognizant of anyone else's presence, so enamored were we with each other. Then I became somewhat of a celebrity on base as word circulated that I was dating one of the most beautiful women in Europe.

At the Bamboo Club I danced for the very first time in my life, though not letting this on to Pat, whizzing her onto the dance floor as though it were old hat and I was a pro.

"You dance divinely," Pat breathed in my ear, her soft rapture warming the cockles of my heart.

Our only problem was in bed. A big problem. On many nights I slept with Pat, awkwardly holding her, stiffly caressing her skin, feeling her satiny touch, the responsive joy surging through her body. I allowed myself to savor her kisses, sweet kisses of warmth from lips softer than they looked, joining tenderly to mine, passionately, with total surrender. But that's as far as I'd go. As far as I dared go. I never made love to her. I couldn't. Not a decent girl. And especially one as decent as Pat. If while taking her back to her hotel I saw that she was already overly amorous, that certain twinkle in her eye, I'd make some excuse not to stay over with her that night.

Pat was baffled by my reluctance in bed. After one particularly festive night of plate smashing in a Greek night club, Pat became so drunk on Oozo—the national Greek liquor, laughing so loudly and silly, that I literally had to carry her out of the club. Outside I sat her down on a curb and sat next to her. She was still laughing, but then her laughter took on a thinner edge, a shrillness that suddenly broke into crying; agonizing crying of confusion, brimming her cheeks with tears.

"I know I'm drunk," she sobbed, "but I'm in love with you. I know you like me too, but something's not right. Are you already married?"

"No, I'm not married."

"Then what is it?... What's going on? Don't tell me you're queer!"

"No. Nothing like that. There's nothing. I like you very much."

"Do you love me?"

"Yes."

"Then why don't you want to make love to me?" Her words were all the more crushing for being soft-spoken. "What's wrong? You remind me of Jake in THE SUN ALSO RISES. Is that it? Is... is that your problem?"

"No." But there were many types of wars.

"Then *what* is it?!"

I couldn't answer. I couldn't tell her the truth. No reason under God's green earth could make me tell her. Or anyone. Those secrets were locked away forever, where they belonged. But Pat stirred them up, making them restless. "Let's get you back to your hotel."

One evening, with only two remaining before she sailed back to England, while we were alone in her flat, Pat, now certain I wasn't married, a queer, or a Jake, and assured that I loved her, exclaimed determinedly. "What I'm going to throw at you tonight no red-blooded man can refuse!" Then, her whole face a vision of unconcealed love, she became actively aroused and emboldened in bed, going all out in her effort to arouse me to make love to her, bringing into play every feminine enticement in the book, and a few innovations of her own.

But I refused. Restrained by complex, strait jacketed feelings, I had no choice but to hop out of bed, get dressed and flee the flat.

The next day, when I visited her, Pat was subdued and sad, at a loss over my panicked behavior the evening before.

"What do you find wrong with me? Am I some monster or something?"

I couldn't answer. My eyes fell away from her, and a deep silence filled the room.

That evening, both our moods dampened, we had dinner at a sidewalk cafe in town, quietly drinking Minos and eating souvlaki—chunks of lamb, goat cheese, lettuce and tomatoes on a flat piece of soft bread rolled up into a half moon.

"Let's keep in touch," Pat said, a peculiar note of dejection in her voice that I hadn't heard before. "Next year I want to tour America."

As soon as she said, "tour America," I was seized by a premonition so strong that it obliterated all else from my mind, except for the knowing that our relationship had to cease that night. She couldn't see me in America. Maybe find out where I came from. It would be too cruel.

"America?" I said, attempting a cheerfulness I didn't feel. "Sure. That would be nice."

She handed me a piece of paper with her England address on it. "Make sure you don't lose my address. You will write, won't you?"

"You know I'll write, Pat."

"I want to believe you will," she said, studying me intently.

"Pat, my feelings for you are more than you'll ever know," I said earnestly. "I'll write."

She finally smiled, finally believing I would. "Good."

Finishing dinner, we strolled down to the waterfront in the night air's stillness, holding hands, viewing the tour ships, the fishing boats, the fish markets. Then we headed back toward the Iraklion Hotel.

"Don, I can't believe that my trip is over. I wish I could stay longer."

"I wish you could too, Pat. I'm going to miss you."

"Tomorrow night will be our last evening together," she said, trying to perk up. "It has to be very special."

I hesitated. Then, "Yes. What would you like to do?"

She paused for a moment, her face reflective. Then, with a note of cheer, she said emphatically, "I'd like to make one last trip to the ruins before dark. Then stop by the Bamboo Club and dance. I like the American music and dancing with you. You make me feel safe and secure while we're dancing. A special feeling. And afterwards we'll come back to the flat. With some Minos," she added, that certain twinkle in her eye. "You wouldn't refuse a girl a parting remembrance, would you?"

"No. I'll pick you up early."

Returning her to her flat, I said, "See you tomorrow."

"Aren't you staying over?"

"I have to begin work an hour early tomorrow." I lied. "I better return to the base tonight."

"I love you."

I kissed her good-bye, squeezing her tightly. A kiss to hold me forever.

The next morning I did arise extra early. But not to work. Not only did I have the day off, but the following one as well. I borrowed Harris' jeep and drove over the road toward Iraklion, coming to a fork I'd approached hundreds of times. The road to the right headed into Iraklion, the one to the left to Saint

Nick's, a city on the opposite end of the island. I turned to the left and drove to Saint Nick's, staring blankly ahead, a permanent catch in my throat, gripping the wheel till my knuckles showed white, all the while fighting to stem an onrushing tide of feelings.

At Saint Nick's I rented a room, got drunk on Minos and didn't leave the room for two days. The second evening there I fell into a turbulent sleep, then was torn asunder by a traumatic medley of old nightmares; the murders of Uncle Gus, the "Wavey Man," Colin Culpepper. Then Daddy burning in hell. Then for the first time in three and a half years the Shadow appeared in my dreams. We were in Shack 17, sitting on the floor, my relatives sitting around me. Across from me was Lurlene. Then she became Patsy. Then Pat. Then Mama.

They all begin yelling at me; "We told ya ya'd be back! We told ya ya'd be back!"

Then everyone disappeared except for the Shadow. The intensity of his black shining eyes was still there, but he seemed older, his face less noble. For the first time ever he spoke to me, a gruff, disconcerting, mocking voice:

"You've been had! ... You've been had! ... You've been had!"

Then he began laughing at me, that loud, horrid, gurgling laugh; incessant, vivacious laughter; infuriating, tormenting, hideous—pouring forth in deafening torrents of shock and aftershock until all was incomprehensible, shattering me awake. And awake I felt so dejected and depressed, so wretched and miserable, that it left nothing inside of me, not even the emotional will to perish.

CHAPTER 20

AFTERWARDS CAME THE pain. Unbearable psychic pain. Pain isolating me after duty to the confines of my barracks. Isolating me to the tormenting questions, over and over and over until they became a haunting:

Would I ever be normal? Could I ever have a normal relationship with a decent girl? Would I forever be cursed by my background and family?

Pat had blown my Crete facade, and though physically I was existing in Crete, emotionally I was living in the shacks again. And with my shack living the anxiety attacks returned. Terrorizing. I'd wake up in the middle of the night with my body totally paralyzed. Only with intense effort could I finally get my fingers to move, then the rest of my muscles, coming out of this paralysis feeling like I'd been shredded through a meat grinder, all the while hearing the Shadow's laughter in some deep recess of my being.

During my isolation, Harris cheerfully dropped by my room each day after work. "Come on, Don," he grinned vigorously, "let's go to town, drink some Minos and if we don't pick up anything we can visit Mad Dog's girlfriend!"

"No. I don't want to go anywhere tonight."

After a week of these invitations, always eliciting my refusal, Harris began pushing harder.

"Don, for Christ fucking sakes, there's no need grieving yourself to death. Let's go out and do the things we used to do. Go to the beach. Go downtown. Party. Anything. Just get out of here!"

I looked at him pointedly, with a pain of blackness. "Harris, you can go to the beach. You can go downtown. You can party. You can even go to hell! But just get the fuck off my case and leave me alone!"

His seamed rugged face suddenly took on a sullen grimace, squeezing his eyes into slits. Then abruptly turning on his heels, he stormed out of the room, mumbling testily. "You dumb son of a bitch!"

Harris never came back to my room. And on those occasions that I saw him while working he refused to speak to me, still bent out of shape by our last exchange.

After three weeks of isolation cabin fever finally got to me. I crawled out of my hiding, burying my pain in a smoke screen of activity to forget Pat. The first order of business was to mollify Harris, after which we hopped in his jeep, drove to town and quickly proceeded to get plastered on Minos, gaily serenaded by the Greeks.

Harris and I were friends again. We resumed our visits to Iraklion. We returned to the Crete prostitutes. We returned to the beach. But we didn't return to partying with normal women. Thoughts of Pat made it impossible. She kept popping into my mind, sometimes making me moody, at other times hitting me with bouts of depression. And I'd vent my pain on Harris, resulting in spats between us.

Harris seemed to understand. In spite of our spats, he was lively and fun to be around, many times lifting my spirits when they were in dire need of elevation. But also he could be downright embarrassing. He delighted in making fun of the Greeks, and while in downtown Iraklion, on several occasions, he'd approach some poor, downtrodden, gullible Greek on the street and pour scorn on him under a soothing pretense of praising him.

In his singular, trademark posture, Harris got right up in the face of the Greek and, smiling broadly, with a soft, placating tone suggesting the greatest fondness and reverence, as though the Greek elicited his utmost admiration, purred:

"You dirty, dumb, filthy scumbag shit-eating, smelly, never-took-a-bath-in-your-life shit for brains moron, why don't you flush your ugly self down a toilet with the rest of your stinking family sewage."

Not understanding a word of English, the poor Greek would fall all over himself, feeling honored, feeling that Harris was paying him the greatest homage.

I always felt Harris was picking on the wrong person. He should have been addressing those remarks to me.

In my efforts to escape myself, escape my pain over Pat, Harris and I roamed all over Crete in his jeep, a cooler full of beer always in the back seat. One weekend we traveled to Saint Nick's and on the way back I drove. The road, high up in a rugged range of jagged mountains, was the most treacherous and formidable one on the island—extremely narrow, dangerously winding, sharp curves suddenly jumping up at you, no protecting barriers along the road's edge. To one side of the road was the sheer steep expanse of the mountain, hard rock towering straight up. To the other side was the steep drop off of a cliff, plunging straight down into a swallowing ravine hundreds of feet below. And all along the route, scattered far beneath the road's cramped, unprotected width, one could see the mangled remnants of many vehicles at the ravine's bottom that had failed to negotiate the treacherous curves.

"Christ, if anyone goes off here, it's bye-bye birdie!" Harris commented a bit uneasily. Too steep! Too far down!" Then a little later, staring down at a large crushed vehicle a particularly ghastly sight, he frowned more uneasily, "I wonder if a whole family was wiped out in that one?"

But I didn't wonder. Nor did I care. At times, with the pain of Pat, I considered myself already dead.

Then, all of a sudden, the Shadow's laughter beginning to ring somewhere in my head, I was back in Shack 13, in Em Kilpatrick's '46 Chevy Coupe. I shifted the jeep out of gear, wanting to see how fast and far it would coast down a long stretch of descending, sharply winding road before us. As the jeep picked up speed, Harris' face began transforming through varying shades of green.

"Don, wha—wha—what the hell you doing?" He breathed gloomily, his face a flash of alarm. "Slow it down! You're going too fast for these curves!"

But I didn't slow it down. I was racing freely again in Kilpatrick's Chevy Coupe, but this time a more thrilling ride, excited by the rush of air hitting my face, pumping me with exhilaration, the sensation of speed a deliciousness vitalizing my being as I let the jeep keep on accelerating, an unharnessed feeling of ecstatic freedom.

"Fucking Christ, Don—you're crazy!" Harris thundered, his eyes maniacally fixed on the road ahead. "Slow it down!" S-L-O-W I-T D-O-W-N! You … You're way too fast for these curves!"

I ignored his pleas, now completely intoxicated by the fast flow of air bombarding against my face like some emotional aphrodisiac. "Don't worry, Harris," I gleamed, the jeep taking on more speed. "I got it!"

"You've got it hell! *Slow it down!*"

I threw him an ever so quick reassuring glance, my eyes catching his, eyes approaching the idiocy of sheer terror.

The jeep had reached a coasting speed of around 70 miles per hour when all at once we were bearing down on a vicious curve abruptly jumping out at us from nowhere. That was cause enough for dread, but coming around that curve, creeping up the side of the mountain, was a wide-bodied, dusty gray truck. The road was much too narrow for both of us to pass. The mountain was to my left, the steep gorge to my right. There was no where to go. If I rammed into the truck, or even grazed it, it was all over. And if I hit the brakes the jeep would immediately skid over the edge of the cliff.

"Unh-oh!" Harris moaned, his face a wilting sheet of white. Then, horror-struck, "Jesus fucking Christ Almighty! Look what you got us *into*!"

"Shut up, Harris. I got it!"

"*HOW!*"

"I don't know." I didn't. We had had it!

"SHIIIITTT!" Then Harris let out a strangled noise from his throat in what was less a scream than a gurgle, bracing for imminent death.

Suddenly the oncoming truck became that thick, gigantic, menacing rattlesnake Daddy had saved me from in Shack 3, returned for another shot at me. "Daddy!... Daddy!—Find the spring that controls your own Universe. Find…"

I swerved to the right as we passed by the truck—groaning around the curve in the slowest crawl—without touching it, the jeep's two outside wheels to the right airborne over the gorge for about 12 feet, then all four wheels miraculously back on the road, jarring loose several boulders sprawling down the mountainside.

There's no way we should have made it. The weight of the jeep when those wheels became airborne should have sent us plunging down into the ravine. But it didn't. And even then the curving road beyond the truck, which I couldn't see, had to curve just right for me to get all four wheels back onto it.

In deathly silence I coasted the jeep for another mile, braking its speed drastically, a thick dust trail fly-up behind us, pulling off to the side of the road at the first wide spot allowing such a maneuver. Harris, incapable of speech at the moment, sat immobilized in his seat, his face, motionless as hard rock, unchanged from the moment he became certain we had met our doom.

Strangely, my first feeling was one of harmony, similar to the harmony I had experienced in Pea River Swamp. Automatically I thought of the ghostlike figures and gave thanks. And with the thanks came sensations of vast satisfaction, the strange euphoric feeling that comes from facing death headon and surviving. The thrill of living on the edge, facing extreme danger, and escaping it. A rare high of the purest, most in distilled pleasure in life. I felt even more ecstatic than when I was speeding down the mountain road.

"Harris, we *made it*!" I shouted gleefully.

That jarred him back to life. "Yeah, you dumb son of a bitch!" He groaned, fixing me with a nebulous stare, the relief almost too much for him. "You almost *killed* us! You should have killed us! I don't know how you didn't kill us!" His words came in gulps and strained sighs of relief as the blood rushed to his face. "Why didn't you slow down like I told you to?"

"Quit your damn griping, Harris," I rejoined with more gleefulness. "We made it and that's all that matters." Cheerfully, I reached into the back seat to the cooler and grabbed two beers, then rammed one of them into his chest. "Let's celebrate. We're alive!"

"You know, Don," Harris said, a startled edge to his voice, "something about you has changed." He hesitated for a moment, then pursued adamantly, "You've turned into one crazy son of a bitch!" He hesitated once more, apparently coming out of his shock. "But you're right. We're alive. And I want to *stay* alive! This is our last trip on this fucking mountain road. Now move over. I'm driving."

After that we stayed clear of the mountains, except for some cave explorations around their edge, dangerous in their own right crawling through spaces with little room, running across the carcasses of sheep that had become wedged in the caves and couldn't get loose. Following the close call on the mountain road—after which my anxiety attacks ceased, most of our out-of-town excursions were limited to visiting remote Crete villages in the fertile valleys between the mountains, the disbelieving looks on the faces of the inhabitants in some of these villages clearly indicating they had never seen a motorized vehicle before. But the Greeks—Harris' warped view of them notwithstanding—were friendly people, and very hospitable, invariably offering us all the grapes we wanted from their vineyards. Grapes and olives, Crete's two major crops, were grown all over the island and the grapes—very large, usually white—had a sweet, delicious, irresistible taste beckoning you to eat more.

But not everything the Greeks offered us was irresistible. Once, while visiting this little old Greek lady in her village house, she insisted, in broken English—one of the few Greeks we ran across speaking any semblance of English-that we join her in coffee and she proceeded to bring us a strange concoction in two small white skinny coffee mugs. Sipping the weird-looking brew, Harris and I both gagged on the stuff, strong enough to keep a horse wired for a year.

"You like?" The old lady beamed, eager to be the perfect hostess.

We both essayed smiles, nodding our heads affirmatively.

"I'll get cookies."

When she left the room, Harris frowned at me and said. "I don't know about you, but I'm not drinking this shit!"

"Remember the orders."

"Fuck the orders!"

"Right."

We both darted for the door, quickly emptied the mug contents outside, and hastened back to our seats. Upon the old lady's return, with cookies, she asked how we liked the coffee. We told her it was the best coffee we had ever tasted in our lives.

Since the Boo-Turkish fez riot, we had been instructed in no uncertain terms by the Air Force regarding the utmost importance of diplomacy in dealing with these outer Crete villagers. And lying was a crucial part of that diplomacy, the best liars becoming ambassadors.

At the end of September Harris and I took a thirty-day leave together and toured Europe. We sailed from Iraklion to Athens, then boarded another boat to Brindisi, Italy. From there we took a train to Munich, Germany.

Trains in southern Italy at that time weren't exactly the Orient Express. The one we boarded was old, noisy and dirty, and we ended up being herded into a cramped compartment with a mob of other people, including families with squawling children, and rotated with them standing up and sitting down on less than a square foot section of hard bench. We were cold and miserable the entire trip, bringing to mind my trips to the storm pits back home.

In northern Italy we got rid of the Italian storm pit. We switched to a German train, one more modern, more comfortable, cleaner, quieter, and allowing you more privacy. And a fantastic view. The train passed high through the mountains, through the Dolomite range, this view of the Italian Alps a view of the magnificence of Creation. Breathtaking. Overawing you with its grandeur; overpowering in its sheer striking picturesque beauty. A majesty of Nature, the towering peaks capped with snow mesmerizing, forever imprinted upon the memory, paling everything else into insignificance by comparison.

I could only gaze at it in wonder, taking deep breaths, the awe of each breath invigorating every cell in my body, harmonizing me, rendering my mental defenses useless. And while useless I thought of Pat rather than fighting to forget her; admitting to myself how much I missed her; admitting that I wished she were here now, with me, to share this grandeur and majesty, become one with it.

Then we arrived in Munich and the Alps were gone, and so was its beauty and power, and my trance dissolved and my defenses sprung back intact, once more getting on with the task of forgetting Pat. The festive mood in Munich offered a smoke screen setting helping me to do just that.

It was Oktoberfest in Munich, a two week massive drunk, Bavarian style, a time of merriment with no holds barred, brass bands and orchestras everywhere, everyone dancing and singing and carousing to their hearts content, the spirit of comradery prevailing, attended by people from every country and every walk of life. An endless sprawl of concession stands, tents, rides and shows. And pretzels and beer. And more beer. Beer consumed in gigantic quantities. Beer dirt cheap.

Drunks were everywhere, and Harris and I joined their ranks, finding everyone to be friendly, particularly the Germans, great lovers of song and great drinking buddies. Before long we found ourselves whimsically shouting, "Achtung!" And clicking our heels.

But the German beer tents proved to be too much for us. There were seven of them. Massive tents. And Harris and I vowed to drink a beer in each one of them, making it a contest, a challenge to our capacity to drink. But these weren't ordinary beers. Each beer was served in a huge Bavarian stein, about 36 ounces. We guzzled through six tents, joining in on the gusty German songs in each one, and headed for the seventh. But by now we weren't walking. We were crawling. And becoming sick. Slurring German lyrics all out of order, crawling up the steps of the seventh tent was as far as we got. Then wham! Harris and I became dizzyingly sick at the same time, rolling over to the edge of the steps and throwing up.

And in my drunken agony I thought of Pat. And again I could hear the Shadow laughing.

Shortly after our thirty-day leave was over, and I was back at the Iraklion Air Force Intelligence Base, I received a letter from Pat, written in her elegant hand.

> Dear Don,
> Hope this letter finds you well and happy. I'm okay. School's in session. Sorry you missed the last night. What happened? Sure you had a good reason. I'll never forget my vacation in Crete. It was wonderful; You were wonderful! I've thought of you every day and I really want to see you again, hopefully in America next summer. That would really be wonderful! As you can see, I miss you very much, so please write and let me know how you feel and what you think of next summer.
>
> Love, Pat
>
> P.S. I loved the plate smashing.

For an instant, the letter brought me a twinge of sadness. But quickly it was dispelled, replaced by the grimace of pain. I wished she hadn't written. Away from the spell of the Alps, my mental defenses wanted whatever there was between us to be finished. It would be unthinkable to answer her letter, or to see her next summer. With Pat's class, education, and proper family upbringing, there was no way I could introduce her to the chaos of my personal life; explain to her the degrading poverty of my crazy backwoods upbringing, or the ignobility of my childhood nightmare existence preventing me from relating normally to a decent girl. No way I could explain that, much less expose her to it. No way!

CHAPTER 21

I N MARCH OF 1965, at the age of 21, after a 15 month tour of duty in Crete, with 21 months remaining to serve on my four year hitch in the Air Force, I left the scenic Greek island to return to the United States, receiving another thirty-day leave before reporting for my new assignment at Kelly Air Force Base in San Antonio, Texas.

My trek home took me from Crete to Athens, then a flight from there to New York, another flight to Atlanta, then one to Columbus, Georgia. Flying back to the states I viewed myself as being both baffling and paradoxical, plagued by doubts that I'd ever be normal, and wondering if, sexually, the only women in my life would be whores.

J.P. and Doris met me at the Columbus airport, with them the Grissett brothers, David and Ricky, my drive-in sneak in buddies from Phenix City Central High School. David was the same as ever—tall, dark and handsome. Ricky, though, had changed. Now six foot, like me he had grown considerably since high school, his face fuller and nicer looking, well structured like his brother's beneath a mane of jet black hair. But he still had that bug-eyed expression, with its hint of wildness.

The game plan for my thirty-day leave was to spend the first two weeks in Alabama, the second two in Mexico, with David, Ricky, and a friend of theirs, Gary, accompanying me to south of the border. But first we needed transportation.

Having saved four hundred dollars for a down payment, I went car shopping. I found what I wanted; a sharp 1962 yellow Corvair Monza, clean, super-looking, fast-driving and at a price I could afford. I bought it, J. P. cosigning for me on the balance.

Every day for the first week of my leave, David, Ricky, I and Gary—a short, stocky lad, blond hair, pleasant face but shifty eyes—would huddle together in Phenix City, most often at J. P.'s house, planning our trip to Mexico. At one of those planning sessions I took out my album of Crete photographs and showed them to the three.

"Who is this, Donald?" David asked curiously, pointing to a photo of Pat. "You never told us you were going out with somebody *like* this! You and her are all over these pictures. She's *beautiful!* Who is she? Where's she from? Why didn't you tell us about her in your letters?"

At that moment Ricky let out a wolf-whistle, pondering over the photos of Pat in an affected, cross-eyed manner. "Beautiful? That *ain't* the word! She's an *angel!* Tell us about her, Don."

The palms of my hand began to moisten. "There's really nothing to tell. We just went out a time or two. No big deal."

"No big deal?" David yelped. "Look at the two of you in the back of this jeep. *That's a big deal!*"

"It... it ... it's nothing," I insisted, an ironic sadness to my eyes. "Really, it's nothing."

"You must be crazy to think that it's nothing!" Ricky countered. "I got eyes. Look at the way you two are looking at each other. Scratch my ass, but that's love, man!"

He had hit a nerve, leaving me naked in my pain. "Forget the pictures! Let's go shoot some pool."

"I knew it. You're in love with her! What happened? She dump you for some double-talking officer?"

"Shut up, Ricky. You're crazy."

"You're the crazy one!"

"Forget who's crazy, forget shooting pool." Gary interjected. Let's get back to Mexico. If you want something beautiful, the streets are lined with them there. All waiting to hop in your pants."

The second week of my leave I went to see Mama and Daddy. They had moved back to Shack 15, where we had been living when Red was caught screwing that mule.

"The Air Force making' ya any different?" Daddy asked, swishing his cigarette back and forth across his mouth with his tongue.

"Not really," I deadpanned.

"Didn't figure." Daddy coughed, then sighed heavily, frowning at my shiny yellow Corvair Monza. "Ya sure ya need that fancy thing?" He was beginning to show the wear of his wild and woolly life, his singular laugh not quite so loud now, his features not lighting up as much.

Mama was more astonished at my physical being. "Lord have mercy!" She screeched. "Look how you've grown! Ya must be six feet now. And look at the meat on yer bones! How much ya weighin'? I'd say at least a hundred, sixty."

"One hundred and sixty-five." I corrected.

"I'm proud," she said nicely, deceptively bland, capable of changing that voice to unkind gritty chalk on a blackboard in an instant. "Yer my favorite, Donald. I always knowed ya'd turn out good!"

"Real good. Mama."

The first two days of my stay at Shack 15 Mama and Daddy went out of their way to make certain they were peaceful, Mama particularly making an effort to cut down on her fighting with Daddy over his drinking, no mean accomplishment. But it was thin consolation, in no way easing my discomfort, or an old restlessness inexorably creeping over me, causing me to feel out of sorts, wistful, lost again in the merciless vexations of my childhood.

Though this was familiar, on the other hand I felt like a stranger in a sordid land, one feeling confused and jittery, volatile and vulnerable, much like a reluctant war veteran revisiting an historical battlefield he'd just as soon never see again, the guns now quiet, the mangled corpses long removed, the splattered blood cleaned up, only the memories of horror vibrating the air. It was here that the war for Pat had been fought and decided, before we ever met.

Then came more beautiful memories, the mountains of Crete, then the Alps, and for a few moments my visualization of the Alps became the loveliness of Pat, and I smiled a sad private smile as tender memories laid siege to my mind.

Out of some weird notion of respect carved from scorn, I planned to stay with Mama and Daddy for a week, but on the third day the peace was broken. Red became plastered, really petulantly and obnoxiously drunk, and Mama tore into him with a vengeance, then tore into Daddy, a chaotic uproar reintroducing me to my darker thoughts, reactivating my anger. That night, the Shadow appeared in a dream.

"Welcome *home*, pal!"

"Leave me alone!"

"Leave you alone?" The Shadow's face then changed to that of Daddy's. "Can't leave ya alone. Ya ain't seen nothin' yet!" Daddy began laughing. Then his face was that of the Shadow's again, the Shadow's horrid laughter, intensifying, becoming deafening. I awoke. Mama was screaming to hit the storm pit. I left the shack right then and there, the day's uproar a clear reminder of why I had left in the first place, something that time had blurred during a long absence.

CHAPTER 22

I WAS SUPPOSED to be on leave, R and R, rest and recuperation, but on my drive back to Phenix City from Shack 15 I could still hear the Shadow's laughter invading my brain, my muscles tense and taut, each mile tightening its grip on me. I never wanted to return to the shacks. Ever!

Arriving in Phenix City, I went to J. P.'s house. Ricky was there. So was my nephew, Roger Dale Riley, Ruby Lee's oldest son—15, white-headed, tall, skinny, very much on the wild side, a heavy boozer, definitely a Riley.

"Let's go out on the town," I said.

Hopping in my car, the three of us set out for a night of carousing. I had several bottles of Seagram's V. 0. Canadian blended whiskey I had brought back from Crete, and Ricky and I hit the bottles heavily. To Roger Dale's chagrin, I refused to let him have a drop.

Like Daddy, I could drink a good amount of liquor without it affecting my judgment or coordination—it took a lot to get me sloppily drunk. But Ricky couldn't. Like Red, when sober, Ricky was a pleasant, good-natured, likable person. But when drunk he was something else. And he got drunk on the V. 0. whiskey. Exceptionally drunk, sneaking Roger Dale a few gulps while I was driving.

With Ricky obviously plastered, me less so, Roger Dale not quite sober, the three of us stopped at a Phenix City nightclub, the Sans Souci, and went in. Immediately we were stopped just inside by a female door attendant, a beefy blonde looking like a Dixie Mafia male bouncer.

"You guys can't come in here!" She growled. "We're not going to serve you. You're too drunk!"

"Dru... Drunk?!" Ricky stammered, his eyes bug-eyed, popping out now more than usual. "Good God Almighty, lady, I'm not drunk!" He slurred, barely able to keep his feet, his V. 0. thick voice becoming uppity. "So give me a drink, honey. A V. 0. with Seven-up." Then looking at me with that glassy fog of one well inebriated, "Whatcha having, Donald?"

"Nothing. She's right, Ricky. Come on, let's go. Let's get out of here. We don't want any trouble."

"No, damnit, Donald, she's... she's not right! We're ... we're ... we'reeeer not drunk! We'reeeer going to stay."

"Get out of here!" Beefy Blonde gritted. "*Go!*"

"Ricky, damnit, the lady doesn't want us here. This is not the only place in town to drink. Let's go! *Now!*"

"She—eeet, Donald!"

I grabbed him by the arm and led him out of the club, Roger Dale right behind us, Ricky complaining. "goddammit. Donald," he protested peevishly, becoming more rowdy, "we'reeeeer not thaaaaat drunk! She had no right ... no. no. no right, to make us leave!"

"She has every right." I informed, opening the Corvair's passenger side door. "So get in the car and let's go."

"Damn, that makes me madder'n hell!"

With that, Ricky broke my grip on his arm, reached down on the floorboard of the front seat, picked up a 12 ounce Coke bottle and, looking around in disgust, smashed it against the windshield of the car parked next to mine.

I couldn't believe it!

Quickly pushing Ricky into the front seat, Roger Dale next to him nearer the driver's side, I slammed the door, hastened around to the wheel and hightailed it out of the club's parking lot in a hurry. We hadn't traveled much more than a block when I caught the flash of a police car's blue light in the rearview mirror.

"Shit."

I pulled over to the side of the road, the police car edging up behind me. Two uniformed policemen exited the car and approached us cautiously on either side. "Get out of the car, boys!" One of them ordered, harsh voice, meaning business.

Immediately I complied, easing out of the car. But Ricky and Roger Dale remained defiantly seated inside.

"Get *out* of the car!" The officer reiterated.

"Go to *hell*!" Ricky blasted. "Nobody's going nowhere!"

"Aw shit, Ricky!" I grimaced. "Shut up and get out of the car for chrissake!"

Ricky glared at me through the open window with that strickened wave of self-pity only drunkenness can affect. "All damn night people's been ... been telling us what we can do. Do this! Do ... do ... do that! I'm tired of it!"

"Yeah, even the pigs are in on it tonight." Roger Dale stupidly piped in.

"I'd advise you boys to keep your mouths shut and get out of the car," the other officer, to Ricky's side of the car, emphasized. "*Now*!"

"*Fuck you*!" Ricky retaliated. "I'm not getting out!"

"Yeah, fuck you!" Roger Dale echoed. "We're not gettin' out!"

Ricky quickly rolled up the car window as the officer grabbed the handle of the passenger side door, attempting to yank it open as Ricky clutched at the inside handle, pulling in, preventing him from doing so. Then with both officers pulling on it the door yanked open and Ricky, cursing, was wrestled out of the car.

"You *sonsabitches*!" Ricky screamed, glaring at the officers, taking a wild swing at one of them, missing with his fist but hitting the officer in the body with his elbow. I grabbed Ricky's arms, preventing him from throwing another punch, while one of the officers handcuffed him.

"You don't go quietly, do you!" The officer said to Ricky, not displeased to use a little force. He pushed Ricky back into me with a stout arm and I held him there.

"Easy, Ricky," I cautioned. "Easy... easy ... easy!"

"Easy, shit! They're mother fuckers! Whore fuckers! Bastards! Pricks! Cunt eaters!"

With Ricky screaming in handcuffs, me trying to hold and calm him down, the officers pulled Roger Dale from the car and put cuffs on him as well. Then all three of us were crammed into the back seat of the police car and hauled off to the city jail.

Christ, when the Air Force gets wind of this they'll kick my ass out of the service in a second, I mused. All I wanted was R and R, not a free-for-all with the police.

The Phenix City Jail was dismal and disheartening, the cells packed with human refuse—livid screams, fuzzy mutterings, violence, even savagery. And the constant, oppressive odor of rancid sweat. After being shoved into a cell, a policeman came and unlocked the door. "You can leave now," he said. "There's no charges against you. The arresting officers said you cooperated, and indeed even helped in subduing the other two. But you're still under the influence so I'm afraid you can't drive. We'll keep your car overnight and you can pick it up in the morning. I suggest you take a cab home."

I did, taking a taxi to J.P.'s.

Unfortunately, Ricky and Roger Dale remained locked up. The next day Roger Dale, being a minor, was turned over to the Juvenile Authorities while Ricky was charged with public drunkenness, disorderly conduct, resisting arrest and striking a police officer. That same day Ricky was released from jail under bond and later, acquiring an excellent attorney, managed to have all charges against him dropped.

He looked and behaved so sweet when sober.

With Ricky out of jail, our planned trip to Mexico got underway as scheduled. We drove to Del Rio, Texas and crossed the border into Acuna, Mexico, our destination. The entire town was a walking whorehouse, prostitutes roaming everywhere, a place where a gringo could live like a padishah with his fill of whores. There were so many of them, mostly pretty women, some quite beautiful, that it was tough deciding where to jump in.

I jumped in with this pretty young thing by the name of Juanita—flowing black hair, hot dazzling dark eyes, leggy, nimble and a body so ripe that it would keep a man from siesta. Without posturing or artifice, she kicked off her shoes, disrobed as if holding a Gold Medal in the event and gave me a bare-toed roll in bed you couldn't put a price tag on.

Later, while David, Ricky, Gary and I were recuperating from some very serious whoremongering in a bar over beer, this stunningly beautiful Mexican lady, early 20s, long, brownish-sweet legs, came prancing up to me at our table and flung herself on my lap.

"I'm Maria," she moaned, a rhythmic voice of good English, squeezing out a bawdy wink as she put her arm around my neck. "I really like your looks. Juanita said you were *hung* like a donkey! Ooohhhh! Come up stairs with me, donkey!

Instantly the other three unhinged into an up and down shaking fit of laughter, tittering so loudly, so hard and so uncontrollably, that I was certain they'd gag themselves.

"No, no," I said above the din of laughing spasms, red-faced with embarrassment. "That's okay."

"For you—free!"

"No, no. That's still okay."

"You sure?"

"I'm sure."

Skillfully, she began rubbing her buttocks against my groin, at the same time plopping her ample tits in my face. "Show you good time you never have before!"

"Hey, hung like a donkey." David chortled, "Go on upstairs and let her show you a good time. I mean, how can you refuse a *donkey* lover?"

I blushed, gently lifted the persistent lady up off my lap, then quickly left the bar. But that wasn't the end of it. Each time we went into a restaurant—or anywhere—after that, either David, Ricky or Gary mocked, "Hung like a donkey, what are you having this time? A little hay, or a jump in the hay!" Then they burst into laughter, laughing at me, reminding me of the Shadow.

And word got around among the senorita whores. Several of them approached me offering their services "free." And I began feeling like some kind of freak. Suddenly I became tired of whores.

After nine days in Acuna, nine days of screwing, drinking and sobering up in the Mexican sunshine, our stay was over. I had to get on to Kelly Air Force Base. David, Ricky, and Gary—as well as myself—were as broke as convicts, having spent all of their money on prostitutes and booze. Unable to afford a bus back to Phenix City, they hitchhiked there.

I arrived at Kelly in San Antonio, Texas in mid April, 1965, and reported for my new assignment. Once back on duty I began missing Harris, still stationed in Crete. But Boo and Dennis—the airman who finished at the head of the Goodfellow AFB training class—were now stationed at Kelly too, and after work we went out together, mostly to these special type bars, known as Texas ice houses, and to drive-in restaurants.

Then I heard from Harris. A disquieting letter. Harris corresponded with Pat's Crete vacationing girlfriend, Anne, and through her Pat had inquired of Harris about me, and Harris passed this inquiry along in his letter.

Painfully trying to forget Pat, her inquiry only intensified my heartache. Reading Harris' letter I finally concluded that the only way to forget a woman was to find a new one. Not a whore. Not a one night stand. Not a short superficial relationship. But a full blown one; commitment, duration, caring—and sex, working through the problems there rather than fleeing them.

Normal or not, that's what I saw myself as having to do. End my pain once and for all through another woman. A lasting relationship. I set out looking for prospects.

One of the drive-in restaurants I frequented often was the Frontier. One night I journeyed to the Frontier with Dennis, the studious type but with a penchant for fun, and pulled in beside a 1957 yellow and white Chevy. Two girls were seated in the car and the one behind the wheel was by far the prettiest— striking me as one hell of a prospect.

We glanced at one another at the same time and sort of locked eyes, her smile soaking me with a warm feeling. Definitely a prospect. Wasting no time, I exited my car and walked around hers to the driver's side, gazing at her with what I hoped was a bewitching smile.

"Hi, I'm Don," I said. "How are you?" I figured the ball game would be in her reply. If it were three strikes and out I'd take solace in a hamburger and french fries.

"I'm great!" She enthused, her tone a great sense of life and vitality. "I'm Linda. And how are you?"

"Fine. Just fiiinnee!" She made me feel fine. A well built blonde, skin a golden bronze, eyes wide and as blue as the Mediterranean, her hair floated about her face in gentle short waves. And she had the softest voice, one that would melt rocks.

"I really love your car," she offered. "It's beautiful!"

"Oh, thanks. I like yours too." But Enough small talk. Now for the question separating the prospects from the non-prospects. "Why don't you and your friend come join me and my buddy Dennis over there and let's go for a ride?"

I could see in her gleam that she wanted to. No strikeout here. Quickly glancing at her girlfriend—just a notch above the plain side, edging toward attractiveness—she said "Ann, what do you think?" Ann nodded her approval and she turned back to me. "Really? You *mean* it?"

"Follow me."

The four of us drove aimlessly around San Antonio, talking and becoming acquainted, from which I learned that Linda was a senior in high school and working part time as a telephone operator. We hit it off well enough to fuel my hope that she'd be my commitment. Subsequently, Linda and I began phoning one another and went out on several dates, social outings developing our relationship. In doing so we discovered that we liked each other, and our relationship began becoming more and more special. Things were moving according to plan.

There was only one thing wrong with my plan; I had no idea how I was going to introduce Linda to my past or to my family, part of the bugaboo that had done me in with Pat. True, Linda didn't possess the class or depth of Pat, but nevertheless she was a decent girl from a normal, respectable family living in a fine, respectable home and community. Still way out of my league.

Having no solution. I deferred that problem until later.

Near the end of June Linda invited me to her graduation. And Ann—also a senior—invited Dennis. On graduation day we picked the girls up, Linda dressed to kill, wearing a long emerald green velvet gown which swept low in the front, exposing the softness of her bosom, swelling invitingly. She was so beautiful, bustling about, her eyes more sparkling than ever, bluer than I had imagined, eliciting the spark of something wonderful wanting to happen again.

On that day, at that time, Linda made me forget about Pat. Everything was going as planned.

Following the graduation ceremony, Dennis, Ann, Linda and I enjoyed dinner at a swank restaurant and afterwards, venturing out into the soft night, drove around for a short while in Dennis' car, an old four-door Plymouth, then parked at a lover's lane. Linda and I in the back seat, a small gleam of moonlight in her eyes.

With Dennis and Ann beginning to make out in the front seat, an impish grin formed on Linda's face as she removed her delicately heeled green slippers, wiggling her stockinged feet in seeming innocence, then moved closer and cuddled up to me in the back. At first it was pure pleasure taking her in my arms, feeling my chest warm and expand, feeling the gentle fullness of her body press against mine, feeling the hardness of her young breasts against my chest, her breath upon my throat. Initially, when our lips first met, the pressure was gentle, exploratory. Then the pressure became crushing, Linda suddenly kissing me as though she were in training for Acuna, such a sudden and unexpected passionate onslaught leaving my mind reeling, automatically raising the old red flag.

She's a decent girl! She's too nice for you! She lives in a nice house! She lives with nice parents! She—

I pulled away from her, beads of sweat forming on my forehead, my heart pounding within my chest.

"What's wrong?" Linda frowned.

"Your eyes are too blue," I answered, my voice cracking.

"What kind of dribble is that?"

Her gentle sarcasm underscored the absurdity of my remark, the absurdity of my situation. What the hell am I doing? I'm defeating my own plan. My determination to be normal. My desire for a lasting relationship. My wish to forget Pat. Forget pain. I set this moment up, I have to see it through.

"Never mind," I said. "Come here, baby!"

Brazenly, I grabbed her in my arms, going on the offensive, kissing her as passionately as she'd kissed me, sucking in her hot breath, kissing her lips, her neck, the crevice of her bodice. She responded by writhing her body hard against mine, her throat emitting little moaning, groaning darts of rapture, her breath becoming hotter, the moans louder, more desperate, coming in gasps, the rawest, most lustful scenario of foreplay I had ever been a party to.

"Feel me!" She groaned, squirming madly. "Suck me! Suck me *all* over!"

My hands squeezed at her breasts, firm bulges throbbing as hard as bricks, drawing their fullness upwards until my lips met with hot skin. She moaned loudly, throatily, grabbing at my penis, that move triggering my panic. Abruptly opening the car's back door, I got out, retreating to the car's rear, leaning on the trunk beneath the stars, slightly misted and seeming so distant. Linda was out of the car too, following me, all hot and bothered. Dennis and Ann, caught up in their own lust in the front seat, paid us no heed.

"My God!" Linda whimpered, bewildered, just a touch surly. "What am I *doing*? What am I doing?!"

It was half time and I was behind. Badly. I couldn't keep on bungling this so attempted to overcome my panic with a rousing inner pep talk:

Don, this is it! It's all on the line! Get in there and fight for the team—fight for normalcy. Get in there and fuck this girl. Fuck! Fuck! Fuck!

"You're doing fine," I deadpanned when I finally spoke, my face drawn and flushed. "I'm just taking a breather. A little too much excitement. But I'm okay now. Let's get back in the car."

"I hope for more than just kissy-kissy."

"You're getting the works, baby," I contemplated aloud.

Back in the car she burbled hot little nothings into my ear, igniting us back into passionate embrace, her body again squirming all over me, but her groans deeper, more expectant, her kisses wild and wanton, begging out of her mind to be made love to, our kisses so fiery and intense that I had cuts and bruises all over my lips for days afterwards.

Becoming frustrated with our prolonged kissing foreplay, Linda took the offensive, running her hands down my back beneath the bottom of my shirt until her hands were tearing at the nakedness of my skin, plundering, grabbing all over my legs, my buttocks, my groin, my penis, my testicles. Then pushing her gown upwards, exposing her panties, she began pulling my hand down toward her crotch, moaning heavily:

"Feel me! Feel me inside! I want you! Take me! Take me anyway you want, but *just* take me!"

"Our first time shouldn't be in the back seat of a car," I sputtered. The game was lost.

She looked at me in dumbfounded question, both puzzling and alarming, her body trembling. "*What?*"

"Our first time making love should be somewhere more private. More dignified. Not here. Not now."

Linda recoiled, like a victim. "What kind of whacko *are you?*"

I returned her stare, the futile pain of paralyzed shock, as though I were another entity, the pain cementing my tongue to iron. I was terrified. She was Pat all over again.

"Oh, *shit*!Aaaauugghhh … ooohhhhhhh!" Her disgruntled squeal jarred my ears. She was almost berserk.

Ann's eyes popped up over the front seat, that well-screwed look beneath a wispy bush of hair all tangled in corkscrews. "Linda, what's *all* the commotion?"

"*Get me home!*"

Linda wouldn't go out with me again. I received another letter from Harris. Pat, through Anne, had made another inquiry about me, wanting me to know that she'd be coming to America soon.

"Oh, God no, Pat! Don't try to look me up!"

At that moment my pain was so intense that I was hurled into uncontrollable sorrow.

CHAPTER 23

I QUIT PURSUING women, the sexual debacle with Linda, the earlier one with Pat, personal disasters I couldn't ignore, making it too clear that I'd never be normal with normal women, those above my cultural station in life. That eliminated most prospects. Gradually I even quit running around with my Air Force buddies after work, my heart no longer in activities with them. This left me with time on my hands, time I filled by seeking a part-time job off the base.

I didn't need the money. It was my version of joining the French Foreign Legion.

In September I made application at the Frontier drive-in restaurant and was hired on the spot as a cook and general helper trainee during the late afternoon and evening, my work assignments involving me almost anywhere I was needed. A few days after I hired on I had the strangest dream involving the Shadow. The dream had a peaceful setting, a green meadow, a golden mellow sun, the rest of the setting rather surrealistic. The Shadow, appearing even civil, the intensity of his eyes subdued, as was his manner, behaved totally out of character. There was no laughing. And he was talkative.

"Who are you?" I asked, as I had countless times before.

This time the Shadow answered. "Let's just say I'm your guardian."

"*Guardian*?! Guardian of *what*?!"

"Your needs."

"My *needs*?! Sorrow? Suffering so with Pat? Linda? Even Patsy?"

"They weren't worthy of you."

"*What*?! . . ."

"You will meet someone who is."

The dream ended. Quietly. No horror. No terror. No torment. Yet when I awoke I somehow felt I had just had my worst nightmare.

A few days later the Frontier hired a new car hop, Sandra Miller, a good-looking, hazel-eyed gal with a clear complexion and splendid movements. Her figure was the gentle fullness of a woman, small waist, well proportioned hips, and her hair was somewhere between a brown and brownish red, depending upon whether it was night or day, and the heaviness of the sun.

One day late in the afternoon, just after I had arrived at the Frontier, Sandra, who came to work earlier in the day, approached me as I swept the floor.

"Hi. How are you doing?" She said, her mouth cornering into a slight smile. Her voice had an earthy vibrance, seeking softness.

"As well as this broom will allow." Her hair was done in a fancy new hairdo, sort of layered on top of her finely shaped head, and I added. "I like your hair."

Her eyes went wide-eyed with excitement, suggesting compliments didn't come that often. "Do you really like it?!"

"Yeah. It looks—well, attention grabbing."

She giggled, breaking into a wider smile. "Thank you. Say, could I ask a favor? I need a ride home. Could you take me home tonight?"

"Sure. Where do you live?"

"On Roosevelt Drive."

"That's right on my way to the base."

But later, Sandra's father, a short potbellied man in cowboy boots, shirt and hat, showed up unexpectedly in an old yellow jeep and took Sandra home instead.

Sandra apologized the next day. "Daddy brings me to work but he's a self-employed musician working a lot at night and usually can't pick me up. Last night was an exception. Can you take me home tonight?"

"As I said, it's right on my way home."

After work, shortly after Sandra was in the Corvair, she said, "We don't have to go straight home."

I wasn't looking for a prospect. "Where to, then?"

"Let's just ride around for awhile and talk."

We did, with Sandra asking me all kinds of questions about myself. I answered them broadly, safely, revealing nothing significant about my civilian background, in our exchange finding out that she was 18 years old and lived in a trailer park with her father, mother, brother and four sisters, she the eldest of the children. My impression was that Sandra had little opportunity to talk much with people, and welcomed any chance to do so.

"As much as I can, I run the household for daddy, cook his meals, and take care of the laundry and kids." Sandra told me. I wondered what her mother did but wasn't that interested to ask.

Finally taking her home I didn't expect the trailer park Sandra lived in to be such an eyesore. Not only was it shoddy, but the rubbish, junk and dismantled old cars—many of them perched haphazardly up on blocks—scattered everywhere made it look like a condemned dump. And most of the trailers, including the one Sandra lived in, were dilapidated, run down, filthy, with broken windows and ripped screens, all of them submerged in a common layer of putrid odors sickening enough to gag a rat, giving me an uneasy feeling of deja vu, the trailers reminding me of my entire childhood. Shacks 1 through 17 all crammed into one small squalid area.

The shabby trailer Sandra lived in consisted of just two bedrooms, one of them doubling as a living room, plus a small kitchen and one bath, much too small for the number of people living in it.

No wonder Sandra was in no hurry to get home, I thought, feeling a strange empathetic affinity toward her.

I found myself taking her home almost every night, often parking on the way to her trailer and just talking, chatting between two fellow employees.

"We had a nice home in Houston." Sandra told me. "On Breland Street. I sure miss it."

"What happened?" I asked.

"Oh, daddy owed the IRS a bunch of back taxes and they just came and took our home away. It killed me! Then daddy built our trailer."

"I can see why you miss your home in Houston."

"The physical home, yes. But not what went on inside."

"What was that?" I asked matter-of-factly, making conversation.

Her answer wasn't so matter-of-fact. "Mama was always drunk," she said, her voice taking on a grave quality, her hazel eyes beginning to brood. "Always running around with other men! And mama and daddy were always fussing about the drinking and the men! I mean, real bad fights. I remember during one fight," Sandra shuddered, "mama grabbed a butcher knife and stabbed daddy in the stomach with it. He almost died!"

I looked at Sandra more pointedly, arching my brows in expression, my interest suddenly less detached. I could see her pain and instantly I identified with it.

"My mama's a hard core alcoholic," Sandra continued, as if needing someone to confide in, "either bordering on insanity or at times actually insane! She does some crazy things! And some mean things! Real cruel things!"

Sandra was much more open talking about her family than I was talking about mine, and the more she spoke of her mother, the more it became apparent that her mother was not just insane but downright evil. The more I learned of what her mother put her through—was still putting her through, and how she survived it, taking care of her younger brothers and sisters while her mother terrorized the family with her alcoholic and insane rampages, the more I began admiring Sandra, viewing her as an unusually sturdy person, one having an underscore of deep strength. I could relate to the turmoil or her life, and to her spunk and determination coping with it, overcome by her inner fortitude against all odds. And I felt a special tenderness for her filling myself within; a tenderness born from being battered myself on a similar path against defeating odds.

"Why does your daddy put up with it?" I asked.

"Us kids, I suppose. I don't know. He has his own problems."

Sandra's father, a one man band traveling all over East Texas to play in beer joints, hit the booze hard too. Several times after work Sandra and I visited a few of the beer dives where her father was working—rowdy places, dark, packed, smelly, noisy, the tables crowded together, people bumping against one another, the air reeking of cigarettes, cigars, slopped beer and dirty dishcloths—to hear him play and sing. He was an excellent musician, able to play any instrument, and he was gifted with a rich, talented singing voice, one that could emulate Johnny Cash perfectly. He had a performer's class written all over him and would have made a successful splash in the music business if he hadn't been straddled with an unhinged, alcoholic wife holding him back and destroying his opportunities.

"Daddy was once set up in a recording studio to cut an important record."

Sandra informed me, her voice sad. "But mama came crashing into the place, all drunk and crazy, smashing everything in the studio to pieces, and ruined his chance to make it big in the recording business. Daddy never tried again after that. He became a drunk."

Then it hit me. Bingo! Suddenly Sandra not only became a prospect, but with her I had struck gold. Someone with a family as bad as mine. Someone just as ashamed of her family as I was of mine. Someone with a family as crazy and mixed up and as destitute as mine. The more Sandra spoke of her parents, her upbringing, the more it became obvious that with her I didn't have to worry about my background; didn't have to hide it from her. Sandra's background was as impoverished and as chaotic as mine; producing as much anguish, anxiety, mistreatment, anger, depression and humiliation. She had contempt for her family and herself, as I had contempt for my family. I started taking Sandra home almost every night and was beginning to enjoy her company a great deal. I did notice that her mother was always holding a baby at the window each time we arrived and I asked her who the baby belonged to. Her answer was always "Oh, Just a friends."

Later, during one of our parking sessions, our hugging and kissing became heatedly intense, arousing my loins from tenderness to the swelling thickness of passion. Unable to contain myself, I pushed to make love to Sandra, confident that, being her equal, with nothing to hide from her, nothing now to be ashamed of, nothing to shock her in my background since hers was just as shocking, I'd be free of sexual problems with her, able to touch every part of her body, taste her completely, have her until she was part of me and I part of her. Totally.

But Sandra steadfastly resisted making love. "I want to very much." She groaned regretfully, anxious lines on her brow, "but believe me—I can't!"

This was an ironic twist. I stared at her in question, perplexed. "Why not?"

Her mouth twitched, dim shadows dulling the brightness of her eyes. "I … I really don't want to tell you—I'm so ashamed," she whimpered, eyes downcast in an air of resignation, "but I figure, sooner or later, I'll have to. I know I'll probably lose you, but I have to tell you. The little girl you saw mama holding is mine."

I sat stiff, startled, stunned, unprepared for that news, her words bringing a resurgence of despair and outrage, and crushing thoughts, so strongly were my feelings on this matter that I had broken off all communication with my sister, Marilyn, for having a baby out of wedlock.

"But I love you, Donald." The delicacy of her lips seemed to give out, hanging her mouth slack like a wound. "What … what do you want to do?"

I quietly allowed the dejection of Sandra's confession to settle within me. Then, "I want to take you home."

"I knew it!" A muted cry. One attempting to hide the tears moistening her eyes.

That night I had a nightmare about Daddy burning in hell. The Shadow flashed an appearance in the dream and, subdued, without laughter, stated, "With

Linda you have no worry about a decent girl." Then he was gone.

I didn't take Sandra home for the next few nights. In fact, I didn't say a word to her, giving her only silent glances at the Frontier. And after work, in my barracks at the base, my nights were nights of fitful sleep, a feeling of weary disaster, a time I was not part of this world. Then on my night off from the Frontier, when I returned to my barracks from duty, I retired to bed early and fell into a startling dream.

I was in a church. A wedding. Linda, dressed in a white gown, was the bride. I was the groom. The Shadow was my best man.

The dream snapped me awake. Bleary-eyed I blinked at the clock. The hands danced, multiplied, finally steadied, 11:04. Sandra would be getting off from work soon. Then the thoughts just came, as if laid out for me. To hell with Sandra having a baby out of wedlock. Time to push those feelings aside and do what's right. Help Sandra! I have to get her out of her atrocious environment. J.P. helped me escape my bad environment. I'll help Sandra escape hers. J.P. was my link to survival, I'll be hers.

Those noble thoughts concluded, I bolted out of my barracks, hopped in my Corvair and sped off to the Frontier, there screeching to a halt in front. Sandra, about to leave work, gawked at me with puzzled gladness.

"Let's go for a ride," I deadpanned.

"But daddy ..."

"Never mind daddy. Hop in! I've something important to say."

We drove to one of our parking spots, a small lane out in the country beneath some large trees, the stillness of the night sighing through them, the stars a quiet, peaceful twinkling, a soft chorus of insects the only sound.

"Sandra, we haven't known each other very long, but I feel I'm in love with you. Something inside me tells me we need each other. That we can help each other. So I wonder if you will marry me."

A breathless sigh engulfed her, then came the sparkling tears. "God, yes! You *know* I will!" Then her eyes went wide and serious. "But how do I know you really mean it. What ..."

"Believe me, I *mean* it!"

We embraced, then kissed, the matter settled.

Immediately we began making plans for our wedding. Sandra, though, strangely hesitant in the planning. Something was bothering her. A couple of days later I found out what it was.

"Don, I have a problem." She said, doleful and highly emotional, lips pale. "I'm only seventeen. I need daddy's consent to get married."

My eyes went blank. Then my jaw muscles rippled. "Seventeen?! You told me you *were* eighteen!"

She bit her lips, suffering a sigh. "I'm sorry." She whimpered. In spite of her valiant efforts the tears made their advance down her cheeks. "But I felt you wouldn't have anything to do with me if you knew I was only seventeen."

"But you shouldn't have lied about it!"

The tears running down her cheeks were now long, grotesque streaks of black. "I know. I'm sorry. I didn't want to lose you! I love you more than you'll ever know!"

"Okay," I replied, feeling a strong chill of emotion. "What else haven't you told me?!"

Her shoulders began shaking pitifully. Without energy she sobbed, "My daddy doesn't approve of you. He … he doesn't like you! He doesn't want us to be married! He's dead set against it!"

"I'll talk to him."

"No. Not yet. I'll make him come around. He owes me!" Then her body convulsed into open uncontrollable sobs, lonely-sobs of underlying goodness reaching out and tearing me apart. Unable to choke back my emotions any longer, tears were trickling down my cheeks as well, and I allowed them to flow freely, without embarrassment.

Three days later Sandra phoned me, ecstatically excited "Come pick me up. I've got tremendous news!"

"What? What is it? Tell me!"

"No, no. I want to tell you in person. Come on. Now! *Hurry!*"

I hightailed it to the trailer park. Sandra, standing in the yard, dashed toward the car, flinging her arms around my neck as soon as I stepped out of it.

"I *love* you!" She singsonged excitedly. "Guess what? Daddy said yes! He's driving me up to Austin tomorrow to get my birth certificate. Can you *believe* that?! He said *yes*! We're *getting* married!"

"Great! That *is* great!"

"It's a miracle! I can't understand it … I … I don't know what happened, but *something* just changed daddy's mind!"

"It was meant to be."

We hugged and kissed, and Sandra began laughing, a deep rhythmic bray radiating into contagious yelps of delight. "Come on," she enthused, bouncing with new spasms of energy, "let's go down to the Frontier and *tell* everybody!"

We set the date of our wedding for October 17, 1965, a month after we had met, and rented a comfortable, simple, well kept, one-bedroom furnished duplex next to Kelly field, on Quintana Drive. I moved into the duplex right away, Sandra to join me after the wedding. Though we were broke, we had fun fixing up the place. The only thing that bothered me about the duplex was that it was located almost on top of where the Air Force maintenance personnel serviced the B-52 bombers, and they were forever revving up the jet engines during all hours of the night, a deafening thundering racket.

The fresh early slant of sunshine turned Saturday, October 16, into a bright glowing golden day in San Antonio. I was waiting for Sandra in the duplex when I heard her drive up in her father's old clunker jeep. Hustling out to meet her, the sight of Sandra sent my hormones staggering. Happy, radiant, smiling, bubbling all over, clad in a pair of tight white short shorts, she was parading her lovely figure in full glory, her step springy, just the right wiggle, more than a mortal man could withstand.

Embracing her, my impatience transparent, I blurted. "Let's get married today. *Right now!*"

Not blinking an eye, she answered. "Okay."

"I'll get the preacher, you get ready!"

It took some searching to find the preacher. He wasn't expecting to marry us until tomorrow. But I found him. Reluctantly, he agreed to marry us at seven o'clock that evening, at the same church we were scheduled to be married in on Sunday. Because of the last minute change of plans, many of the people from the base and from the Frontier, invited to attend the wedding on Sunday, couldn't be reached so missed the Saturday ceremony. A handful of friends, those we hurriedly rounded up, plus Sandra's shabbily dressed family, were those in attendance.

There was no reception following the wedding—that had been planned for the next day, so after receiving the congratulations and well wishes of those in attendance, Sandra and I dashed off to our duplex, sent off by the ominous warning of Sandra's father to me in parting:

"If you mistreat my daughter I'll beat the *hell* out of you!"

"Don't worry." I replied, "I'll take *good* care of her!"

At the duplex Sandra and I nervously prepared for our honeymoon bed, both of us apprehensive. Stepping out of her wedding dress, Sandra popped her solid, firm body into a plain white gown, one of those simple wispy things heightening a woman's sexiness. Then, moving slowly, like music, she curled up on the bed, a double bed with a white coverlet. Moseying over to the bed's side, I disrobed as Sandra watched bright-eyed, rolled up onto an elbow, an oh-my-God look enlarging her eyes as she caught sight of my huge erection.

"I can't believe we're married." Sandra said breathily. "We're *actually* married!"

I smiled, gleaming, almost gloating. Sitting down on the bed, I replied in matching euphony. "Come over here and let me hold you and let's see if this is all for real.

She slid over to me. It was for real.

We leaned back, eyes half closed, and eased into our parking foreplay of hugging and kissing. Then, as a sweet, steady undercurrent of sensuousness aroused us, we slipped beyond our hugging and kissing, going where we hadn't gone before. I ended up hovering over her, pushing up her gown, the hardness of my groin against the firm young flesh of her thigh.

I was ready. Finally! That one, big, long-awaited magic moment! The bare, vibrating, soft, magic mound before me.

But the pure majesty of that moment was suddenly wiped out by the grinding blast of a B-52's jet engines, jarring us, becoming louder, until the revving thrust of the engines rocked the air with deafening assault.

Damn!

But undaunted, with the shattering noise of the jet engines serenading us, slowly, gently, I entered Sandra, hoping not to hurt her. She reacted by drawing me in deeper, giving of herself—moving—squirming—groaning. Then she let out a little scream of physical pain.

"Oohh … careful … easy … not all the way in … it hurts!

She couldn't take all of me. I was too big for her. I modified my thrusts, easing up, and eventually we reached a union of sexual tenderness and closeness satisfying to both of us.

For the first time in my life, other than with a whore, I had normal sex with a woman while feeling normal throughout. No fear or reluctance beforehand. No shame or guilt afterwards. And normal, enjoyable pleasure in between.

After having sex with Sandra I almost felt normal. But not quite. A fuzzy nagging sensation still tugged at me; a subdued, crepuscular feeling, almost ominous, like an open wound, only now with a little less salt.

Before falling asleep that night a phrase of Dylan Thomas' popped into my head:

"Do not go gentle into this good night."

I did not fall asleep gently. When I did I had a dream in which I was a noble knight on a horse, rescuing Sandra from a terrible dragon. Then suddenly I turned into that dragon. Then I was immediately into another dream. The Shadow was there, but he was no longer subdued, his black shining eyes burning more intently than ever. Then Sandra appeared it the dream tied to a stake, and the Shadow began chuckling at her. Then Sandra began transforming herself, slowly becoming Mama. Helpless. Defenseless.

"Now you can take your revenge!" The Shadow said hideously. Then he began his horrid laughter, the most deafening and tormenting yet.

CHAPTER 24

SUNDAY MORNING, OCTOBER 17, dawned into brightness, promising another day of brilliant sun. When I awoke, Sandra was stirring, not quite awake yet. I leaned over and kissed her, recalling our honeymoon lovemaking the evening before.

Her eyes popped open, their hazelness expanding in wonder. "I love you," she sighed, returning my kiss. Then, "Oh, did you have trouble sleeping last night? I felt you thrashing about. Who were you yelling at?"

"Just a bad dream," I said. I hugged her, sliding my hand down the fine curves of her spine. "Time to get up!" I cried, attempting joviality, slapping her on the rump.

"Get up for what?" She drawled sleepily.

"Breakfast. Then we make love."

Reluctantly, Sandra dragged herself out of bed and went into the bathroom. Emerging, she frowned, "I don't know about making love. I've got a bad bladder infection."

Sandra's mother kept Sandra's seven-month-old daughter, Donna, for the next several weeks, and during that time Sandra and I adjusted to one another in married life, confident that the two of us could beat the world; confident that Sandra's bothersome infections following sex would soon cease. But then, when Donna came to live with us, the confidence waned, disenchantment set in and the peaceful atmosphere in our duplex began deteriorating rapidly, until finally it became devoid of loving family harmony altogether. Donna not only was a constant reminder of my sister Marilyn's illegitimate child but, more disturbing, not being an offspring from Sandra and I, as Red and Inez were not offspring's of Mama and Daddy, Donna served too as a reminder that Red and Inez were the result of Mama's sexual indiscretions with Hubert.

It was beyond my capacity to handle, releasing in me a spring I hadn't anticipated. Donna reactivated all of those shameful and humiliating memories, as well as my fury against Mama. Subsequently, I never saw anything good in her. Only bad. And that bad consistently elicited my wrath, keeping me continually angry at the infant; invariably yelling at her with uncontrollable spite over the most petty of things.

Without warning, I had transformed into a black-visaged demon. The terrible dragon in the dream. Sandra was shocked, but it was just as much a shock for me. My infuriated behavior toward Donna kept Sandra on edge, and she was forever apologizing to me on behalf of Donna for the child upsetting me. But my rage at Donna continued.

Then, two weeks after Donna came to live with us, Sandra became the focus of my wrath—smoldering pouts, crazed glares, elevated eyebrows shot up in disdain. I began finding faults with her in everything she did; her care of Donna, her ironing, her cooking, her cleaning. Anything. Nothing hinting at the slightest disarray escaped my sharp scrutiny. Again, Sandra, her manner deferential, apologized for what I found wrong in her, or in what she was doing. But again her apologies were to no avail, leaving her confused and shaken.

Then my gleams became more violent, the anger lurking barely beneath their surface suddenly unleashing itself, escalating my fury into rabid temper tantrums; screaming and hurling objects fitfully about the duplex—ashtrays, plates, whatever was in my reach that wasn't nailed down, converting our home into a war zone.

"What's wrong with you? What's wrong?!" Sandra cried, horror struck. "Oh, God ... God!"

These verbal battles every day.

A month after Donna came to live with us, Sandra visited a beauty parlor and had her hair frosted—bands of blonde streaking through her naturally brown hair. One glance at this mutilation—in my eyes—and I became uncorked.

"Why in *fucking, goddamned hell* did you *mess* your hair up like that?" I screamed sanctimoniously, like Mama used to scream at me, my voice cracking across the room like the boom of a low-flying B-52. "What was wrong with your regular fucking hair?! Now you look like some damn *cheap floozy whore!*"

"I ... I just wanted a change," Sandra quavered, looking at me incredulously, a dark sad concern about her eyes. "Tha ... that's all. Mary Ann and Bob said it looked good! I'm sorry you don't like it."

"Fuck Mary Ann and Bob!" I screamed, waving a fist at her. Then picking up a nearby vase, I hurled it vengefully at Sandra, shouting, "Here's what I *think* of your goddamned floozy whore hair!"

Sandra jumped aside, the vase zooming past her and crashing against a wall, puffing her face in alarm. "God, *that's* it! I'm leaving, Donald! I've *had it* with you!" She was breathing heavily, a note of something very much like hysteria in her voice.

"Oh, yeah! Where in *hell* you going?"

"Back home to *my* daddy!"

I let out a bitter chuckle. "Back home? That's a laugh! A dump! There's nothing there for you! When you tire of filth you'll be back!" I added maliciously.

"I'd rather live with filth than you!" She shrieked heatedly, her neck puffing up like an adder's. Her words came in gulps, her hands shaking. "I want a *divorce!*"

Sandra took Donna and left. She didn't come back. After a few days I went over to her father's trailer where she had fled with Donna, remembering what her father had told me; "If you mistreat my daughter I'll beat the hell out of you!" I was prepared to do battle with him.

But when Sandra retreated home she did not bad mouth me, so her father was not worked up. Now cooled down, tired of the trailer chaos, Sandra readily came out to the car and we sat in it and talked.

"I apologize for being such an asshole!" I said, quickly warming up to Sandra, my deep, down-home baritone pouring the words out glibly like honey over biscuits. "Things will get better! We'll just have to work at it. It'll take a little time. This is all so new to me."

Mollified, Sandra sighed, "I believe you, so I'm willing to give it another try. I do love you very much and want to make it work with all my heart! So let's go work on it."

Sandra and Donna moved back into the duplex. In no time I felt like a live voltage wire that had just been cut, flipping sporadically on the ground, wild and loose, a dangerous charge of energy suddenly released, unmanaged, unable to focus where it was designed to be focused. But for a month I kept a reign on my emotions and there was peace. We even bought a new car, trading the Corvair in on a '65 Mustang. Then late one day, as dusk was rapidly seeping into the sky, I came home and found the iron still plugged into the socket, setting in an up position on the ironing board, ready to burn anything that touched it. Sandra had finished her ironing and forgot to unplug it.

That's all it took to ignite me, a wild charge of anger leaping out. "Sandra, you *crazy idiot*, you *left* the iron on! *Burning!* How can you be *such* a moron! Don't you know how *dangerous* this *is*!"

"Not *again!*"

I saw that I-should-have-stayed-home-with-daddy look on Sandra's face. And seeing it I puffed up, my lips going tight, my breathing becoming choppy, cramming the released anger back inside. With the squelching of the anger, the anxiety hit, the beginning of an anxiety attack.

Sandra can't *see* this!

I barged out of the duplex in quick strides, my whole body perspiring, and jumped into the Mustang. Hastily, I squealed out of the neighborhood, heading for the interstate highway. By the time I was on the interstate, my anxiety was so intense, my nerves so singing like wires, that I was ready to burst. Then I felt the suffocation and paralysis begin to set in. I rolled the car windows down, letting in more clearly the bright gimlet gaze of the early evening stars. Then, out of desperation, I opened the Mustang up, and as it accelerated in speed, the air rushing in, sweeping around my face, my anxiety began diminishing, and with it the suffocation and paralysis. I was back on that mountain road in Crete again, the sensation of speed pumping me with a delicious sensation of exhilaration, kicking out all of the anxiety from my body. I was intoxicated. Charged with the grandest emotional high vitalizing my whole being.

Euphoria!

The mesmerizing thrill of living on the edge! The rarest, purest, most in distilled pleasure. An unharnessed feeling of freedom. From *everything*!

Ecstatic!

Zooming along the highway like a rocket, my eyes were suddenly drawn to the rearview mirror, catching sight of the flashing dome light sparkling through the night. A damn Texas State Police Patrol car! I pulled over. Soon a Texas State

Trooper, a big, tall fellow of simian proportions, about six-foot-six, came walking up to my car.

"Hey, buddy, we don't want you killing yourself," the trooper said, his voice deep, gravelly. "Can't have that." There was something disturbingly familiar in his voice. That disconcerting edge. Taking my eyes off of the road ahead, annoyed at the disruption of my euphoria, I took a close look at his face, then froze in disbelief. I was looking into two shining black eyes; a rugged-looking noble face with that aquiline nose. The trooper was a dead ringer for the Shadow. "May I see your driver's license, please?"

Transfixed, I took my license out of my wallet and handed it to him. He barely glanced at it, heavy furrows outlining his forehead and eyes. Then he said gruffly, "Hey, fella, what's going on here?! Having troubles?"

"My wife and I had a little spat," I found myself saying. "I'm just riding it off."

He shot me a mirthful gleam, one suggesting he was on the verge of breaking into that horrid laughter any moment. "She's no good to you if you're dead. Do you realize how fast you were going?"

"Sixty-five or seventy, maybe."

He cast me a sideways eye, his grizzly hunk silhouetted against the cars speeding past us like swishing shadows. "Not even close. You were over a hundred." His eyes now were laughing hilariously.

"There's no way in hell I was doing a hundred miles an hour!"

"You sure as hell were!" He let out a laugh, as though all of this was amusing.

I felt my skin color change, the irritation clutching at my throat. "There's no *goddamned way* you're going to tell me I was doing a hundred miles an hour! In fact, at least a dozen speeders have passed us going faster than I was while you've been standing there. Why don't you go *after* them?!

Immediately the trooper's eyes narrowed into two black pools of shining penetration, a strange and empathetic intensity. "They're not my concern. You are. The problem with your wife is more important than speedsters, and more important than giving you a speeding ticket. So I have a suggestion for you; work it out *right* with her, not *wrong!* And don't let me catch you speeding again! Now get the hell out of here!"

Uneasily, I obliged, driving back home at a much slower speed, shaking my head and pondering disbelievingly at what had transpired. No! Impossible! He couldn't have been the Shadow in my dreams. Still? What the hell was happening?

CHAPTER 25

"**W**ORK IT OUT *right* with her, not *wrong!*"
My problem with Sandra was how to ventilate my anger at her—thus preventing anxiety attacks, but not drive her off again. To meet this problem I changed tactics. During the next several months my spats with Sandra, my verbal jumps down her throat, my complaints about Donna, were not continuous, but spaced, and paced, coming in spells, hot and cold periods, the insults tempered, cunningly arranged so as not to overly exasperate Sandra. My temper tantrums weren't as frightening; my throwing of things not as destructive, but allowing enough expression of anger to ward off anxiety attacks. Still, my tactics weren't foolproof, and on several occasions Sandra threatened to leave again, even threatened divorce. But these threats weren't out of a wits end desperation, as before, enabling me to nip her action in the bud with placative, honey-over-biscuits sweet talk, followed by a period of peaceful pleasantness. Then I'd result back to finding fault, insults, arguing, temper tantrums and throwing things, then cool it off again upon Sandra's next threat of leaving.

But this anger-out then anger-suppressed-again strategy wrung emotional havoc with myself, especially during my cooled off periods, leaving me wretched, a throbbing vein in one temple, my throat twitching every few moments, my muscles and eyelids always tightened, keeping me in states of anxiety and depression, menacing me with threats of the suffocation and paralysis of anxiety attacks.

It became too much. I had to free myself from this havoc. Get away from Sandra and Donna for a much needed breather. Recovery. Peace of mind. In October of 1966, after Sandra and I had been married a year, I drove she and Donna to southern Alabama and dropped them off at Mama and Daddy's shack. My plan was to leave them there for two months, until December, when I was to be discharged from the Air Force.

Mama wasted no time indoctrinating Sandra to the storm pit, the hellish fighting with Daddy, the shack chaos, and other grueling debasements. And Daddy introduced her to the toil of moonshining. He and Red also introduced her to something else; sexual harassment bordering on attempted rape, sharecropper style. Daddy and Red keeping Sandra in a furious motion of tension with their continued drunken passes at her, chasing her all over the place. Red going so far as to corner Sandra in the outhouse, as though just having corralled his favorite mule, and not letting her out.

A few harrowing weeks at the shack was the limit of what Sandra could take. She then phoned me from Union Springs, indignant with outrage, demanding that I come pick her up at once.

"Oh, what's wrong?" I asked innocently, playing stupid.

"You know damn well what's wrong! Get in the car and come get us right now!"

So much for my breather.

I drove to Alabama and snatched Sandra and Donna from the clutches of Mama and Daddy's shack life. While in that area, in anticipation of my discharge from the Air Force. I swung over to Columbus, Georgia and visited the unemployment office there, discovering that Blue Cross/Blue Shield had an opening for a computer operator trainee. An interview for the job was arranged right away for me, during which time I was asked to take a data processing aptitude test. After my return to San Antonio I received a letter informing me that I had done exceptionally well on the test, and Blue Cross/Blue Shield offered me a job following my release from the Air Force.

I accepted the offer, and in December, 1966, at the age of 22, I was discharged from the Air Force and went to work for Blue Cross/Blue Shield, foreseeing working with computers in a civilian capacity as offering the new horizon I was seeking. The office I was to work in was in Columbus, Georgia—right across the river from my old stomping grounds in Phenix City, Alabama—and I found a furnished, two-bedroom apartment just down the street from it. Larger than our duplex in San Antonio, the apartment, part of a red brick complex, seemed quite suitable for Sandra, Donna, and myself.

As in the Air Force, I had no problems in my work situation, the only difference being that I was more over poised, and dressed more like an aspiring sophisticate, determined to prove that I was of competent timber. During my first three months with the Blue Cross/Blue Shield office I operated an IBM business computer. Then in March, a month after I turned 23, I was promoted to programming, which I had a flare for, thus picked up easily.

The disharmony at home, though, continued as it was in San Antonio; intermittent hell and alienation! It was draining me and unraveling Sandra, and I had no desire to continue the havoc. Sandra and I both needed a break from it. The only solution was for me to remain away from Sandra and Donna as much as possible—my breathers, thereby avoiding the anger generated around them, and the spurning outbursts that followed. And avoiding too the additional emotional upheaval on myself when that anger had to be suppressed so as to keep Sandra from becoming so totally implacable that she'd leave.

With Mama it was escapes. With Sandra it was breathers. The two one and the same.

With my attention taken by both a new job and a new home environment, the breathers, at first, were slow in coming, meaning that anxiety and the threat of anxiety attacks were ever present. To ward these off, whenever I could I raced around in my Ford Mustang, speeding on the streets and the highways. And every chance I got, I teamed up again with my former drinking buddies and whore-escapade companions to Acuna, Mexico, the Grissett brothers, David and Ricky. Then, as summer approached, another breather. The office had an official softball team and I became one of its players. While playing softball during the summer, I expanded my Mustang speeding into a fabulous breather; drag racing. After a game, on my way home, I'd be sitting in my Mustang at a red light, and some young lion in a souped up hot rod would pull up beside me, gun his motor in a challenge to race, I'd accept, and when the light turned green we both roared off in a madding dash down the street, wheels squealing, engines screaming. But usually I'd lose the race, my Mustang too slow in acceleration to be a match for the hopped-up cars I was racing against.

Instead of reducing my anxiety, these losing outcomes intensified it, a blow to my competitive spirit, leaving me pounding my wheel and cursing under my breath, my guts twisting into an acid mood.

Finally I became fed up with losing, resolving to become the drag race champion of Columbus. To accomplish this I began a tenacious search for another car. A drag race winner. And in August I found it. A spanking-new 1967 two-door Chevelle SS-396 hardtop Super Sport. A 396 cubic-inch engine. Three hundred and twenty-five horsepower. Light blue top, white body, wide oversized tires, raised hood section. It had the look of power. A look of speed.

It looked awesome!

I bought the car on the spot. Its interior was light blue, rich and elegant, enhanced by its soft, sweet new car aroma, making it the epitome of automotive racing luxury. But it was on the road, while listening to the melodic purr of the SS-396's engine, while savoring the smooth powerful feel of its ride, that the car displayed its true beauty. Truly it was built to fly. The top speed on the speedometer registered at 120, but its maximum velocity exceeded that. And the Super Sport's acceleration from standstill was tremendous, reaching a high speed quickly, effortlessly. When I floored the accelerator, the engine's purr ceased and its roar began, like the starting sound of the Daytona 500, the pressure from the sudden powerful acceleration flinging me back against the seat, and in seconds I was screaming down the highway at an incredible speed.

Ultimate euphoria!

Ecstatic!

Reducing all anxiety and worries to impotency.

I knew no one would beat me drag racing in this car. And no one did. I took on all comers on any of the three main drag racing streets in Columbus—Victory Drive, Macon Road, and Fourth Avenue. I beat them all.

Sandra was fit to be tied when she discovered I had bought the car. She hated the Chevelle SS-396. She hated me drag racing. But her hate was my love. I needed the automobile. A saving breather. Needed not only the drag racing, but the car's sheer speed. I opened it up on all the country roads, soaring past featureless geometric shapes in my climbing invigoration, leaving a capricious swarm of dust trailing behind me, just as Leon Golden—the wild speed demon on the back roads during my shack days, used to do back home. Now I was the new menace, and barrel-assing down one of those country roads—at a faster speed than any of Leon's cars could ever move. I was back on that mountain road in

Crete again, but now more exhilarated, more vitalized, more emotionally intoxicated, the fantastic velocity of the Chevelle SS-396 mesmerizing me, the thrill of living on the edge now honed to razor thin sharpness, releasing an unharnessed feeling of freedom putting even greater distance between me and my emotional pain, pushing my secrets behind me.

Magical. I was alive! No burdens. No concerns. Sayonara to the mundane troubles of existence. All the delicious pleasures of the Cosmos condensed into one. An exotic, sensuous, spiritual quality, both elating and reposing my being at the same time.

The greatest possible high!

On September 15, Sandra gave birth to a girl, our first child together, and we named her Michelle. I felt proud being a father but my emotional circumstances and the circumstances of the marriage were in such turmoil that Michelle's birth could do little to change it, or change the surfeit of swift crosscurrents already set in motion. Sandra insisted that I dispose of the Chevelle SS-396. I refused, becoming intractable, thus exacerbating the vicious circle between us, alienating us further, causing me to need more breathers, and need them more often.

So, in early 1968, when I was 24, I intensified my breathers and seldom was home at night, developing a certain obliquity of conscience and an elastic attitude toward the truth, untrammeled by romantic notions of ethics. By now I was frequently in the company of David and Ricky Grissett coming across from Phenix City—particularly Ricky, who was invariably gung ho for mischievous activity. That year, in Columbus, the three of us became the city's three musketeers of carousing, partying, boozing, drag racing and just plain hell-raising, keeping the police on their toes and giving full vent to my wild and loose energies keeping my anxiety at bay. When we didn't have something outrageous planned, or weren't drag racing or speeding around in the Super Sport, the three of us usually ended up at a pool hall or at the Buccaneer Drive-in Restaurant in Columbus, guzzling V.O. whiskey and Seven-Up.

Sandra didn't sit around moping and waiting for me when I wasn't home evenings. Finding someone to watch the kids, she came looking for me! Those few times she could find me she usually tracked me down in a pool hall or at the Buccaneer, where I'd be with David and Ricky, the three of us joking and getting drunk and pursuing ribald things in a light and airy manner.

Strutting rudely up to us, Sandra, a frumpy look, black-circled eyes, feisty defiance, glaring at me, would interrupt, "What are you doing here? Why aren't you home like you said you'd be—instead of gallivanting with these bozos!"

If it was one of my anger out nights, the color would begin in the back of my neck, and my jaw muscles would ripple, leaving my body without a drop of patience, and a battle royal would erupt, during which David, in that macho-masculine abruptness of his, would grimace, commenting:

"Don, Sandra's crazy! Let's go find you a sane broad!"

At other times, if I were suppressing my anger, there would be no battle, and

I'd answer Sandra calmly with an impassive look. But holding my anger back, my anxiety would be reactivated, demanding a release. Sandra, having found me, not letting me out of her sight for a moment, would be in the Super Sport with me, usually on our way back home, when I obtained that release. All it took was someone pulling up beside me at a light and gunning their motor in challenge.

Sandra instantly flashed me that quick look of alarm, not quite sullen yet but quickly on her way there. "Don't you *dare!*" She'd squeal. "Don't you dare do this *again!* I'm … I'm *telling* you—don't you *dare!*"

I didn't say a word. But when the light turned green, I floored the accelerator, the engine's purr instantly turning to a roar, and the race was on, Sandra suddenly flung back against the seat to the sound of Daytona 500 as the Chevelle SS-396 accelerated at tremendous speed, roaring off into the throat of the night, a whoosh of air, quickly leaving the lights of the challenger behind.

"*Damnit,* I told you not to *do that!*" Sandra screamed, approaching hysterics. "Stop this car! Damnit, stop! I'm getting out! You're going to *kill us* some day! Let me out!"

"Come on, Sandra, don't you …"

"I said *stop!* I mean it, damnit! *Stop this car! Let me out! Stop!*"

She was working herself into a frenzy, emotional hyperbole, her chin visibly sagging, her face all puffy, forcing me to bring the car to a quick halt. Sandra then jumped out, a pallid figure, hair becoming frowsy, all the while I'm pleading with her to remain in the car. Once out, I'd try coaxing her back into the car. Occasionally she would get back in, but often, cocking her head belligerently at me, eyes popping, she'd refuse and walk home. Or sometimes I'd circle the block, letting her cool off, then approach her again, pulling up beside her as she strutted in the direction of home, then spend from 30 to 45 minutes talking to her—my voice ending up hoarse, attempting to coax her back into the car. Sometimes she'd get in; sometimes she wouldn't.

At other times when Sandra was in the car with me, and no drag racing was involved, I'd be driving so fast and reckless, a strange vengeful gleam in my eye, that she'd become frightened and begin thrashing about in the car, terrified, screaming:

"*Stop!* Let me *out!* You're going to *kill* us!"

I'd stop, let her out, and she'd either walk home or I'd go through 30 to 45 minutes coaxing her back into the car.

In September, 1968, a year after Michelle was born, Sandra and I purchased our first home, a red brick ranch house in Columbus, three bedrooms, the house sitting up on a small knoll, an inclining driveway approaching it, to either side a nice lawn enclosed by a chain-link fence, providing a rustic, country appeal. It cost a little under five thousand dollars to furnish the place—a tidy sum of cash in those days, and we went into debt to do it.

We bought the home partly because of the children, but also because we thought the home would improve the marriage relationship. It didn't. I wouldn't get rid of my Super Sport. But compared to our apartment the home was a definite step up in ambiance, far surpassing any of the shacks I grew up in, and nicer than J.P.'s home in Phenix City.

Though our new home didn't improve matters between Sandra and me, I did make an effort to be with her more in the evenings, my anxiety permitting. And being home more often, David and Ricky, because I was no longer so much on the loose, began dropping by occasionally, then more frequently, until they were at the house night and day, practically living there.

At first, Sandra frowned at their presence. She particularly disliked David, not only because he called her "crazy"—Sandra did have spunk and fight and a temper, not one easily pushed around—but also because when she caught David in a lie, usually about my whereabouts or activities, David, looking her squarely in the eye, would never own up to it, but persisted instead, rather stoically, that the lie was the truth. Ricky, on the other hand, when caught in a lie by Sandra, would own up to it and be straightforward with her, causing Sandra to overlook his peccadillo. And, unlike David, who's manner was more reckless and self-gratifying, Ricky, when not drunk, had such a sweet, innocent, likable way about him, sort of a model-pretty, erotically-contented look generating gleeful, rabble-rousing excitement, that Sandra couldn't help but like him, even though he was my partner in carousing, partying, boozing, drag racing and general hell-raising, all of which Sandra detested.

But Sandra also liked Ricky because he kept her kitchen filled with groceries and meats, and provided her with items for the rest of the house—all of these items stolen! Sandra had but just to mention to Ricky that she needed something and Ricky, unknown to Sandra, would go out and steal it.

Ricky was a master at stealing. He would have made an excellent cat burglar. While watching him every second, Ricky could steal things without you ever seeing him do it. I would go with Ricky into a Seven-Eleven store and watch his every movement, never seeing anything suspicious. But when Ricky came out of the store, a sheepish look on his face, the inside of his shirt, all around his belt, would be packed with packages of hams. Ricky loved stealing hams, and I never knew how he did it. I could never detect him stealing, even though my eyes were continually glued on him. He was a magician.

I'd say to him, "Ricky, you should quit stealing things. Some day you're going to get caught, and when you are, this time you'll stay in jail!"

Ricky would just look at me with that unflappable, likable, boy-of-the-world expression, an incipient enigmatic grin dismissing his misdeeds.

"I tell you, you're going to get caught one of these days!"

His grin would smooth into a bad-boy prankster smirk, one saying, "Wanna bet?"

Christmas came, then New Year's Day, and we were into 1969. Then I turned 25. My anguish continued, as did the misery for Sandra. Mentally and emotionally, she was buckling, the strain taking its toll, unnerving her in every direction. Her premarital happy vitality around me was now totally converted to nervous, restless and irritable energies, rendering her increasingly tiresome and harboring sentiments toward me similar to those one holds for Caligula or Jack the Ripper.

In March of 1969 I was still going through the gears of the Chevelle SS-396 on the streets, roads and highways. And David and Ricky, perennial visitors from Phenix City, were still practically living at our house, Sandra grudgingly feeding them. By now, Sandra, in an effort to help keep us going with our escalating life-style—mainly mine, had obtained a job as a clerk at a bank, working long hours, about 12 hours a day, and this necessitated my help taking care of the children, primarily picking them up at the baby-sitter's next door after I finished work and bringing them home and watching them until Sandra arrived.

One day, instead of picking the children up when I came home from work, I left them at the baby-sitter's and scrawled out a short, two sentence note for Sandra:

I've left. I'll be back later.

Coming home, finding the children not at home, reading my vague note, Sandra went into orbit.

Meanwhile, Ricky and I had rooted ourselves at the Buccaneer for a long night of serious drinking and roguish contemplation of hell-raising, not returning to the house until 4 a.m., both of us, by anyone's measure, rather drunk.

Slithering up to the kitchen door with the early morning dew, we planned to steal away into the house as quietly as possible. But as soon as we crept through the door, our creeping abruptly ended. Sitting at the kitchen table, waiting for us, was Sandra, mad as a puckered owl and pointing a 12-gauge shotgun at us.

"You drunk son of bitches aren't coming in this house!" She snapped brusquely, tightening her hold on the shotgun. "Not *tonight*, you aren't!"

"Sandra," I gulped, "hold on a minute. Let's be reasonable about this!"

"Yeeeaaaaahhhh ... Sandra ..." Ricky interjected, attempting to stabilize a slurring twang, "let's ... let's be reeeeasonable about this, god ... god ... goddamit."

"*Reasonable*? My fuckin' *ass* reasonable! You call coming in here at four in the morning, drunk as Cooter Brown, *reasonable*?" Her screaming made the whole house thump and vibrate. "I want you two to stare down this shotgun barrel a while! *That's* reasonable! If either one of you does anything I don't like, I'll *blow your asses* into a million pieces!"

"Holy shiiiit!" Ricky sputtered, seeing that she meant it.

"Damn, Sandra," I beseeched, sobering fast, my voice softening to a lilt, attempting the sweet talk approach, "put the gun down and let us come into the house."

I started to move toward her. She jumped to her feet, eyes blazing in a surly yellow sneer, her finger poised more tightly on the trigger. "You better *watch it*! I don't *like* that! I advise the two of you to stand still and watch it and *keep* your damn mouths shut—or I'm *blowing you away!*"

Ricky and I froze, barely making a move for two hours, saying nothing, dissuaded by the malevolent glint of the shotgun's barrel encircling the cold dark hole of death. As drunk as we were, neither Ricky nor I were as drunk as to want to end up a shooting statistic in some small story on a back page of the newspaper. But much more terrorizing, if she pulled that trigger I could see myself burning in hell. Daddy's hell!

There was trouble brewing in River City.

Finally, with dawn waiting to peek over the horizon, Sandra said, "I've got to get a few hours sleep. I've got to work." Then, nodding at me, "Get your stuff I've got stacked over there and put it in your car and you two get out of here!"

I peered wearily at some boxes, packed with my clothes, a few loose shirts scattered over them. Feeling woozy and fatigued, I hauled the boxes out to the Super Sport, pushed them haphazardly in the back, then, with Ricky sprawled out beside me, turned on the car's ignition. Nothing! The damn battery was dead.

Cursing, I exited the car and gazed warily at Sandra, still holding the shotgun on us. "Sandra, it won't start." I groaned.

"Push the damn thing to the street! Just *get* the hell off my property! And don't *bother me* no more!"

Ricky and I pushed the car out into the street, then crawled into it. Exhausted, every muscle in our bodies stiff, cramped and tired, we fell asleep immediately. And immediately I was into a dream. Sandra was tied to a stake with rope, and I was flogging her with a long, black, heavy whip. Then Sandra began untying herself, and as she did, Sandra became Mama.

"I'll git ya for this!" Mama yelled.

Then the Shadow yelled at me; "You're still not doing it *right*!"

CHAPTER 26

I NEVER MISSED picking up the kids again. And Ricky stole some extra nice things for Sandra. By May both of us were on better terms with her. Good enough terms for Sandra, David, Ricky and I to take a trip together, without the children, to Panama City Beach in Florida. We checked into a motel five miles from the water, and the next day slipped our bathing suits on under our clothes and made our way to the beach in the Super Sport. Ricky, with his deceptive boyish charm, wasted no time latching onto some sweet little thing in a narrow bikini of white ruffles, leaving Sandra, David and I soaking up the sun and sucking in the briny smell of the air on a blanket not far from the water's edge, enthralled by the sight and sound of the white-capped waves curving in from the gulf.

The sun was brilliant, the day hot and sticky, the humidity terrible. "Shit," David squawked, "let's get some cold beers before this sun dries us up!"

Leaving Sandra sunning on the blanket, David and I eased through the sand, long stretches of clear, pure white grains glistening under the sun, heading for the concession stand, a good hike down the beach. Reaching our destination we bought our beers and headed back in the direction of Sandra. On our way we spotted Ricky lying on a towel on the beach with his sweet little thing.

"Let's go over there and talk to them." David suggested, a drooling half smile playing about his mouth. "Maybe there's more where she came from."

Grinning good-humoredly, we sauntered over to where Ricky and the girl were lying, and began chatting with them, drinking our beer, intending just a short visit. But soon, four more young leggy women, friends of Ricky's sweet little thing, unexpected breathers, had joined us, all of them golden sun-glowing sweeties in little sopping bikinis, and all of them trim and fit, curvaceous where it counted, definitely a credit to the female species, easily diverting one's mind from the sticky humidity of a hot day's blazing sun.

With David and me blinking like friendly old parrots, attempting to make an elegant presentation of ourselves, our conversation with the girls became gay and lively. Before long we were all giggling, laughing and joking, slapstick fun, roguishly carrying on like adolescents. One impulse gesture led to another and the eight of us ended up lying on the beach together, the musky-sweet, pungent smelling sweet little thing next to me, Lisa, unusually cozy, comfy and cuddly in her vividly orange bikini, her broad bright lips and lovely fun-sparkle eyes the kind of golden bubble pastime that makes you lose track of time.

But Sandra wasn't losing track of time, well aware that David and I had been gone for about an hour, and miffed about it. Heading toward the concession stand, she set out in search of us, finally spotting us—mostly me, caught up in the enduring crow-caw laughter of Lisa, Sandra convinced she was a gal David had lined up for me, something he was always threatening to do in her presence.

Angry, Sandra returned to her blanket, picked it up and headed for the parking lot, taking with her the keys to the Super Sport, plus my clothes, shoes, wallet and money, and David and Ricky's as well. She left nothing behind.

Meanwhile, up the beach a ways, David and I were in hog heaven, continuing our pleasurable interlude with Ricky and the girls, lost in the happy merriment of the moment. Lisa purring into my throat, warming the blood.

Suddenly I rose up from the sand. "Jesus, we better get back to Sandra!" I frowned, banishing our gaiety and good humor.

"Aw, fuck Sandra!" David grimaced. "You got it much better with Lisa here."

"Come on. Let's git!"

"Shit."

Returning to the spot where we had left Sandra, seeing that she was gone, taking everything with her, my mind did some quick gymnastics. "We've been gone too damn long. She must have come looking for us. Saw us. Come on, David, let's get to the parking lot. Maybe we can catch her there."

What we found at the parking lot was the Chevelle SS-396 gone.

"Shit!" David snarled.

Returning to Ricky on the beach, I apprised him of our predicament. "She's pissed off! We'll have to walk back to the motel!"

Ricky let out a long whistle. "Hope to hell she left the shotgun at home!" Then pondering that possibility for a moment, he added. "You guys go on to the motel. I'll get a ride there later."

"I can drive you fellows back to the motel," Lisa offered, her smile eager to please.

"Oh, no!" I sputtered, staring at her with an air of expectant caution. "There'll probably be enough hell to pay for this without you coming on the scene making it worse!"

David and I began the five mile trek back to our motel on foot—literally on foot, we had no shoes, David mumbling bitterly and angrily, his long dark hair curling in the heat and humidity. Hot and thirsty, clad only in our swim trunks, dripping in sweat, we were drooping, captive figures silhouetted against the torturing bonfire of the sky, the broiling sun mercilessly roasting our skin, sun burning us to the crisp reddish shade of roof tiles. And the only place to walk was on the hot concrete of the road, burning the bottoms of our feet like scalding coals, leaving large sores and abrasions. And we kept picking up sand spurs in our feet, adding more to our scorching misery.

Finally, with an expectation of saving relief, looking like stragglers from the Bataan death march, we staggered up to our motel, the Super Sport parked out in front. Stumbling to our motel room door, we found it locked. Dehydrated, sore, aching, crippled, totally exhausted, sun-mauled to a flaming tender burnt dryness, in no further mood for Sandra's sadistic, jealous whims, we began pounding on the door, yelling, cursing, murderous looks contorting our faces.

But Sandra wouldn't unlock the door.

"Goddamnit, Sandra." I demanded, "open this fucking door or we're busting it down!"

"Screw you! I'm not opening it!" Sandra hissed on the other side. A determined growl. "So fuck off!"

David returned her growl. "I'll kill her!"

"Sandra, what the hell's gotten *into* you?!"

"I'll tell you what's gotten into me! Those damn floozies I saw you messing with on the beach. What were you *doing* with those girls?"

I recalled my diplomatic warnings on Crete, regarding this as another Turkish fez. "Nothing, Sandra. Just chatting."

"Chatting my *ass*! You were *doing more* than chatting! With that one hussy— that one that damn David fixed you up with, you were doing everything but sucking her tits! And that's only because they were too big for your mouth!"

My eyes, mouth and throat all seemed to pop at once. She was twisting things a little, the way women can do. But now I needed to do a little twisting. Appealing to her maternal instinct, I said, "Open the door and look at us! Look at our feet! Look at the shape we're in! We've been baked to ashes walking back here! If there had been anything to those girls, don't you think they'd have given us a ride back?"

A few moments of silence. Then Sandra finally unlocked and opened the door, just a little, peeking through the crack, a frumpy look but slightly mollified, studying us curiously. We really looked a beaten sight, two unwrapped mummy candidates for some metropolitan museum. "Well ... maybe." She said sulkily, leaning toward giving us the benefit of the doubt.

But David couldn't hold still. "Damn, Sandra, you're crazy as hell! You need to be locked up somewhere!"

"Crazy, uh? Mister Grissett, if you keep messing with me, your ass will *walk* all the way back to Phenix City!"

David hesitated, then with a little lift and fall of his shoulders, he gave up, knowing she meant it. "Shit."

This incident illustrated too clearly how out of hand Sandra was becoming. She was trying too much to keep me in check. Besides the anger and anxiety her presence elicited, I just couldn't enjoy myself and have fun with her around. In June of 1969, the employees at the Blue Cross/Blue Shield office in Columbus put on a large gala party for the workers and their spouses. But not wanting Sandra to attend it with me, I told her that the affair was a bachelor's gathering— which she believed, and attended the party without her. The following week Sandra was sitting up in the stands at the ballpark where our office team played its softball games, watching me play against one of the other teams.

A lady sitting next to Sandra in the stands casually commented to her, "Sorry you were sick last Saturday night and couldn't make it to the party with Don."

"Sick? I *wasn't* sick! He told me that was a bachelor's party."

"No. It was for both husbands and wives. I was there."

Sandra's face stiffened. Then the more she thought about it the more her eyes fumed until, finally, she leaped out of her seat and descended down out of the stands and onto the ball field. At that moment our office team was up to bat and I was a runner on third base, and Sandra, in a tawdry march, headed straight for me, stopping play of the game.

Reaching third base, arms akimbo, fixing me with a stare tougher than any agitated umpire's, she thundered. "You've got til when you cross that plate up there to come up with an answer as to why you *went* to that party *without* me!"

The third baseman for the other team—a short, stocky fellow, standing close by, overhearing Sandra—as everyone in the ballpark had, chortled, "Ain't love grand!"

"Let's get this ball game under way!" Bellowed the umpire behind the plate, gawking impatiently in our direction. "Let's play ball again!"

In a huff, Sandra turned away from me and walked back toward the stands. With the game back in play, the next batter singled, sending me in to score. As soon as I crossed home plate, I trotted over to where Sandra was standing at the edge of the stands, serenaded by the sudden affected yells and clapping of the fans.

"Take her to a party for Chrissake!" Someone yelled.

"Hey, tootsie, you can come to my party!" Another shouted.

"Hell, put her in for an inning!" Came a cry.

Ignoring the fans, I looked at Sandra calmly, one of my suppressed anger moods. By now she had cooled down. "Okay, I'll tell you. I didn't *want* to take you! I wanted to go by myself."

This set the stage for further tension and vitriolic hassles between Sandra and me, in turn increasing my depression and anxiety and making me vulnerable to even more reckless breathers.

A couple of weeks following this embarrassing scene in the ballpark, David, noticing how edgy and down I had become grimaced, "Hey, man, what's with this bad trip?"

"Nothing. Just nothing."

"Hell you say. Man. You need some new life! You need some of these *uppers!*" He showed me some white pills. Amphetamines. Speed. "Believe me, these little white buggers will make you *feel better* than you ever have in your life! You'll want to *party* all night long! You'll never run out of energy!"

"Shit."

"Take one. You'll see."

I did. David was right. The pill accelerated the respiratory and circulatory systems while giving a tremendous psyched-up feeling. I was ready to fly to the moon, the pill's effect taking the edge off my nerves and boosting me into an euphoric feeling where I felt I could do anything.

Vibrant, regenerated, recharged, from that point I cut loose on a wild and reckless three month upper binge, continually countering the speed's depressed aftereffects by replenishing my energy with more amphetamines. But it left me nervous and erratic as well, and during this time my home life deteriorated into a new agony of dissension, as did every other facet of my life—except for my work. There, amazingly, I could function, managing to keep my mind a constant of perceptive appraisal, never lessening.

It was while driving the Super Sport that the effects of speed were the most dangerous, stripping me of all caution and intensifying my reckless impulses, this state reaching the zenith of its peril in August. Ricky and I, and another friend, were out speeding around in the Chevelle SS-396. All three of us were drunk, and still drinking as we drove. Making matters worse, I also was spaced out on amphetamines. Speeding on speed. Combined with alcohol, a fatal combination, pushing living on the edge beyond the limit and into the jaws of catastrophe.

We had just roared across the lower bridge in Columbus, going through the gears at over one hundred and twenty miles per hour. Then I turned the car around and came back across the bridge at a speed equally as fast, my mind twirling erratically with surrealistic images, my ears pounding with the noises of mocking laughter and maniacal crowds, my eyes caught in a sickly glare of dislocation. Then my head seemed to pop like a broken drain and suddenly, rising up out of these spaced out sensations, naked and unadorned, was the irresistible urge to whip the Super Sport into a sharp turn on the very next exit after crossing the bridge, but turning onto the road of that exit an impossibility to do at the speed I was traveling.

Ricky, though drunk out of his gourd, sensed, through a silent, elliptical kind of communication between us, what I was about to do, jarring him to the realization that if I attempted that turn the car would never stop flipping over until it came splattering against the Houston Astros farm team stadium wall, by then the three of us dismembered corpses.

"*No, Donald!*" He screeched to the bulge of his eyes. "*Don't do it!*" Then he let out a strangled scream.

And with the scream I saw it. The Texas State Police Patrol car, suddenly parked at the shoulder of the road where I was bent on turning. What the hell was it doing in Georgia? But the patrol car altered my action. Instead of trying to make the turn I zoomed by the exit like a shooting star, then slowed the car's speed drastically, trembling. The Shadow.

That was it! My amphetamine days were over. I quit uppers cold turkey, even though it heightened my anxiety and depression, and left me sordid and withdrawn, more edgy, sometimes shaking, at times my ears ringing, my eyes blurry. Still, I wouldn't touch another speed pill. And I had more than these effects of quitting speed cold turkey and the Shadow to preoccupy my mind. By this time the cost of a new house, new furniture, new clothes, combined with the cost of the Super Sport, carousing, partying, boozing, hell-raising, popping "speed" and other items, had buried me so deep into financial trouble that we were going under.

We couldn't pay our bills!

I began searching for a new job, one with more pay. When Bickerstaff Clay Products in Columbus offered me significantly more money to come work for them, I accepted. But the increased pay of the new job was too little too late, unable to forestall the creditor hounds beginning their siege of harassment, forcing Sandra and me, in October, 1969, to file for bankruptcy under Chapter 11. When the chief honchos at Bickerstaff Clay Products found out about the bankruptcy, they regarded it as a sign of irresponsibility and no longer wanted me as an employee. Thus, in early November, I was ungraciously fired from my job at Bickerstaff, even though I had written and implemented a complete multi state system for them in a short time, a system which they were exceedingly pleased with.

At first my firing left me stunned. Then angered. Then I settled into sort of a wistful, lost expression, unable to fathom the gossamer organizational dysfunction producing such blatant ungratefulness. I phoned Blue Cross/Blue Shield to see if I could get my old job back. No dice. The bottom line of their thinking; "You'll leave again the next time somebody offers you fifty dollars more."

My new horizon had just disintegrated. Shaken to the core, I felt like a persona non grata. I was bankrupt. No job. No money. No credit. My emotional life in shambles. My marriage a mess. Sandra pregnant again. And we were on the verge of losing our possessions.

All had been for naught, the reach of my sharecropper's legacy suffocating me, claiming me, leaving me feeling vacant and unseeing. And again, as in my childhood, I felt like a being without substance.

The portrait in the Shadow's dream.

CHAPTER 27

I HAD FAILED miserably. I had lost control. Everything was collapsing around me, overcoming me with draining helplessness. An overwhelming emptiness sweeping me away. Emotionally, I was living in the shacks again, with the same choice as always; fold or try to escape. My whole life had been a conditioning toward escape. Now that conditioning was instinct. I resorted to that instinct.

To escape, I had to find a job. Quickly. A job in computers. But here I was at a disadvantage. I lacked a college degree. My only hope was that my experience—and my tenacious intellect—would make up for this lack.

I queried my business contacts. An IBM representative suggested that I apply at the Service Bureau Company in Atlanta. On November 10, 1969. I drove to Atlanta and rented a room. The next morning, after sprucing myself up the best I could, I set out for the Service Bureau Company.

I managed to arrange an interview with Al Kruzek, the company's Programming Manager. Scholarly looking in a three-button traditional suit, he had an uncanny likeness to my Air Force buddy, Harris. Same features. Same build.

"No college degree, uh," he frowned slightly, blinking his patient eyes sadly. "Well, I don't know if …"

"Mister Kruzek, I have good experience in programming," I emphasized assuredly, then outlined to him what I had done at Blue Cross/Blue Shield and Bickerstaff Clay Products.

Hearing me out, he paused and reflected a moment. Then, furrowing his brows in question, he said in a frank, concerned tone, "Let's do this. Before we talk further I want you to take a programming test."

I hadn't counted on that. My Adam's apple jumped up and I swallowed it back. "Okay."

But it wasn't okay. Usually I was a whiz on tests. Today, though, my intellect wasn't up to par. It was mangled. I was still suffering the withdrawal effects from amphetamines, leaving my mind still foggy, my head feeling like a gigantic festering sponge. Compounding this disability was my anger at the Bickerstaff people for their unceremonious dismissal of myself in view of what I had done for them, this disability helped along by unhappy thoughts popping in and out of my mind on my bankruptcy in progress bringing about that dismissal. In short, I was hazy, upset and frustrated. Also, my mind was warped by the pressure I was under. Too much pressure. I was out of a job with a family to support. And Mama and Daddy, and especially J.P., had this illusory notion that I was setting the world on fire, placing me on a high pedestal I didn't deserve. All of these seamy distractions combined were engaging me in an inward wrestling match prompting a renewed, uncontrollable restlessness. An unsettled desperation leaving me too out of sorts to sufficiently relax and concentrate on taking a test.

Taking the exam, I felt all my muscles go limp and knew right then I didn't stand a chance. In keeping with my emotional state, I failed the test miserably.

Studying the test results, Kruzek looked at me a bit dumbfounded. With professional gravity, he said, "You sure you've worked with computers?"

The nape of my neck horripilated with embarrassment. "Yes. Quite a bit."

"These results don't show it."

"Look, Mister Kruzek, I know you people place a lot of confidence in that test, but I *can program*! Give me a chance to *show* you! This was just an off day for me taking a test. *Believe* me!"

I could see in his eyes that he did. An instinctual grasping of the clarity and force behind my words rather than the words themselves. That extra savvy. "Okay," Kruzek said, "let's go see Bill Hale."

Bill Hale was the Service Bureau Company's Branch Manager. Slim and trim, about five-eight, bald-headed, dressed in an expensive, conservative-cut suit, he presented the elegant corporate image. His split-shine demeanor also gave the impression of a sergeant in the Air Force or Marines.

"Bill, this is Mister Donald Oakes from Columbus, ex-Air Force Intelligence," Kruzek said. "He did lousy on our programming test but insists that he can program. I'm inclined to believe him."

Hale shook my hand, baring straight strong teeth, looking at me with a commanding gaze, one suggesting that I should snap to attention. "Air Force, huh," he said with a glint. He even sounded like a sergeant, his tone that of authority, deep and fluid. "Where were you stationed?"

"Iraklion in Crete. Then Kelly in San Antonio."

"Good assignments." Then looking at Kruzek, Hale said with aplomb, "Al, you know how I trust your judgment. If you think Mister Oakes can program, let him!"

The blood surged in my throat. My needed escape. In thanks, I vowed they wouldn't be sorry. I was hired on a trial basis, as a supplemental programmer, at five dollars an hour, with no fringe benefits.

Returning to Columbus, I told Sandra of my new job. But she didn't share my excitement, something strangely dismal about her. "We'll sell the house"— our only possession not affected by the bankruptcy—"and get an apartment in Atlanta," I enthused.

"No." She said tiredly, "*You* get an apartment in Atlanta!"

"What? … What are you talking about?"

She gave me a deep-breath weary look, that kind of haggard expression when you've struggled with something momentous and finally resolved it in your mind. "Don, I simply can't take our marriage any longer," she announced dejected, launching into a collected speech she'd obviously rehearsed in my absence. But her voice was squeaky, desolate, no fire, without histrionics, her words coming in gulps. "I've finally had it." Her hands began shaking. "Had it with your flaky attitude. Letting everything go to hell! Never home. Running all over hell-raising. Showing no signs of changing. No commitment to me. No caring. No depth of good feeling. You don't want to be married. So let's break it off now. A good time. I'll take the kids to Texas and you go to Atlanta. I just don't have the will to fight anymore!"

Then, her hair whipping across her face, she added, "And please, don't try to sweet talk me out of it this time. It won't work!"

My cheer gone, I stared at her blankly, flat out and fatigued, suddenly feeling diminished and impotent, grappling with my thoughts. My face a bit ashen, I recalled the Shadow's reproach in my dream:

"You're still not doing it *right*!"

Soberly, straightforwardly, without my honey-over-biscuits tone, I found myself mouthing hitherto unconcerned family convictions. "Sandra, I promise if you come to Atlanta with me, I'll cut out the running around. Completely. I'll be home every night. No more hell-raising. No more drag racing. No more boozing. No more David and Ricky—or their likes. That's the commitment I'll make to you. Family. Us. Nothing else."

Sandra never expected to hear me say that, and she gazed at me startled, as if her eyes were debating with her ears. I was a little startled myself. I'd never before made such a promise to her. Such a commitment. "You mean that, Donald? Your word?"

"Yes. My word. I promise."

"And the Super Sport?" Her haggard appearance was dissolving.

"I'll get rid of it."

"When?" She pursued, watching me intently.

"After we move to Atlanta. After this bankruptcy mess is straightened out."

"Promise?"

"Promise."

The darkness of wear under her eyes began fading, replaced by a sparkling glow to her pupils that had long been extinguished. "Donald, that would make me so happy!" She exclaimed, seemingly coming out of a daze, her voice low but joyous. "It's … it's almost too wonderful to believe!"

"Believe it!" I said with extraordinary potency, unsuccessfully trying to grin.

She knew I meant it. She flung her arms about me, giving me a robust hug. "Thank you! I love you!"

I located a suitable furnished apartment in Atlanta and moved the family in. Then I returned to Columbus to attend the court hearing on my bankruptcy organizational plan. All my creditors were there, most of them looking stiff and grim. The expression of the man from GMAC—the company financing the Chevelle—was particularly troubled. A lackluster-fellow, necktie askew, looking like a wrestler fallen on hard times, he informed me quite rigidly, throatily, that if I didn't bring my car payment up to date—a ninety dollar payment I was a month behind on, right then and there on the spot, I had to surrender the car to him that day, even before the hearing was over. Like now.

I was already nervous, but now I became frantic. I didn't have ninety dollars. No where close to it. And without the Super Sport I had no transportation back to Atlanta. More critical, I'd have no transportation to my new job.

Rather forlorn, I turned to Mr. Johnson, another of my creditors from the Beneficial Finance Company. He was one of the few pleasant creditors there, one I had been on excellent business terms with before the bankruptcy. "Mister Johnson, can you do anything to help me out with my car? I need ninety dollars or they're going to take it!"

In a display of compassion, uncharacteristically breaking rank with the grimness of the other creditors, he said affably, "Mister Oakes, I'd be glad to loan you ninety dollars—or even more if you need it!"

My eyes glittered as he reached into his back pocket, pulled out his wallet, counted out ninety dollars in cash like he was dispensing blue ribbons for peach preserves at a country fair, and handed it to me.

"Thanks!" I rejoiced. "I'll pay you back! You'll be the first! Rest assured!"

I intended to pay all of my creditors back. Every last cent.

My creditors approved my reorganization plan and I returned to Atlanta. There, with the dedication of a perfectionist temperament, welcoming my new escape, pushed by new meaning, guided by an undertone of determination. I began working long hours at the Service Bureau Company, developing programs on computers, working from 80 to 100 hours a week, paid on an hourly basis, and the money from all of the overtime, plus the little we made on the sale of our home in Columbus, helped me to begin getting back on my feet financially; and I began paying off my creditors as arranged under the reorganization plan. And, as I had promised Sandra, I came straight home every night after work.

"What about the Super Sport?" Sandra asked me. "You promised after the bankruptcy was settled you'd get rid of it. "Well? ..."

I sighed. "This week."

Two days later, after work, a couple of work buddies and I went on a trout fishing trip on the Chattahoochee River, having beforehand informed Sandra of the trip and obtaining her approval. After the fishing was over, after we returned to Atlanta. I opened the Chevelle up on an unfamiliar street reeling the Super Sport deserved one final majestic flash of glory. Putting it through the gears, I rounded a curve with loose gravel and lost control of the vehicle. The car skidded sideways over a hundred feet, rammed into a telephone pole, then lunged into a ditch.

A fitting good-bye to the last of my breathers.

I experienced cracked ribs in the wreck—not enough to keep me out of work, and the other two in the car suffered only minor bruises.

The Super Sport had been given its proper funeral. That done, Sandra insisted that we buy a nice, slow, safe family car. A Volkswagen. We bought it. And I croaked. The recalcitrant rebel brought into line. The harbinger to a new horror.

CHAPTER 28

AUGUST OF 1969 was when I first became aware of it. Daddy had lung cancer. During November his condition began deteriorating rapidly, and he became so incapacitated that by December, J.P. rented a house in Phenix City, moved Daddy and Mama into it, and shortly afterwards Daddy was admitted to Phenix City's Cobb Memorial Hospital.

From December through January, 1970, I received urgent phone calls, usually in the middle of the night, from J.P. or other members of the family, frantically stating:

"They don't think Daddy's going to make it through the night! Better come!"

After each call, Sandra and I would hop out of bed, quickly dress, jump in the car and head for Phenix City, either taking Donna and Michelle with us, or quickly finding a neighbor to watch them.

But the next morning Daddy would still be alive, holding onto life with his indomitable spirit. At the hospital I stared at him dolefully, my mouth as dry as a tomb, the man I was looking at a shrinking skeletal stranger to the substantial, hearty and cheerful Daddy I had known; the one with the broad, earthy strong face who was a bull of strength and endurance; the one who's granite spirit had cheated death 19 years before following his car accident. But not this time, Daddy had run out of miracles. He was dying, wilted away to nothing, the cancer reducing him to skin and bone, covering him with the faint sour smell of mortal illness.

I hesitated a long time before speaking to him, trying to find the right words. There were none. "You need anything, Daddy?" I asked, a hard lump squeezing my throat. "Can I do anything for you?"

"No." He grimaced. He spoke in a wane, almost muted rasp, a hollow metallic sound from thin bloodless lips, his mouth quivering as he spoke. His breathing was labored and shallow, his eyes sunk into darkened lugubrious pits, his entire face a sallow expression of excruciating pain. "I'll be better in a few days."

My heart leaped into the middle of my throat when he said that. Knowing there was no hope for him, all I could do was to grimace at him helplessly, then grimace even more as he gawked sightlessly at the ceiling in a defocused stare, shaking like a leaf on a tree during a storm. Then he'd break into loud, uncontrollable chest-racking sobs, weeping bitterly at the pain.

Mama, with a fatalistic calm, finally resolved to his fate, was with Daddy every moment. But I couldn't remain calm. Not watching this. Not watching the last painful throes of Daddy dying. It settled a fear around my heart, deep and dreadful, and my legs almost buckled. Death still terrified me, and looking at him lying so pitiful and hapless in his hospital bed, the face of death itself, I'd break out in cold sweats and have to leave the hospital room's sepulchral atmosphere, scuttling over the shiny gray vinyl floors of the hospital and out of the building, walking around aimlessly, absently, on the grounds wrapped in a trance, trembling all over, eyes wide and starry, trying to pull myself together. I had to remain strong and not lose it. But I was losing it, gripped in another of my old terrorizing fears; Daddy burning in Mama's hell!

Daddy didn't deserve to go like this; go in such terrible, agonizing pain, a hell in itself. Then, after dying, to continue agonizing in hell's incomputable pain for all time.

That vision ripped me apart inside.

Somehow I'd manage to regain a tenuous composure and return to Daddy in his room, presenting a facade of strength, my voice modulated again. And looking at Mama sitting by his bed, the one who had cursed Daddy to hell all my growing life, now ready to open hell's gates and push him in, my hate for her intensified, knowing no bounds.

After each urgent trip to the hospital in Phenix City, Sandra and I would return exhausted to our Cindy Courts apartment in Tucker, Georgia, a suburb of Atlanta, 12 miles from work. In between those visits I began having horrifying nightmares again of Daddy going to hell after he died, and I'd wake up in the middle of the night in a cold, trembling sweat. Then came the anxiety attack. The suffocation. The paralysis.

During this period of spur-of-the-moment visits to the hospital, my work at the Service Bureau Company never suffered. I made up for the time I lost due to Daddy's illness by working extra hours when I was at work. And often I went to work with little sleep, usually no more than three hours—that sleep fitful and thin, sometimes no sleep at all, my eyes baggy and sunken, cheeks hollow and gray and bristling.

In between the turbulent trips to see Daddy, there were other pressing matters to be dealt with. One was my work situation. My job was only temporary, on a trial basis, with no fringe benefits. But with Sandra pregnant, I needed more security, including fringe benefits, especially insurance.

In January I approached Bill Hale on the possibility of being given a permanent position. He looked at me for a few moments, his eyes seeming opaque, his expression unreadable. Then he replied. "Don, this is a bad time for programmers in our company. Even for those who have permanent positions. We're closing our large "490" division in Dallas and hundreds of programmers are being let go. But let me see what I can do for you."

I had little hope for my request. But a few days later, after one of my hospital trips to Phenix City, Bill called me into his office. "Don, because we like what you're doing for us, I went to bat for you. I told the higher-ups what a tremendous asset you've been to us in programming, and they agreed. So good news! Effective February first, you'll become a permanent employee, retroactive back to November eleventh, the day we hired you on. A day, I might add, we're pleased you decided to drop by. Congratulations! Well earned!"

On the first of February I became a permanent employee, placed on salary, with full fringe benefits. Fifteen days later, on February 16, eleven days after I turned 26 years of age, Daddy's breathing finally snagged and stopped.

An era in the legacy gone. His laughter at life no more, as though there was nothing else to laugh at so he said to hell with it and died, leaving behind only dimming memories, his life an obscure cameo testament to the reality that we are all insignificant, comical, slapstick creatures bungling our way through life on a journey toward death, and those seeing that journey as noble rather than as a joke living the greatest folly of all.

It was a taut wintry sky the day of Daddy's funeral, the sun a dim orange glow. Services were held in Josie, Alabama, at the Ramah Baptist Church, the church which Mama pronounced "Ramer" and made so infamous with us kids by shouting that she'd rather be dead and buried there than having to keep putting up with Daddy—and the rest of us. But now that she no longer had Daddy to put up with she sang a different tune, a bizarre tune of disembodied grief.

At the funeral, with all the family members there—pale worn, dusty-looking, a partially congealed din of quieted voices, Mama became totally unraveled, completely losing her mind.

"Oh, Jesus God no!" Mama screamed, her eyeballs a flashing, disjointed panic. "Joe! . . . Joe! … Joe! … No. Joe … No! … No! … No! … No! Dear Jesus—nooooooooo! Oh, No! Jesus God … Joe … No! No, Joe! No! Joe! Joe! No! Please! No. Joe! Nooooo! Pleeeeeeaaaaaaaasssssssseeeee!"

Quickly she sank into delirious derangement beyond any sense of rational thought. "Ya can't be dead. Joe! No! No! No! Ya not dead, Joe! Please don't be dead, Joe! Please. Not dead! Pleeeeeaaaaaaasssssssseeeeeeee!! No, Joe! EEOWWEERRRR!! NO! NO! NOT DEAD, JOE! YAAAAAAAAAAAAAAAAAAAAAAAAAA!"

Shaking uncontrollably, Mama waved her arms without purpose, sinking into a torturing realm of her own, beyond grief and despair, her utterances no longer words but a chilling, primitive hollering lashing out like a whip; a dreadful bellowing, screeching and piercing; a wailing echoing and reverberating, ripping through the air in frightening, lost, bloodcurdling terror, as if witness to the world's fiery end.

Her eyes changed color, a yellow, glowing hissing glare, as if her mind and emotions and total being had left this earth and entered another world, following Daddy into that flesh-eating, meat-scorching, black-embered hell she had created for him; and now, through her chilling, primitive bellowing, suffering all of his agonizing torment with him.

Through it all my guts tightened into a mass of hot rivulets. It was too much for me to see, to feel, to experience—Mama so much out of control, putting me out of control, leaving me petrified, my breath racing and my body twitching and jiggling and shuddering, the inside of my head becoming a sound track for Mama's dissonant walling, an eerie pounding symphony making contact with the labyrinthine reaches of irrational energies and fears buried deep inside my heart; a graphic reliving of the fears and terror and turbulence and nightmares of my entire childhood. The iron scream again behind my lips. Horrible impressions passing unsummoned through my mind.

I wanted to run. Hide. Anywhere. Escape this ordeal. But I had to stay put, dreary, empty of color, my muscles feeling like piano wire. I had to look strong. Act comforting. The dead bringing out the absurdity in the living. Daddy's last laugh, finally free of the snarling, slashing frenzied reproaches of Mama, the joke now on her. Daddy's death was his last laugh and joke on all of us, his laughter ringing with the wind as he was lowered into his grave, then fading with the sun's lengthening shadows lowering into the darkening gray-blue edge of night.

CHAPTER 29

MAMA'S HELL FOR Daddy was now mine.
And the Shadow, whether or not he appeared in my nightmares, was always with me. I felt his presence, night and day, an invisible force pushing me, tormenting me, bringing to mind the Zen passage:

> "As I was going up a stair, I met a man who wasn't there. He wasn't there again today. I wish to God he'd go away."

The city of my escape from Columbus, Atlanta, Georgia, was the gateway to the Southeast. The city, surrounded by the wooded foothills of the Blue Ridge Mountains, was more than a Southern city, more than the South's chief railroad, airline and professional sports center. The dynamic metropolis of Atlanta, thriving and bursting with growth, was an international city. A corporate city. The center of commerce, industry, transportation and finance in the Southeast. And unlike other major cities, Atlanta wasn't hard and forbidding—at least not in 1969, but possessed a soft, sensuous grace, especially in the spring, the flowers blooming in radiant colors, exotic aromatic scents, lovely deep green everywhere; and, as in Pea River Swamp, the dogwood trees gracing everything with their greenish-white flowers beautifully set off by bright red drupes.

Atlanta was unique in the spring—thick green masses of hickory and pine and maple trees, blending with the sparkling colorful contrast of dogwoods, shading and landscaping most of its streets and avenues with a magic of their own. And again, unlike other large cities, Atlanta's air, like the air in southern Alabama, was clean and clear and almost pure, relatively free of pollution. The rich greenery, beneath unsullied, clear bright skies, in and of itself, made Atlanta and its vicinity, similar to Pea River and Pea River Swamp, a place of Nature's bliss, only a different version of its majesty.

And there was nothing as lovely as Peachtree Street at night, with its enchanting stillness or its cool evening breezes. Winding easily through the heart of Atlanta, then spiraling picturesquely outward from it, dotted with bustling cafes and shops, Peachtree Street was a gentle street, its warmth the warmth of Atlanta.

In this city of warmth, in this unpolluted place of Nature's bliss, a modern Camelot of sensuous grace, a sight-seeing paradise with the almost year around honeysuckle aroma of spring, I was out of sync, feeling disembodied, propelled by a megalomania cal swashbuckling psychic force out of my awareness that would embark me on a 15 year reign of vengeance against Mama through Sandra.

Daddy's death and the loss of my breathers set this reign in motion. The unsettling shock at Daddy's funeral reintroduced me to traumatizing nightmares in my sleep, the same nightmare, night after night; Daddy's corpse, the faint gassy stink of decay, hearing his screaming as he roasted alive, a flaming pyre in the roaring inferno of Mama's hell, the nightmare so intense as to wake me up in the night, trembling, a cold sweat, the room closing in on me. Then came the anxiety attack; the paralysis.

Following Daddy's funeral I poured myself into my job, working nights and weekends, whatever it took to get the work, always a copious amount, out. Since going on salary my pay for overtime ceased, though my workload and number of hours worked didn't. But I welcomed the extra hours. Work was the only breather from my hell that I had. It was my childhood all over again, only rather than school it was work my great escape. But unlike my childhood, I had no escapes from home. When not working, I was nailed there. My promise to Sandra.

By April I had made a large dent in paying off most of the debts forcing me into bankruptcy. On April 2, 1970, Sandra gave birth to another girl. We named her April. The infant was two months premature, weighing only a little over four pounds, and she had to be placed in an incubator until she gained more weight. A hard birth for Sandra, she acquired phlebothrombosis as a result, and a warning from her doctor that giving birth again would probably kill her. She underwent surgery to prevent another pregnancy.

It wasn't until just past mid 1970 that the effects of being without my breathers began evidencing itself at home. They began simple enough. A creeping sardonic demeanor. Snide disdain. An edge to my voice. Petty gripes. Moodiness. Then a restless obstinacy of clipped, strangled tones making me unpleasant to be around and keeping Sandra's and my life at a distance from quotidian things.

Not enjoying these effects, to escape being around them, Sandra enrolled at DeKalb Tech on a two year nursing program at the same time obtaining a job as a nurse's aid at the Doctor's Hospital in Tucker where we lived.

Meanwhile, at the Service Bureau Company, my work was hard, the hours long, and my performance noticed. Impressed with my efforts, Bill Hale provided me with avuncular encouragement which I responded to with the soft-voiced sincerity of a 26-year-old, prompting me to work all that more determined.

Beginning in 1971, after I had turned 27, my moodiness and petty gripes and obstinacy at home escalated to an acid-etched gaucherie of yelling at Sandra and the kids, finding fault with them, dishing out insults, picking fights, starting arguments over nothing, and just being ornery in general. Then, in 1972, when I was 28, I graduated back to temper tantrums and throwing things, dangerous leaps making my disposition much meaner. In response, Sandra became bilious, yelling back at me with hot, dark-eyed hostility, evolving our relationship at home into thunderous verbal war, but not fierce enough to make her leave. For one thing, I had kept my promises. All of them. When not working, I was home at nights, and keeping my promises to her increased Sandra's tolerance for my tantrums and angry outbursts and flinging things about, as long as this frenzy remained in bounds—not reaching the pitch of a madman.

To be sure, Sandra made threats of leaving, but threats in the heat of battle, threats forgotten when she calmed down, when her cooler head prevailed.

As in childhood, I was unfolding into an embodied paradox. As much as the home situation was becoming bleaker, the work situation was becoming brighter. On the job I was displaying such a formidable talent and acumen for programming, such a tenacity to stick to difficult programming projects until they were finished, and finished to the satisfaction of my superiors—sometimes dazzling and amazing them, revealing a knack for bringing off the near miraculous, that my efforts had garnered the attention of the Service Bureau Company's Headquarters' Manager in Greenwich, Connecticut, Roger Cole. In 1972 he flew to Atlanta to confer with me and two other programmers.

"Don, I'm forming a new national programming group within the company and I'd like you to become a charter member of that group," Cole said. Thirty-three, round face with dark-rimmed glasses, balding on top, thin black hair on the sides, sober and dignified, dressed in the same elegant executive tailoring as Bill Hale, Roger Cole was an articulate, dynamic person reflecting commitment and trim habits of mind, yet having the flare of persuasion and appeal. "As you know, all twenty-eight of our offices nationally have their own programming staffs. But I want to get out of this mode and do all of our programming in one location. Headquarters has decided upon Atlanta as this location and as a charter member you'd be in on the ground floor of the new operation, meaning more responsibility, but also advancement and more money!

"Would you like to become a part of this?"

I drew in a sudden breath, a victorious roar welling up in my intellect. "Yes!" I smiled unctuously, unable to contain my exuberance. "Most definitely! I want to move forward with this company!"

"Consider yourself so moved."

With my new advancement and hike in pay, in November, 1972, I moved the family into a townhouse in the Plantation Apartments in Clarkston, Georgia, right below Tucker and three miles from our old apartment. It was a much nicer apartment complex, and the townhouse, three bedrooms, was larger and more elaborate than our apartment flat in Tucker, homier, almost inviting, more accommodating to the size of our family, and more appropriate to the new horizon opening up for me at the Service Bureau Company.

By now, Sandra had finished her nursing course at DeKalb Tech and was functioning as a LPN. Wanting to further her career, and needing an escape from me at home now more than ever, she began taking courses at Brenau College in Gainesville, Georgia, there working towards her RN.

We were both into our careers. As for mine, I was now operating from a management level, the scope of my work expanded nationwide. On January 13, 1973, the Service Bureau Company, a subsidiary of IBM, was sold to Control Data, and I assumed more management responsibility, developing powerful parameter driven accounting applications through 1975.

During that same period, and beyond, my anger and anxiety, with no breathers for release, were streaking toward full orbit of release on Sandra at home, converting my demeanor to viciousness, becoming more vicious, making Sandra incensed and perplexed, and leaving her increasingly harried.

It now was not just a matter of my temper tantrums and throwing things. It was the demented impetuous verbal rages accompanying those tantrums and fits. Vicious waves of resentment, their churning fury so incredibly intense and volatile, so loathing, that I really had no control of myself, browbeating and disparaging Sandra with my violence like some deranged Sun Belt Captain Bligh.

I had reached the pitch of a madman.

"You're *crazy!*" Sandra screamed. "A maniac! *I want a divorce!*"

Instantly I metamorphosed into a kind being of peace and tranquility. And just as instantly the anxiety and depression bulged inside of me. But when I changed, Sandra changed, overcome by a sweet melancholy of forgiving sadness, that urge of love to forgive. She'd forgotten about the divorce. Then after a period of making up, a period where I'd attempt to narcotize the disruptive emotions I had stirred up in her, a period usually lasting for weeks, sometimes months, I'd start in on her all over again, pushing my verbal abuse on her until once more she was pushed over the edge, divorce her only out. And once more I'd cool it and she'd forgive.

In my dreams I'd have Mama tied more securely to the stake, slashing mercilessly at her with my whip, the Shadow exhorting; "Now you're *doing it right!*"

Sandra's and my relationship kept ebbing and flowing, hot and cold, hopping from one extreme to the other, no long term consistency to either extremity, except for a madness turning me into a yo-yo Jeckyl and Hyde personality at home.

During my periodic stints of peace and tranquility, when ostensibly I was the kind Dr. Jeckyl, on the surface Sandra and I had some good times. We managed a good deal of traveling together, sight-seeing to Helen, Georgia, taking in the colorful German culture; visiting the white, crispy ski slopes of Gatlinburg, Tennessee; hopping off to New Orleans a couple of times, there enjoying the spirited jazz music atmosphere and the Creole cuisine. We made several trips to Texas, and several to the silver daylight of Florida's crystal clear waters, exploring the beaches together in the fading light of evening.

> *"And hand in hand,*
> *to the edge of the sand,*
> *we danced to the light of the moon."*

Sandra even surprised me in 1975 with a pleasant cruise in the Caribbean.

But during these times my anger, lurking just below the surface, kept me on a razor's edge, a certain reserved callousness, a frigidity of tone, and my voice distant and atonic. The anxiety and depression worsened with each trip, torturing me, the Shadow clawing away at me with torment. All I could do was choke on it and grit a measured smile—until my next eruption of vengeful anger, when Mr. Hyde was turned loose, each of his succeeding eruptions becoming more vicious.

While my married life was periodic hell, my work life was constant heaven. In May of 1976, when I was 32 years old, I was promoted to Development Product Manager, responsible for implementing an enormous amount of complex computer software, and developing and maintaining powerful IBM mainframe computers. With the position came a staff of eight people reporting to me and a beginning salary of thirty-five thousand dollars a year.

With this new promotion and more money, in July of 1976 I purchased four acres of land in Maysville, Georgia, in Jackson County, 52 miles from work, with the intention of building a new home there. Until the home was built, I bought a large 70 foot used mobile home trailer, placed it on the four acres and moved the family into it.

Finally I was overcoming my roots. Beating the legacy. Or so I thought.

CHAPTER 30

OFTEN, AFTER MY vengeful brawls with Sandra, usually the next day while at work when my mind and intellect were in their best shape. I'd think whimsically; Mankind's mistake is getting out of bed. That's when its madness begins.

But my madness began before then. In my sleep. Painful, graphic, frightening nightmares of Daddy burning in hell.

"Donald, save me! God, save me!"

"I'm trying. Daddy! I'm trying! But I'm burning too!"

And there'd be other childhood nightmares—the murders-reactivated since Daddy's death. The Shadow began making his appearances again in the nightmares, beginning to laugh at me again, and I'd wake up from my dreams in a cold sweat, always a cold sweat, followed by the paralysis of an anxiety attack.

So when I got out of bed it wasn't my madness beginning it was my madness continuing. If I was in a Mr. Hyde period, my continuing madness was in the form of violent temper tantrums and throwing things and anger outbursts at Sandra. If in a Dr. Jeckyl period, it was anxiety, anxiety attacks and depression continuing at home when I was around Sandra.

During our peaceful periods Sandra tried helping me. Unable to keep from noticing my anxiety paralysis in bed, and my pronounced nervousness and anxiety out of bed, she put me on Valium pills, hoping to calm me down. And although I'd promised her I'd quit my heavy boozing—my all night drunken binges on hard whiskey, which I had done, she didn't mind me drinking beer at home to relax me. Also, knowing how I loved to hunt, she encouraged me to go on hunting trips, hoping that would calm me.

These helped some but reduced the overall madness very little. My legacy, my childhood fears and rage, the Shadow—these called the shots, and Valium and beer and hunting trips addressed them not at all.

October 16, 1976, our eleventh wedding anniversary, hit during one of my Dr. Jeckyl periods, and to celebrate Sandra and I grilled some steaks, tossed a salad and drank a few beers.

"I love you," Sandra toasted, smiling peacefully.

I returned her smile, mumbling something inanely back about love, then the smile dwindled as my darker side thought of a more enthusiastic toast:

I love you too, darling. I can hardly wait to throw an ashtray at you! Or better, a knife!

But even my madness didn't dare carry the revenge that far, the reason I'd never be rid of my anxiety.

That night of our anniversary my down slope into sleep descended me on into the terror of my nightmares, this night a severely frightening dream of Daddy roasting alive in hell.

Then I became Daddy, and I was roasting. Then I was out of hell, now alone and scared and trapped in my tall office building where I worked, engulfed in raging, crackling fire. A thick mushroom of smoke hung above that, slowly distending and dissolving in a breeze. Then the building suddenly collapsed, me with it, the Shadow laughing as everything crashed to the ground in a colossal sonic boom, my flesh rotting and melting and dripping off my bones.

The dream's trauma jerked me from sleep. It was before dawn, a rainy morning, my hands clutched into fists, my mouth dry, my cold sweat and hot anxiety greeted by the cool touch of the predawn air. I was amazed I was alive. I could still feel the scorching burning, for a moment convinced I had brought the fires of Daddy's hell and the office building out of the nightmares with me. An excruciating pain flamed inside of me, feeling like a bed of red hot fire coals in my upper abdomen penetrating through the backbone. Then came the extreme nausea. And I began vomiting. And I couldn't quit.

Frightened, Sandra summoned our next door neighbor, Hollis. He looked at me aghast. "Better get you to a hospital!"

My back felt hinged, and when I straightened to walk the pain became unbearable. Assisting me out into the dark rainy overcast weather, Hollis practically carried me to his decrepit '64 Chevy, then rushed me to the Emergency Room at the hospital in Commerce, a nearby town. By now the fiery pain in my upper abdomen felt so intense that I feared I was on the verge of spontaneous combustion. Still, I had to suffer in this agony for over an hour before a doctor saw me. When one did the doctor spent no more than three minutes with me.

"What did you have to eat last night?" He asked.

"Steak, salad … couple of beers," I grimaced, groaning, not only in pain but fighting a merciless pounding in my skull.

"Indigestion!" The doctor diagnosed rapidly.

"But doctor, I'm in terrible pain! It has to be more than indigestion."

"Naw, naw—indigestion," he readily dismissed. "See it every day. But I'll give you an injection for the pain. And some pills for the nausea. You'll be feeling better in an hour or so."

Whew! Only indigestion. And I thought I had something serious.

I left the hospital still in pain, still nauseous and still vomiting, but looking expectantly ahead to an hour or so. The doctor said I'd then be feeling much better.

The ride back to the trailer in Hollis' Chevy was just as miserable as the bouncy ride to the hospital. Two hours later I was in more pain. I waited another hour. The pain grew worse.

"That doctor's full of shit!" I scowled at Sandra in disgust, feeling I was about to expire. "God. I feel like I'm dying!"

"Let's get you to another doctor!" She frowned, alarmed. Sandra got on the phone, calling a Dr. Dyckman, a professional acquaintance of hers, and he agreed to see me at the Emergency Room at Northside Hospital, 60 miles away on the outskirts of Atlanta near Sandy Springs.

The long ride to Northside was continuing painful torture but I was willing to undergo any suffering that would rid me of the pain. Dr. Dyckman was waiting for me at the hospital and immediately started a thorough workup, including a blood test giving an Amylase count. The count was extremely elevated, identifying my problem.

Pancreatitis!

This diagnosis got me a bed in the hospital pronto, where I was given a strong dosage of Demerol, quickly easing my pain. Then an NG tube was inserted through my nose, down my throat and into my stomach, a painful, highly uncomfortable procedure, but one effective in relaxing the stomach facilitating critical drainage. For the next several days, pumped up on Demerol, I was free of the burning pain, but not allowed to have anything by mouth. After a week my physical health appeared to be back to normal and I was allowed to leave the hospital.

But the pain could return so I was referred to Dr. Rodzewicz, a specialist in pancreatic disorders. His mission: discover the cause of my attack of pancreatitis.

"Mister Oakes," Dr. Rodzewicz said to me at our first meeting, "pancreatitis attacks are caused by either alcoholism, trauma, or blockage between the gall bladder and pancreas, with by far—I mean almost all—the majority of attacks caused by alcoholism." He paused a moment, then looking at me coolly and appraisingly, asked, "Are you an alcoholic?"

My eyes narrowed and I grunted, "Why, no. No. Of course not. I have a few beers, but I haven't done any heavy drinking for seven years."

"Hmmmnmmmmmmmmm. Seven years, uh? You sure?"

"I'm sure."

Convinced he was staring into boozy eyes, he gave me that I-think-you're-lying look, frowned, and said, "Well, I suggest then we do a procedure called ERCP to analyze for possible blocked ducts.

The procedure, a very painful one, was performed, but with no definitive results.

"I'm unable to penetrate the needed area because of some blockage," Dr. Rodzewicz explained.

"What blockage?" I groaned.

"I'm not sure what it is, but in your case I don't think it's significant." He reassured in a peremptory tone. "I'm sure your attacks are caused by your drinking. Cut that out, or reduce it substantially, and I believe you'll have no more attacks."

"But I don't drink."

He gave me that why-keep-lying-to-me look, overcoming me with a weird feeling, bringing on a sense of foreboding. What was the mysterious blockage?

Though I wasn't an alcoholic, I took no chances. I quit drinking even my few beers. It made no difference. I kept having acute pancreatitis attacks. And I kept being rushed to the hospital, socked continuously with bland diets, taking

25 pills and tablets daily—Demerol pills for pain, Valium pills for nervousness and anxiety, and diet supplement pills to prevent aggravation of my pancreatic condition. I was a walking pharmacy.

The attacks continued, angering me, eventually persuading me that I had an unknown disease, convinced the doctors had blown it. A new fear! What was my unknown disease? Not knowing gave me cold chills, frightening me, making my body shake all over, at times my eyes dilating and darting. And with this new fear came additional nervousness and anxiety, extra anxiety for the next three years, a period during which my work at the Service Bureau Company would be interrupted days at a time, sometimes weeks, by many pancreatitis attacks, several hospitalizations, immense dosages of medication, much physical pain, and the fear of an unknown disease. And during this time, at my insistence, Dr. Rodzewicz would attempt the painful ERCP procedure numerous times to see if I had any duct blockage that could explain my pancreatitis attacks, with always the same inconclusive result; the procedure couldn't be completed because of a mysterious blockage, one Rodzewicz had no inclination to pursue because he was convinced my attacks were caused by alcohol, and the blockage, whatever it was, of no consequence.

During these three years all I heard from the doctors was; "Quit that drinking." Or, "Cut down the drinking."

That was their solution to the attacks. And regardless of my protests that I wasn't drinking, the doctors wouldn't look beyond alcoholism as the cause.

In the spring of 1978 I experienced a particularly painful and disquieting pancreatitis attack and was again hospitalized. The day following my discharge, while driving in dense bumper to bumper traffic on Interstate 85, a large tow truck rammed hard into the rear of my car, the jolting impact hurling me forward and caved my abdomen in against the steering wheel. The excruciating burning pain began again and the next day I was rehospitalized with the most severe pancreatitis attack yet.

For the umpteenth time, the disgusting NG tube was shoved down my nose and throat and into my stomach for the lifesaving drainage and I began another hated stint in the hospital.

Ten days later I returned to work but began losing weight steadily, feeling in more pain than ever, in spite of huge dosages of medication and a strict diet.

Back to the hospital. An ultrasound procedure disclosed that a pseudocyst had formed around my pancreas requiring surgery. The surgeon who would perform the operation instructed me to wait 30 days to allow the cyst to firm. I did, and at the end of that time I was so weak that I could barely walk and I weighed less than 120 pounds. Then, on the day of the surgery a routine blood test indicated that my white blood count was dangerously low, necessitating the administration of huge amounts of blood during my operation. Convalescence from the surgery required a few weeks before I could return to work. As soon as I did I was hit with another pancreatitis attack, and it was back to the hospital.

Medication, sleep, nightmares, the Shadow laughing at me.

And the more bedraggled I became by my havoc, the more the Shadow laughed. Before, that havoc was the hurt of emotional pain. Now, on top of it, I was hurting with equal physical pain. This pain, combined with endless hospitalizations, large dosages of medication and a strict diet were pulverizing me down to a senseless agonizing pulp. On the home front, when not in the hospital, with my Dr. Jeckyl-Mr. Hyde periods continuing to alternate, the extra stress of my mysterious pancreatic problem, my heavy doses of medication, and my fear of an unknown disease made the anxiety and depression of my Dr. Jeckyl periods almost unbearable and the anger outbursts of my Mr. Hyde periods exceptionally vicious and outrageous. As Dr. Jeckyl I was totally a nervous wreck. As Mr. Hyde I was just about impossible to live with.

Work was my only sanctuary. There seemed to be a protecting shield around my intellect, and at my office I was still able to function competently, even though I was getting less sleep. But outside my office everything was a war zone.

By 1979 I didn't know what was going to happen to me. Because I was physically sick so much, in continuous pain and consistently "pilled" up, the combination of the 52 mile drive from Maysville to work, then the return trip home afterwards, was becoming impossible to manage. I had to be closer to work. And being so sick, figuring I could be struck down any moment by my unknown disease, I also was concerned about bringing my family closer to Atlanta—during my Dr. Jeckyl periods, developing a strong worry about the welfare of Sandra and the kids when they weren't in my sight, fearing that if anything happened to me they would be left stranded in Maysville, mostly rural country.

My illness dictated that I abandon my dream of building a new home in Maysville. I sold our trailer and bought a new house in Duluth, Georgia, much closer to Atlanta and to work. On February 2, 1979, three days before I turned 35, I moved the family into our new home on a verdant wooded lot, a spacious, four-bedroom natural red cedar home with a drive carefully winding along the edge of an expansive lawn blending with the umbrella of gracefully towering pine and oak trees almost hiding the house from the street. An elegant kidney-shaped swimming pool, a beautiful veranda and exquisite landscaping graced the back. And inside the house were all the modern salient features and special accoutrements of an executive home. Not exactly a sharecropper's shack.

But enjoying it was another matter. With nightmares, anxiety attacks, pancreatitis attacks, severe depression, Mr. Hyde, doped up on medication and fearing an unknown disease, the best I could do was to slump in my expensive, early American easy chair in front of my home's beautiful field stone fireplace, surrounded by plush furnishings and advanced electronic marvels, and sit there dazed like some tiresome, sluggish beast licking the fang and claw marks of its own self inflicted wounds.

I felt so tiresome I wanted to hide from people, so I began growing a full length beard. As it was approaching abundant bloom, a woman at work said to me:

"You have the looks for TV or the movies."

I was told that by other women and a few men as well. People say the craziest things, I thought, not considering my looks as being that appealing. Average at best.

During my Dr. Jeckyl periods my only breather from my anxiety and depression was my hunting trips. On a frigid Saturday morning in November of 1979 I awakened from my nightmares in my usual cold sweat, followed by an anxiety attack. The burning pain in my abdomen was more fierce than usual so, once I recovered from my anxiety attack and struggled out of bed, I took an extra Darvon pill with my morning cup of coffee. Then with Hollis and another friend, I set out on a deer hunting trip.

We drove to some woods, one of my favorite hunting spots, and sounding like a walking medicine cabinet with all the rattling of pill bottles stuffed in my pockets, I climbed up about 20 feet into a familiar tree stand a little after daybreak, the air crisp and cold, the wind singing through the pines. Then as the sunlight filtered down through the trees, easing the chill of the air into morning freshness, very rapidly I became drowsy.

I had overdosed on the Darvon.

For the next two hours I clung haplessly to the stand, fading in and out of consciousness, all I could do to keep from falling out of the tree. Then the overdose elapsed and, very weakly, very gingerly, very slowly, I managed to struggle down to the ground, realizing how miraculous it was that I hadn't fallen out of the tree and possibly broken my neck.

That was it! I had had enough of all this pain and medication and overdosing and living like this. Hot under the collar, I phoned Dr. Rodzewicz the following Monday morning and demanded to see him right away. He responded by slipping me into his schedule that day.

"Doctor Rodzewicz, I don't know what, I don't know how—but something has got to be done about all these attacks and hospitalizations and being kept on heavy medication," I insisted with irritable impatience.

Surprise stiffened his face, a sort of strange, startled, sanctimonious doctor's look implying that I was unappreciative of all his efforts on my behalf. His jaw firmed up. "Don, quit your drinking and all of that will stop."

"I don't drink!" I objected, my voice suddenly high and squeaky with astonishment that he kept on persisting that I did. "Will you ever believe that? There's something else going on here!"

His eyes leaped at me a little uppity, as though saying, Why keep lying to me? "Don, we're doing everything humanly possible for you." He rejoined dispassionately. "If you don't follow my advice I don't know what's left."

"I do. What about that mysterious blockage you seem unconcerned about pursuing? I think we should get to the bottom of it. Find out what it is."

Patently exasperated, he paused, sighed and thought a moment, his expression subtly shading into a why-not-pacify-this-drunk look. Then he said, "Would you be willing to travel to Cleveland, Ohio?"

"Yes. Anything!"

"The Cleveland Clinic there has all the necessary apparatus to pursue what you have in mind. If there's anything to that blockage"—his tone indicating that he was quite convinced that there wasn't—"they'll pinpoint it. Let's send you there to ease your mind."

"Right." If ever a mind needed easing, it was mine.

The Cleveland Clinic was one of those sprawling medical complex affairs with a busy atmosphere, everyone running around efficiently doing their duty. Dr. Griffin—no relation to my collaborator—was in charge of my examination visit and wasted no time scheduling several special tests for me. The first was an Upper GI. The barium was awful going down, and it was all I could do to keep from gagging. Then, while lying supine on a table, wall monitors tracing the flow of barium, my insides suddenly felt like a needle-hot meteorite exploding inside of me, the pain becoming so excruciating that the test had to be aborted. The unbearable pain finally lessened, but I was left out of whack for further testing. Disappointed and frustrated, convinced that it was only a matter of time before my unknown disease did me in, sending me to join Daddy in hell, I returned to Atlanta.

A few days later I received a surprise phone call at work from Dr. Griffin in Cleveland. "Mister Oakes, I don't know what we have here, but something suspicious was recorded during the aborted GI test," he informed in the polished tone of some college professor. "Could you come back for a closer look?"

The next day I was back at the Clinic in Cleveland, a fixed, almost obsessed expression on my face. With further testing, Dr. Griffin zeroed in on the suspicious findings.

"You have a little pocket-like growth on your small bowel located at the head of your pancreas," Dr. Griffin said, incredulous. "During the upper GI test, barium filled the pocket, causing it to stretch over the pancreas. That little growth is your mysterious blockage. The villain triggering your pancreatitis attacks. Good thing we found ..."

My face suddenly became slightly mottled and puffy, a far off look of derision. All I could think of was three years of painful physical hell that could have been prevented with proper diagnosis.

"... it when we did. It can be removed by surgery. Doctor Rodzewicz is to be complemented on his persistence in this case. Pancreatitis caused by a small bowel blockage like this is so uniquely rare that it's medical news!

"Mister Oakes, I think you've just made medical history!"

"Fuck the history. Get me into surgery."

Surgery was performed on January 22, 1980, and the pocket-like growth was removed from my small bowel. Almost immediately my burning pains diminished without the use of Demerol. But there was an unforeseen complication. The doctors overlooked the fact that I had been on Valium steadily for over three years and they took me off of the drug cold turkey.

I went berserk! First, I was thrown into an anxiety state of complete paralysis.

Then, recovering, I became rowdy and unpredictable. "Some foreign object has been left *inside* of me!" I screamed at Sandra from my hospital bed, coming out of my sedative mist the night following surgery. "Go get a doctor! ... A damn doctor!"

I was so convincing and demanding that Sandra persuaded a surgeon to come to my room and perform an on the spot examination. Nothing was found left inside of me from the surgery. After the surgeon left, my eyes flitted into restless exploration trips around the room, nervous and itchy. Then that restlessness exploded. I jerked out my NG and IV tubes, jumped out of bed and began pacing and cursing and lamenting.

"Donald, stop ... stop it!" Sandra blanched, her voice tight, panic in her eyes.

Finally she persuaded me to get back into bed, where I began talking sporadically, frighteningly, about things that happened in the past.

"Those poor fuckin' bastards! A bad wreck! ... Bad wreck! That damn mountain road!" My voice was trembling, my face quivering, my eyes ranging desperately about. "God! ... God! Help them! Help them! Not them! . . . Not them! It should have been me *dead* on that mountain! Why am I alive! Why am I alive! ..."

Shortly after I left the island of Crete, four U.S. airmen there plunged their vehicle off the mountain road, where Harris and I confronted the truck, and were killed.

The doctors quickly realized their error and put me back on Valium, calming me down, then gradually weaned me from the drug over the next few months.

Eleven days after my surgery I returned to work—Control Data now having changed the name of the Service Bureau Company to Control Data Business Centers—and my pancreatitis attacks, burning pain, hospitalizations, heavy dosages of medication, special diets and fear of an unknown disease were all things of the past. But in their place I was left with an intense anger—anger at three years of unnecessary hell and unneeded diets and missing work and physically draining myself to raw nerves because of the doctors' conviction that my pancreatitis attacks were caused by alcoholism, the insistent, fast-shooting illusion, in my case, of a fixed medical mentality in spite of my objections.

This new anger combined with my ever ongoing anger to make my Mr. Hyde periods with Sandra so vicious as to be insufferable and unconscionable— in spite of the fact that during my three years of physical illness she had kept the faith, stuck by me, put up with my Mr. Hyde tantrums, my impossible moodiness because of huge doses of medication, prepared special diets for me, raised three children, held down a full time LPN position and attended Brenau College carrying a full load in pursuit of becoming an RN.

But her true grit made no difference now that I was free of the problems and distractions of my pancreatitis attacks. With the Shadow's torment increasing in my dreams, the nightmares of Daddy screaming in hell becoming more agonizing, my temper tantrums, throwing things and acid insults came back into play with greater force. Sandra, now more committed to the family, more entrenched to the habit of marriage, with her own escapes from the wrath and disaster of Mr. Hyde—she graduated as an RN in 1982 and worked herself up to third shift assistant Unit Manager in the hectic Northside Hospital Emergency Room, her more peaceful times with Dr. Jeckyl sufficient enough to keep her from leaving, was now willing to put up with more.

And more she got over the next four years.

By 1983, at the age of 39, my nightmares of Daddy in hell screaming for my help became so horrendous, the Shadow's laughter at my anguish so tormenting and terrorizing, that I'd awake to the most suffocating anxiety attacks I'd ever experienced. To prevent these attacks I quit sleeping altogether. I'd lie in bed awake all night, eyes popped open apprehensively, soaking in anxiety, not daring to drift off into slumber and into the shattering torment of the Shadow and the devastatingly horrible and frightening nightmares awaiting me, then be jolted awake and thrown into the grueling trauma of a most hideously suffocating anxiety attack. Better not to sleep. I didn't. At work, without sleep, I functioned on nervous energy alone.

In 1984, when I was 40, Control Data Business Centers named me to manage a newly formed department called the National Response Center, at a salary of over sixty thousand dollars a year, the demanding responsibilities of this position requiring me to implement special software for large accounts on a national basis.

But despite the promotion, the money, things sailing smoothly and upward at work, in 1984 I had deteriorated into such a physical-mental-emotional wreck that my disintegration was beyond my ability to decipher.

My brother Red was in and out of the hospital for several years due to the severe punishment of alcohol. Many doctors pleaded with him and stated that his drinking would eventually kill him. They were correct because he was admitted in early May of 1984 and rapidly deterioated. He passed away about two weeks later at the age of 49 suffering from cirrhosis of the liver. Mama took it very hard and never really got ovet his death. J.P. and I were asked to make a decision as to whether or not to take him off life support. After many days of struggling with the issue, we concurred that there was no hope so we gave the go-ahead. Mama stayed by his side night and day which contributed to our decision. She finally concurred to take him off life support.

After leaving work most days my body began breaking into cold sweats. My head started throbbing and my neck began feeling as though someone was working on it with a dull hatchet. My vision became blurry and lines edged my eyes. I felt faint, my energy waning, no longer having vitality, walking as though stooped and in pain, leadened with fatigue, dazed, damn near destroyed. Outside of work I suddenly found myself unable to cope, either alone or in crowds. I especially had difficulty dealing with noisy crowds, becoming completely miserable in such settings. I developed constant diarrhea. And I hadn't slept for over a year. Literally, I hadn't slept one wink.

All of these were signs that the anxiety during my Dr. Jeckyl periods was devouring me, intensifying exponentially to the point of becoming virtually unbearable, no longer being allayed by Mr. Hyde's outbursts. I eliminated the Dr. Jeckyl periods entirely. From now on it was all Mr. Hyde, one furious motion of teeming vindictive energy, a deadly verbal bomb of continued, constant predation, with no let up, blinding me to all consequences. To get rid of my worsening anxiety, Mr. Hyde put Sandra through the most crazed fusillade of temper tantrums and anger outbursts and wild hurling of objects this side of a soccer riot, coming as close as I dared to treacherously throwing that knife. My outpourings of pugnacious rancor toward Sandra became so profuse, so ferocious and vicious, so locked with personal and marital desecration, as to throw her into a sickness beyond all desolation and despondency; a harrowed blackness destroying the beauty of her eyes, circles beneath them, dark and deep, deadening her face.

She glanced at me from deep within her soul. "Donald, oh, God! You're still so ill! But not physical!"

Like a piece of hard black coal, my eyes suddenly blazed with a sickly yellow glare. "What <u>do you know</u>?!" I hissed, my voice a thick thunder invading the air, a film of sweat pouring from my face. Then between clenched teeth in sinister emphasis. "About <u>any fucking thing</u>!!"

But as savage as my anger outbursts had become with Sandra, they were now insufficient to ward off the anxiety pulverizing me and breaking out on all fronts. My anxiety and depression were now continuous, coming in suffocating doses, slicing through me from every angle, unable to be allayed by directing my anger toward Sandra. Then, for the first time, the anxiety hit me at work. My madness encroached my office.

On December 11, 1984, I was sitting at my desk in my office when my feet suddenly became cold and numb. My body stiffened. My shoulders knotted. My face became like stone. Then my ears began buzzing with a loud roar. All at once I was stunned, disoriented, debilitated, the room spiraling. I reached for the phone, taking the longest time to pick it up, icy in my hand, a harsh breath in my throat.

Jerkily, I dialed a number, heard the ring, the party answered. "Sandra, I don't know what's happening to me, but I'm...I'm strangely dizzy—and have the weirdest sensations!" I said unsteadily, lips sucked flat, my voice sounding embarrassingly frantic to my own ears, a slightly deranged ring to it, unheard of at work where, until recently, I was the charming elegance of dignity and intensity, guided by the linear logic of detached thought. "Call Doctor Dyckman. Get me into the hospital! Something's physically wrong with me again!"

Sandra phoned Dr. Dyckman and I was immediately admitted to Northside Hospital. There, with Sandra with me, I was given a thorough medical examination. Afterwards, Dr. Dyckman shook his head.

"Donald, there's not a thing wrong with you physically. Not even a suggestion of anything. I think what you need is a psychiatrist!"

"May I see my husband alone, Doctor Dyckman?" Sandra asked.

"Certainly."

Dyckman left us.

"Donald. Doctor Dyckman is right," Sandra began, speaking calmly, tiredly, but a thin edge to her voice. Her eyes were melancholy, moistened. She wanted to cry but didn't, her underscore of deep strength smothering it. Instead she looked fully into my face with obvious question. "You need to see a psychiatrist. I love you very deeply and very much. But I can't help you. You can't help you. And neither one of us can go through this any longer. If you don't agree to get psychiatric help, I'm leaving you. I...we...have no choice. The marriage is finished. And I'm afraid you're finished too. God help you!"

There was an unmistakable wits end finality to her tone that I couldn't misread. I fixed a long, cheerless stare on her, realizing I had no leverage left. I was in deep psychic trouble. My belief that I could master my emotional problems myself, fight them myself, beat them myself had to be recognized as the illusion it was. An illusion that could no longer be dismissed by rigid rationalizations. Rather than my frantic efforts alleviating these problems they were intensifying them beyond my means to cope with their accelerating self-destruction. Sandra's ultimatum couldn't be ignored. She was correct. And I knew it.

And gazing at her, trembling with brittle reaction, overcome with an old underprivileged feeling, a squalid, backward, dumpy solemnity, another thing was clear. I was unable to figure out who I was. My legacy had me by the throat! For attempting the impossible; trying to make a purse out of a sow's ear.

My mind recoiled unto itself, and who I was, I finally reflected, was still that scrawny, miserable, undernourished, pip-squeak sharecropper kid now turned into some wayward, monstrous, back bush demon torn asunder in its own emotional wasteland and unfit for the living Universe.

CHAPTER 31

I WAS QUITE pessimistic about anyone else being able to help me but I made the commitment to Sandra and myself not only to seek psychiatric help but to see it through, no matter what, not knowing then what that really entailed. On December 13, 1984, my toddling steps into the psychiatric world began when I was admitted to the Ridgeview Institute, a private psychiatric hospital in Atlanta, for two weeks of evaluation and what best can be described as a mental-emotional shakedown.

Ridgeview Institute was a pleasant enough looking place—neat, tidy, modern milieu with nice furniture and relaxing colors, all the appeal of a high roller funeral home for the living. But there the appeal ended. Aside from the doctors and staff, the inhabitants of Ridgeview were the pick of the emotional basket cases, most of them either outright psychotics or those driven in that direction by severe alcoholism or drug abuse.

I was totally unprepared for confinement with such a crazy mob of patients. Suddenly being yanked from the real world and thrust into this controlled environment of loonies was a new trauma, leaving me in mute shock and sagging my mouth in stupefaction.

God, what have I let myself in for?

Ridgeview was the modern version of the Snake Pit, a good many of its patients vocalizing and externalizing their craziness every minute of the day. They came in all unhinged varieties, a throated din of painful screamers, moaners, pleaders, loud sobbers, talkers to the walls, deteriorated alcoholic mumblers, catatonic glarers, agitated paranoids, manic schemers, hallucinators, pathetic and fatuous grinners in step with a mirth outside this world, people hearing voices in their heads, and disoriented drug abusers swearing their flesh was crawling off their bones.

In contrast, I was one of the few patients externally appearing normal, conspicuous by my calmness, capable of sane reactions and normal conversation, my brand of emotional turmoil rigidly under control, internalized, a grand facade of peacefulness while I was away from Sandra and didn't journey back into sleep.

During my two week stay at the institute I was provided a modest room which I shared with another patient, a fumbling, stumbling man strung out on drugs; a blunt-nosed, slobbery-mouthed person with confused, disoriented eyes that sort of popped out of his head, his voice a rasping, cooled-out throaty eroticism suggesting he was constantly exhaling marijuana smoke. Withdrawn and listless, the man was poor company—not that I was the greatest, seeming lost in bored resignation and relating to me with dull indifference.

My first two days at Ridgeview were taken up mostly with psychological testing—intelligence, coordination and a battery of emotional and personality tests, highlighted by the Rorschach, the famous ink blot test, ten cards, vague forms on each one, either in dull black and white or in blazing, inglorious flaming colors, a razzle-dazzle of operatic blotches appearing as though painted by an artist unable to make up his mind on concept, none of the blotches making sense but my task to make sense out of them.

Two days following completion of the tests I was called into an office shared by visiting doctors stopping by for conferences with their patients. My doctor, Dr. Nancy Engel, a psychiatrist, the one with whom I would begin psychotherapy once I left Ridgeview, was there to consult with me.

A balanced person of careful perceptions, Dr. Engel was a soft, pretty woman in her thirties, smartly dressed, well proportioned lithe figure, her hair an attractive veil of brownish-blonde, her face angular, with unexpected freckles. Beginning our conference, looking squarely at me with startling sherry brown eyes—clear, lively, almost a tan, she announced:

"Mister Oakes, the tests disclose you're suffering from severe depression and anxiety." Her voice was pleasant, a supple grace, a certain soothing quality to it, her manner down-to-earth, personable, direct, and low key.

Irritated by where I was, sleepless nights ravaging my disposition, my first thought; Tell me something new, doctor. How's this broad possibly going to help me? Then, "Okay, so you know what's wrong with me," I growled, a bit obnoxious. "How long will it take you to fix me?"

"Mister Oakes," she replied quietly, calmly, gazing at me with speculative appraisal, "I can't fix you. I'm not in the people fixing business. I will, however, help you help yourself. The first thing you have to do is to come to terms with the fact that you have a problem."

"It's pretty *obvious* I have a problem! Otherwise I wouldn't be sitting here in this *mad house*! Now, can we get started? How long's it going to take?"

"We've already started. And I can't tell you how long it's going to take."

"*Wait a minute*! You mean to tell me you've never treated anybody like me before?" I challenged, radiating skepticism. "With the same symptoms?"

"Mister Oakes, everybody is different. Different circumstances. Different environment. Different layers of stress. I sense you have a lot of layers to peel off. It's up to you how long it takes. Depends on how hard you work at it."

"You mean to tell me we're about to start something and you have *no idea* how long its going to take?! You've got to be *kidding me*, Doctor Engel! Can't you at least give me a ballpark?"

She shook her head, stating emphatically, "It's impossible to predict. It could take as little as one year, or five. Maybe more."

I stared at her more than weary. "You mean to tell me that I'm going to feel like this for maybe five years?"

"That's exactly what I'm telling you. Maybe longer."

My eyes drooped, drawing my brows together. I began stroking my beard, considering her protracted prognosis, none too pleased with the indefinite time frame for my therapy.

Years? My God! What have I let myself in for?

The remainder of my time at Ridgeview was taken up by group therapy and other types of group involvement, including educational classes and physical exercises—a cluster of around-the-clock probing, pushing, coaxing activities so regimented that I had to account for my whereabouts every minute. I hated it. No free time except to sleep. But my sleep was worse than the institute regimen. Dr. Engel prescribed an antidepressant for me to help me sleep and the first night I dozed off—my first sleep in over a year—the Shadow was waiting for me. He seemed to have grown older, but still there was that majestic sweep of flesh on either side of his nose, curving like an eagle's beak. And those eyes were still the same—black marble eyes, two glaring discs, glistening, piercing, possessing.

"Welcome back, pal!" Then the Shadow began his deep, unhinged, fiendish laughter.

"Why are you laughing at me?"

His only answer was his loud, tormenting, mocking laughter.

"Damnit, tell me! *Tell me*! Why do you keep laughing at me?!"

His laughter became more deafening, a bristling, monstrous, thundering roar. I awoke from my sleep screaming, then the horrible anxiety attack. My screaming awakened my roommate, and in the throes of my attack I could hear him mutter. "Crazy, man!"

Dr. Engel didn't have a chance against the Shadow.

An elderly, swarthy-backed patient at Ridgeview, Elizabeth, depressed, a yellowish look to her skin, approached me one day and from clouded little eyes said in a quavering little old voice, "Mister Oakes, you look like a very intelligent and reserved gentleman. What are you doing in here?"

I looked at her with consuming humility. "Elizabeth, you can't imagine the internal pain I'm going through."

On another occasion a staff member commented to me. "Mister Oakes, you could easily be mistaken for one of the doctors around here. Are you sure you're sick?"

"I'm sure."

On December 27, after two weeks at the institute—sort of a subdued, drawn-out, psychiatric pep rally for psychotherapy, I left Ridgeview, looking and feeling like a dissipated owl, and began my psychotherapy with Dr. Engel, one or two sessions a week, depending on how often I felt I needed to come in. Her office was on Peachtree Street in Atlanta, the Buckhead area. Plushy furnished in professional taste, green plants everywhere, the office presented a comfortable decor and soft colors, obviously for its soothing affect on patients. But on my first visit, anxious lines on my brows, the tenseness of anxiety stiffening my jaws, I felt none too soothed.

With both of us seated in chairs facing one another. I began our first session of therapy filled with a heavy air of resignation, gawking at Dr. Engel and asking, "What should we talk about?"

"Whatever you want to talk about."

"What do you mean, whatever I want to talk about?" I yelped testily, guarded and self-conscious, feeling stunned to verbal inaction by a combination of undefined anxious fury and draining helplessness. "Aren't there specific things you need to know so you can help me?"

"We'll eventually get to them once you begin talking." She answered cryptically, the quiet assurance of the statement somehow disturbing.

I frowned with an odd type of resistance. "I … I can't just start talking with no topic."

"Choose one."

"Come on. You choose one."

"You choose it." Engel reiterated, indicating that the burden of communication was placed on me.

"Shit!" I squirmed. "We're getting nowhere!"

"Perhaps you don't want to get anywhere."

"What the hell do you mean?! Why in fu—why do you think I'm here, for Christ sakes?"

"That's for you to decide."

"What is this shit? We're wasting time!"

"It's your hour. You can do anything with it you want."

I fell stiffly silent for a moment. Then, drawing in a short breath, I said, "What I want is for you to help me—if you can. So far all you're doing is aggravating me!"

"Why are you aggravated?"

"Why? Shit, you're not helping me!"

"Why are you aggravated?"

I began breathing heavily. "Damnit, I just told you! You're not helping me!"

"You're not helping you."

I looked aghast. "Me? If I could help myself I wouldn't be here! You're the *damn* doctor! So start helping—if you can!"

"Why do you feel you need to keep challenging me?"

"Challenging you? I'm not challenging you. I'm just saying you're not helping me!"

"You're aggravated. That's something."

"*That's help?*"

"That's a beginning. Why are you so aggravated?"

"We're going in circles, that's why!"

"They're your circles. Why are you aggravated?"

"Because you won't tell me what to talk about!"

"I sense you're easily aggravated."

"What's that got to do with anything?"

"You tell me."

"Shit! We're getting nowhere!"

"We'll only get somewhere when you decide we will."

"I've decided, goddamnit!" Shaking my head in perplexity. "Why do you think I'm *here?*"

"Why are you aggravated?"

Suddenly, a feeling of such helpless worthlessness seized me that I exploded. "Because it's a *lousy, fucking* world!"

"Tell me about it."

"Don't you know about it?" I snorted gloomily, my eyes wounded and void.

"Not your world. Tell me about it."

My eyes now turned dark and fathomless. "It's not worth talking about."

"It is if you want me to help you."

The first two months of psychotherapy proceeded like this, rigid defiance on my part, refusing to offer little beyond name, rank and serial number. Then, very superficially, I was eased into a safe area. I began talking about my work.

"How does your wife feel about that?" Engel asked me on some work related matter that touched upon home.

I felt outraged at this probing. "What does it matter? She has nothing to do with my work decisions!"

"What does she have to do with?"

Suddenly I was glaring at her, my eyes steaming. "Not a goddamned thing!"

In her calm, low-key, patient way, Engel kept pressing me about Sandra and it wasn't long until I became aggravated and began yelling at Engel each time she did, yelling at her the same as I used to yell at Sandra.

"You're stupid to keep asking me about Sandra!" I shrieked.

"Come on, doctor, get your damn act together! Let's talk about things that are important, for Christ sakes! Why do you fucking women always have to stick together! That's not what I'm here for! Now, damnit, quit asking about Sandra! Earn your money! Is that asking too much from your one-track brain?"

The more I yelled at Engel in our therapy sessions, the less aggravated and touchy I became with Sandra at home, and the more the relationship between Sandra and me began to improve. I began to even sleep a little better, though still sporadically. The nightmares of Daddy burning in hell were still waiting for me, as was the Shadow. And the anxiety attacks still awaited me when the dreams jarred me awake. My depression, though, thanks to the antidepressant Engle had prescribed for me, hand diminished.

It was when Engel weaseled me into the area of my childhood that the sparks in our therapy sessions really began to fly. I resisted saying anything significant about growing up in the shacks, offering a torrent of trivia that shielded anything meaningful. Yet, just touching upon events in my childhood, as superficial as they were, still brought a cold stiffness to my heart, frustrating me, aggravating me. I'd become noticeably nervous, my sentences faltering under a bubble of sourness in my throat.

Swallowing it back, strangely feeling a victim, one not part of this world, I'd counter Engel, "We're in a rut! I've been over that again and again and again. Let's move on to something else!"

But we'd zero back in on my childhood. And I'd become more frustrated and aggravated. And impatiently anxious to flee the subject.

"You're never going to pinpoint my problem if we keep wasting time talking about my childhood!"

But we kept thrashing back and forth about it, and I was tiring of discussing my childhood, even on the surface, becoming wearisome of the seedy events such discussion reminded me of, making me more irritable and impatient. And it was beginning to become very threatening.

"We've covered everything that could possibly be a cause of my problem! There's nothing left to talk about!"

"What about your mother?" Engel pursued.

A chill hit me in the pit of my stomach. Discussing Mama was absolutely and automatically verboten. "Leave Mama alone." I warned, my skin stretching a bit tighter, lips receding to a razorblade thinness, an unmistakable message that no further questions about Mama would—or could—be tolerated.

"We can't," Engel emphasized.

My rage, my fear, my horror, more cool and controlled a moment ago, now erupted irrepressibly. "No! … No! … No!" I unexpectedly thundered, my voice pitched higher by the poignant fear that possessed me. Suddenly I jumped up from my chair, quavering, looking glassily about, my face harrowed, emanating rapid pulses of panic, my knees about to buckle. "I'm quitting seeing you!" I spat back, my tone sharp and mocking now, a slightly deranged ring to it, a sickness in my throat. "I'm going to find someone who can help me! You're a quack! A goddamned fucking hussy quack!"

An emotionally traumatic threat born of throbbing agony in my head, the flowing and tormenting mush in my brain. A threat I'd repeat many times in sessions to come, but always I'd come back. The commitment to Sandra. To myself.

But the sessions were stormy. As soon as Engel got back to the area of Mama I became inimical to her. Even the thought of discussing Mama brought a painful and agonizing twinge, then a noticeable spasm would tear through my body. Each time Engel asked me about Mama I was thrown into the siege mentality of a desolate diatribe, each time my yelling at her becoming more vicious in its rage.

At night, at home, when I chose to sleep, I began having a new dream. I was in Dr. Engel's office, seated, talking with her. Suddenly I'd jump up from my chair and began cursing at her, grabbing my whip and slashing at her with it. Then Dr. Engel transformed into the Shadow, and I dropped my whip, paralyzed, the Shadow crucifying me with his laughter.

"Why are you laughing? … Why?... Why?... Why!"

My answer would be harder laughter snapping me out of my sleep, trembling in a cold sweat, only to be devoured by an anxiety attack.

At the beginning of 1987, after two years of psychotherapy, Engel hadn't come close to penetrating even the first layer of my psychic defenses. They were too heavily fortified, making me totally intractable, silenced by the painful emotional cacophony of a restless sharecropping legacy insisting upon my fealty to it. Insisting that I forever remain that scrawny-face, fly-squashing, cotton-picking, mule-plowing nervous wreck.

For Dr. Engel it was far from any joy ride. For two years she had to put up with my aggravation and impatience with her. Two years of my anger unleashed upon her. Two years of yelling and screaming at her like some wild demented beast. Two years of denouncing her with tangible bitterness. Two years of refusing to explore anything significant about my childhood or Mama. All those secrets were still locked away, guarded fiercely.

For all the insults and verbal abuse I had hurled at her, I thought I'd become an implacable enemy to Engel and she would have kicked me out of her office long ago, giving up on me as an outrageous blunder. But through all of my railing and denouncing and rudeness and insults, Engel remained accepting, tolerant, low-key, patient, totally lacking in temperamental ego, never becoming unnerved, and never even hinting that I quit seeing her.

Finally becoming just too stunned and bewildered over her refusal to reject me, feeling it was grossly unfair for her to continue putting up with my outrageous therapy behavior in her office, one night, before I fell asleep, I decided to inform Dr. Engel the next day that I was quitting my psychotherapy with her. This time for real. Regardless of my commitment, I'd just have to tell Sandra that after two years of psychiatric treatment, any continuance of it was hopeless. A waste of time and money.

Finally falling asleep, I dreamed. I was in Dr. Engel's office but she wasn't there. Instead, in her chair sat the Shadow.

"Just you and me now, pal." He smirked in that awful disconcerting voice. Then he commenced laughing.

"Why are you always laughing at me? Why?... Why?…"

The Shadow's answer was more laughter—louder, harder; that horrid gurgling incessant vivacious laughter, hideous and infuriating and tormenting. Deafening.

"Why don't you *ever* help me instead of laughing at me?"

The Shadow abruptly stopped laughing, his black shining eyes taking on a sudden sobering intensity burning right through me, almost empathetic. "Remember the swamp."

I awoke. But I wasn't trembling. There was no cold sweat. No anxiety attack.

Remember the swamp? What the hell did he mean?

The next day, in my therapy session with Engel, I said. "Doctor Engel, this is my last day. I'm quitting therapy."

"Another escape from Mama?"

I jumped up from my chair, becoming unglued, making Engel the object of one of my meanest temper tantrums. In the midst of it, the Shadow's words took hold of me. "Remember the swamp." Immediately I quieted, uttering:

"Find the spring that controls your own Universe."

For the first time Engel displayed emotion towards me, tears coming into her eyes as she softly glanced at me, tears full of warmth and mothering. "You broke your tantrum. You quieted down on your own. Your hard work is paying off."

That moment was overwhelming. Seeing the heady brew of empathy welling in her eyes—consuming, almost spiritual—I knew then that Dr. Engel harbored a deep-rooted, genuine concern for me. In a way, Mama finally showing me love. Instantly, something inside of me, something caged up within the deepest recess of my spirit, was set free and reached out to her, as though some light had suddenly sprung forth from the darkness, one that had never been lit before but now illuminating with a thousand sparks of brightness.

My new reaching out allied with Engel's genuine humane empathy was too potent a combination for me to resist. I continued my psychotherapy with her and our sessions took on a new determination. A new spirit within a new atmosphere. No more yelling and screaming. No more insults. No more denunciations. No more rigid resistance. In their place was a new openness. A new willingness to explore within myself. A new trust. Dr. Engel was now someone I could confide in free of judgment or rejection, her understanding—consoling without presuming to advise—bestowing importance and meaning, encouraging and allowing me to talk in earnest about my childhood, about Mama. Deftly, skillfully, sensing all my emotional difficulty antedating my ability to speak, Dr. Engel paved the way for me to wander courageously into the disarray of my inner emotions; ever more deeply whisking me into the seamy poisons reigning in those areas—into the shame, guilt, humiliation, chaos, torture, anger, rage, torment, fear and terror, all defying feral logic.

And as Engel moved me through the mazes of these inner psychic regions with intensifying clarity, yanking them to the forefront, every yank like inching forward on a beachhead against the blazing weapons of a formidable foe, more and more I was able to sleep better, no longer running on nervous energy. And my nightmares toned down, though those of Daddy burning in hell persisted. Oddly, the Shadow no longer appeared in my dreams. And with him and his tormenting laughter gone, my anxiety and anxiety attacks diminished, and as they lessened, I began to think more clearly, my emotions calmer, less frightening. I was able to tolerate crowds. I had periodic spasms of energy. Then I began sharing with Sandra what I was pursuing with Dr. Engel in my therapy sessions, this sharing bonding us, improving our communication with one another, gradually transforming our relationship into a special communion previously lacking in our marriage.

A new way of thinking, of feeling, of living, was opening up to me.

In therapy I was now able to zero in on Mama as the main architect of my emotional woes, taking a hard, deep, uneasy look at myself in relation to her, seeing how instrumental she was in molding my emotions—my feelings of unworthiness, my shame, my fears, my terror, my nightmares, my feelings of inner torment. And my anger. The terrible rage. The leading culprits in producing my anxiety and anxiety attacks and depression; my anxiety attack paralysis really a paralysis of my awareness of my death wish for Mama, vengeance against her for brutalizing my youth, the reason behind my terrorizing fear of death, Sandra, a substitute for Mama, the object for carrying out my revenge.

Mama made me feel the way I did and I finally stopped her!

With my progress here I began relating to Sandra as a woman in her own right rather than as a punching bag substitute for Mama. The result; Sandra and I discovered one another for the first time. It wasn't just a matter of an improved relationship. It was a totally new relationship-loving, meaningful, mature. Happy. Relating jocosely to one another. Something we never had. Something our children had never seen.

At the beginning of 1988, in one of our therapy sessions, calmly, earnestly, with a certain flash of bonhomie, I asked Dr. Engel. "How much longer, Doctor Engel?" My upper teeth were clamped ecstatically on my lower lip because the tenseness of my jaws was no longer there.

She smiled at me, shaking her head, looking surprised, then impressed, blinking her eyes as though floating in a pleasant dream. She had never seen me this calm and assured.

"Don, I don't know. But you will know when the time comes."

I now looked forward to our sessions. I was no longer just talking about Mama and my childhood. The whole world was my oyster. I talked about anything. By May of 1988, after three and one half years of psychotherapy, my anger, depression, anxiety and anxiety attacks had all vanished. And my only nightmare remaining was the one of Daddy burning in hell. Confidently I was looking forward with lingering waves of new expectancy for the normal life I now could live.

"It's time," I announced to Engel at a session in May, graduation day, that session our last. At the end of it Dr. Engel and I both stood up, both of us suddenly subdued by this leave-taking. Somehow Engel now seemed more feminine. She held out her hand to shake mine. But touching my hand she shoved it aside and gave me a long, hardy hug, her eyes all watery.

"Don, I'm glad things worked out for you," she soothed. Squeezing me tightly, a message from the heart. "I'm going to *miss* you! Do take care of yourself."

My heart was in my throat. I hugged her in return, sharing our satisfaction given in full measure. "I will, doctor. Thank you. For everything. *Everything!*"

CHAPTER 32

DR. ENGEL'S PARTING words; "Now you are your own therapist."

Leaving her office for the last time, walking out into the charm of Peachtree Street, thinking of those words I felt none too charmed. I suddenly felt incomplete. A void within me. And I didn't know why. Or what. Emotionally, mentally, physically, I never felt better, ready to join the ranks of normal people and finally begin living a normal life. I should be dancing on the street. I wasn't.

Of course, I knew psychotherapy hadn't cured everything. I still had worries and problems to face, but now I had a solid grip on them. I still had fears and dreads, but psychotherapy had scaled them down and given me the great edge in resolving them myself. Finishing them off on my own. But the one thing psychotherapy hadn't done was to clear up my fear of death and hell, and my nightmares of Daddy roasting alive in it. And psychotherapy had totally failed to even begin explaining away the Shadow.

That evening I was quiet and subdued with Sandra. When she asked me why, I told her of the strange, incomplete feeling overtaking me as I left Dr. Engel's office.

"That's natural," she said. "Your reaction to ending therapy. An important influence in your life is suddenly over."

That explanation had crossed my mind. But I knew that wasn't it. Something else. A beginning, not an end. Something having nothing to do with psychotherapy. Mama, the turmoil of the shacks or the sharecropping legacy. But it was much too vague to identify, as mysterious as the morning mist.

That evening, in bed, I was still thinking of it. Maybe the feeling is nothing at all, I concluded. Then I fell into calm, peaceful sleep; and into a dream. In the dream I faced a tall, ranging wall of stone. Then on the wall appeared a black shadow, and it quickly transformed into the figure of a man, very vague at first but then very clear; the Shadow. He began aging quickly, rapidly deteriorating into a draggled brawny form, drooping porcine eyes, no longer piercing or shining, his nose now nothing but a hook, his hair powder white, disheveled and scraggly, bouncing on his skull, the majestic sweep of flesh of his face old and wrinkled, sagging, tired and diminished, reduced to an extremely silly manner, that of a fizzled-out buffoon.

"What are you doing?" I asked astonished.

The Shadow began giggling childishly at me. "I'm disappearing, pal." Then his eyes took on a blackish sardonic glow of aristocratic authority changing his childish demeanor to a ravaging sneer. Then he spat out a massive wad of phlegm at me.

"Why'd you do *that?*" I recoiled.

"You drip!" He reproached. "The fun of tormenting you is gone!"

Then he began laughing throatily, a harsh vulgar laughter of loud mockery. A steady barrage.

"Then why are you laughing at me?"

"For all your years of self-hate … years of anguish and torment … years in psychotherapy to recover." The Shadow scowled, cackling in lipcurling contempt. "They were all so unnecessary! The joke's on you! You've been *duped!*"

The Shadow's laughter became louder and louder, deeper in derision, a final hurrah. Then in a parting glance of disdain he became the black shadow on the wall again, and the shadow disappeared, disappeared into the stone of the wall, its laughter trailing after it. Then the stone wall disappeared and total silence, like the sound of one hand clapping.

My eyes opened slowly to that silence, and I awakened as calm and peaceful as I had fallen asleep, the Shadow's parting words still caressing me. "You've been *duped!*" I knew then that finally just being normal wasn't enough. Something was still missing. Something vital. Central. All encompassing.

The reason I had been duped.

CHAPTER 33

ONE OF THE pressing tasks now of self-therapy, of being my own therapist, was trying to discover why I had been duped. But who did it? When? How? What had I been duped about? I had no idea of what I was searching for or where to begin. But whatever it was it seemed it had to be rooted in my past.

With this my only clue—and I wasn't even certain it was a clue, I began making notes on my life history, hoping maybe this would uncover some hint, putting down on paper all the significant events and feelings of my life, including those which I had worked through in psychotherapy, events and feelings that for most of my life I wouldn't dare mention to a soul—or even remind myself of, much less write of them in a personal chronicle. I kept adding to the story, putting down things which I hadn't explored with Dr. Engel, a good deal of it relating to the Shadow. And once I got into this I became consumed by the task, becoming painstakingly exhaustive, leaving no stone unturned. This all-out effort led to a decision to return to the shacks where I had grown up; there to see what additional information and feelings could be elicited by being in the environment giving rise to my once maligned psyche.

This trip back to the area of the shacks I took alone. Since the 17 shacks I was raised in were all located within a six mile radius of one another in southern Alabama, I would not have far to travel to visit each one once I arrived in the Josie-Corinth area where they were grouped. But once I arrived there, to my chagrin, there were no shacks, as if they never existed. Save one. Shack 11, the old Garret place. The rest of the shacks—except for Shack 5, with only its chimney remaining, poking into the sky with defying tribute had vanished completely, swallowed by age, as though time had tired of their era.

All I had was Shack 11 to help me in the continuance of my search. The shack was vacant, decrepit, on its last legs, barely holding up as if in anticipation of my visit, after which it would crumble and disappear, its purpose served. Walking up to the shack I was greeted by the lengthening shadows, a golden cast now tingling the afternoon light. Inside, Shack 11 had that dusty, moldy, old sour smell of age, cobwebs everywhere, the place completely empty except for a makeshift cot in one of the rooms, apparently used recently by some wandering hobo. And the shack was deathly silent except for a curious sub aural echo, a lingering sound by the ghosts of the past.

It had been 33 years since I had lived in this shack. I was 11 years old, in the sixth grade, Lurlene my girlfriend in school. Shack 11 also was where I had experienced my worst asthma attacks, and where Mr. Thompson rescued me from them with his miraculous little breathing gadget.

But in the here and now of the present, Shack 11 elicited no particular feelings or emotions, offering me no new clues to my search, my emotional state neutral, my mind looking upon the awful memories of the time I lived here as being the experiences of someone else, foreign and inconsequential to me now.

No help here. Nothing to add to my written story. Drawing in a long sigh, disappointed in my journey, I returned to my car in the gracefully cooling temperature, prepared to head back to Atlanta. It was then that a little chill drifted across the back of my mind, then mushroomed into an eerie feeling. Uncanny. A sort of parasensual sense intercepting subliminal vibrations around me, vaguely directing me.

Without thought, without a reason, I drove back to the site of where Shack 1 had been located. It was the cool end of the day when I got out of the car, still and quiet, the fading light of dusk beginning to settle, only a few minutes of sunlight left.

Not only was Shack 1 gone, but so were the other shacks that had been in the neighborhood. All that remained was the old dirt road. I had no idea what I was doing here. There was nothing to see, and the eerie feeling with its directed vibrations had left me.

From where Shack 1 once stood I was staring sightlessly across the road to the grassy field where peanuts used to be grown when, inexplicably, I sensed I was somewhere else. In another dimension. Then I saw them; that long string of ghostlike figures, very clear, hands joined, floating a few feet off the ground, eyeless, facing me, an irregular mass of cloud-like forms, pulsating in grayish-white luminous transparency. Seemingly it was the same string of ghostlike figures I had seen here when I was five years old, the figures that had so frightened Mama, Ruby Lee and Inez, and sent the dogs into a weird, abnormal frenzy of barking.

The ghostlike figures were moving across the field toward the woods, and as 39 years before they seemed harmless and wanting to communicate. I was standing there motionless, watching them, not making a sound, when three of the figures suddenly took on eyes, then identities, startling me.

One of them was Daddy. Next to him was Nat Mitchell. And next to Nat was the Shadow.

Immediately I was immersed in an overwhelming calm, transported, sensing a harmonious communion so vivid and so directed and so strong that my own volition was suspended. I was to return to Shack 11.

The next thing I knew I was back in my car driving toward Shack 11, arriving there as the emerging stars began their glitter over the stillness of the night. Taking a couple of candles with me from the car, I entered the shack, lit the candles and searched about, waiting. I didn't know for what but feeling in the hold of the shack.

Then it hit me suddenly, the drowsy, sleepy sensations, feeling so exhausted that I went into the room with the makeshift cot and laid down on it. Within moments after my head hit the cot I fell into a deep sleep, and into a dream. I was facing a walnut coffin with a fawn satin lining, its lid open, and all around there were instrumental strings of soft blissful music to a backdrop of bright golden light. Daddy sprung up to a sitting position in the coffin, garbed in his grungy overalls, his eyes boozy drunk and puffy, teeth gleaming, that ingenious, enigmatic grin on his face, flipping a cigarette across his mouth in a wad of nasty spit, the fiery embers of its end lighting up the mirthfulness of his features and the deep swarthy laugh lines giving it character as he reached down to his crotch, rubbing shamelessly his rupture.

"Daddy, why aren't you burning in hell?"

He beamed at me gibingly, then broke into his loud, bellowing, garrulous impresario bray of laughter, answering merrily, "Because thar ain't no damn hell, son! Thar ain't no heaven, either. Time you wised up! Stop all this frettin' over it. Over me. Over anything."

Then Daddy increased his bray of laughter by several decibels, great gurgling sounds, great seizures of laughter, tears in his eyes as he shook up and down, a bouncing fit, laughing so uncontrollably that he fell out of his coffin, then jumped nimbly to his feet with effortless agility, laughing harder, sheer exuberance. Daddy's laughter wasn't mockery, but had the joyful euphony of celebration. He wasn't laughing at me. He was laughing for me.

Finally calming his laughter to snickering hilarity, Daddy quirked with amusement, his features suddenly becoming an immaculately barbered face, "Son, ya don't ever have to cry. Over nothin'." Then his snickering stopped and he smiled benignly, "Life ain't meant for tears. It's not what it seems. Quit taking yer lot so seriously. Hot a mighty! It don't matter."

"But, Daddy, I've been *duped*!"

"Y'all have. From somethin' in all yer reach."

"*What*?!"

"Ya'll see."

"But how?"

"Go to Pea River Swamp."

Daddy and the coffin disappeared.

CHAPTER 34

IT WAS LATE morning when I awoke to the deafening quietude of Shack 11. I never felt so peaceful. For a few moments I remained on the cot quietly, barely stirring, flabbergasted. Then feeling released from the shack's hold I jumped up, left the shack, went to my car and drove to Pea River Swamp.

It was a clear, calm fall day and Pea River Swamp, usually breezy and restless this time of year, was uncharacteristically peaceful, the sun above an orange autumn glow, turning the clouds golden, their reflections enhancing even more the wheat-colored golden expanse of the swamp, a special enchantment, a magical affect, illuminating Shakespeare's words:

> *"This other Eden, demi paradise*
> *This fortress built by nature for herself."*

And this was my childhood paradise, its native son returned, a stranger to its surrounding inhabitants because I was from another world, making a salary approaching a six digit figure, owning a sprawling beautiful home, four new automobiles, a condominium at Panama Beach in Florida, and involved in partnerships and stocks and other investments. But I wasn't a stranger to this fortress. Given my legacy, the swamp's glistening luminosity seemed to salute me for such impossible accomplishments, seemingly taking pride and celebrating that, in some small measure, it provided the inspiration helping me to escape the impoverishment of that legacy.

Invigorated by the swamp's pure sweet air, I felt the invisible presence of the ghostlike figures, prompting me to state aloud:

"Find the spring that controls your own Universe."

Suddenly the swamp opened up to me. A special communion. A special peacefulness. A special harmony. A special oneness with it. Standing there, surveying its richly fertile soil, its thick masses of timber, its flights of blue jays and crows, I could feel it. Feel the swamp giving up its secrets, the secrets of Nature, now suffusing me, uplifting me to a loftier dimension of awareness, a keener dimension of communication, an ultimate dimension of experiencing and being. A pure, rich dimension of the soul; birth, living, death, afterwards all the same. One continuum never ending.

And sensing this continuum, an awareness within me coming from without, coming from the soft slight breeze caressing me, from all of Nature surrounding me, I felt both my own significance and my own insignificance. And they were both the same. My significance and insignificance didn't matter. Just the fact that I lived, the circumstances of that living unimportant.

I sighed in awe as this special communion continued, revealing more secrets sighing quietly through the oaks, poplars and pines of Pea River Swamp, whispering around its brush and over its sloughs of water, flat ribbons of sparkling pools mirroring the trees and twinkling in answer to the sun, all a flowing motion of stillness mixing the life of Nature together, then separating it into its components making their own individual runs, then returning each to all the others, to be mixed all together again, everything one with everything, then separating into their individual journeys, only to be joined once more.

Unending.

My body swelled with supreme harmony, the same harmony I experienced with the ghostlike figures the evening before, and in that ecstatic communion I was let in on another secret transforming me. Awesome sensations of vitality, overwhelming yet exhilarating and reassuring. Suddenly I felt so alive! So vibrant! So thankful! A sensation of rebirth. A sensation so immense that I could feel my blood skipping daintily around in my veins, dancing to a new melody, new feelings, producing an effect of tingling warmth in my stomach while my heart seemed to dissolve.

Finally I knew the meaning of joy!

And with that joy I felt the presence of the Greater Harmony outside of me, all around, shooting up to the sky and the sun and beyond. I vocalized my thanks to It, the effect of my tongue being caught with joy between my teeth as I cheered helter-skelter heavenward, yelling goggle-eyed in swooping leaping utterances carrying the joy of my deliverance.

CHAPTER 35

AFTER PEA RIVER Swamp my life was never the same. It couldn't be.

My smile became quick and bright, my laughter deep and true, fully opening me to life, drawing me into it, a zestful awakening to people, to fun, to a jolly good time, enjoying every second of living, not wasting one precious moment on worry—so unnecessary, propelled to act and react from a new realm of sensing, one honest to myself and to others. Life was to be savored every day; every ounce of meaning and enjoyment to be coaxed out of it without being robbed of that meaning and enjoyment by wasteful distracting burdens.

The secret.

And I never felt such a strong sense of my own emotional integrity. I was openly and expressively in touch with my feelings, handling them with mirth, a mirth evolving into a crusty, good-natured humor. I had new energy, new insights, a new capacity to tell those close to me that I loved them, and meant it. I had an eagerness to explore new horizons. A new desire to seek out people, to become personable, engaging, and entertaining, with a wide shoulder of tolerance.

The secret.

It allowed me to accept life's tragedies in harmonized stride and to gracefully accept the inevitable cycle of Nature's ongoing purpose.

Mama finally filled her purpose in this plan. On January 1, 1989, at the age of 73, she died. Cancer of the colon.

In December of 1988 I knew Mama wouldn't be able to whip it. She was in too much pain, the cancer eating her up. She had no appetite and was losing weight and the chemotherapy she was undergoing was of no help to her. Mama's condition rapidly deteriorated, leaving her hunched and withered, looking like a little old gray ghost, her vitality gone, her hail without luster, her delicate face deadened into a strained, hollowed, sallow expression, the pallor of fatal sickness.

Mama had mellowed and tamed down in her last few years, taking a special delight and excitement in seeing me. And since my psychotherapy I was able to accept her for what she was. But since Pea River Swamp I had quickly forgiven her, loving her as a person, regardless of her hang-ups and their consequences on me. That no longer mattered. In her last month I enjoyed rubbing her head, hugging and kissing her, she enjoying my affection in return.

"I'm gonna git better," Mama kept repeating to me in the last two months of her life. "I'll be all right in a few days."

She was going to get better. But not in this life.

What I felt badly about was the pain she was suffering. The day before her death, on New Year's Eve, 1988, I visited her in the hospital. It was evening and she was speaking incoherently, in terrible pain, the doctors unable to relieve it. Suddenly Mama became silent and gripped my hand, squeezing it with a strength seemingly impossible for her frail, fragile condition. In that grip I sensed her dying message to me:

I love you very much and I'm sorry for what I did to you.

I squeezed her hand back, the warmth filling my heart. My message:

I love you very much too, and no apologies necessary. I understand. Everything. Something wonderful awaits you.

Faintly she smiled, an inward expression, a split second of vividness in her eyes. Then it was gone and she gasped with a slight rattle, a slight spasm, into unconsciousness, dying a few hours later, around six a.m. in the morning, her pain no more, leaving me with a flickering of sadness that she had not known the secret in this life.

Mama's funeral was on January 3, 1989, at Ramah Church in Josie. She was buried next to Daddy in the church's graveyard. It was a sunny day, but with a fierce, howling wind. At the graveside Mama's casket was opened and it and her corpse were whipped about in jerky movements by the strong wind, shooting an uncanny chill down my spine, visualizing the wind as the force from Daddy's laughter.

Mama was now laughing with him.

The day after the funeral I watched the sun rise and a new day come to life, and I was thankful.

Previously I had thought of my job with Control Data Business Centers—the name changed to Control Data Business Management Services in 1987—as my final horizon. Where I had to be. My career. Where I'd end up professionally. But now those feelings had dramatically changed, guided by harmonized awareness and understanding, a quest of actualization directing my professional strivings toward endeavors worthy of failing rather than toward those simply offering monetary success.

At our company's annual national Sales Organization One Hundred Percent Club gathering, an out of town affair for elite salesmen which I attended as Response Center Manager, there was a video crew hopping about, busily taking videos of all of us in various activities, keeping their camera in furious motion. I happened to be in many of the shots and one of the video crew members commented to me:

"You should get into TV or movies. You're so photogenic."

His opinion was shared by the other crew members, and some of the salesmen as well.

That again? But now I listened more seriously.

Returning to Atlanta I had no idea how one got into TV or movies. When in doubt turn to the Yellow Pages. I did. Searching through them I found nothing under several categories. Then, under "Modeling," I spotted this agency's ad; TV Acting and Commercials. I phoned and was invited to come to the agency's offices. There, after a quick glance of appraisal, a lady told me:

"By all means, you certainly have potential. A tremendous look with those blue eyes and graying hair and nice facial features. You definitely have a market. But your beard will have to go! It will hold you back in this business. Facial hair is frowned upon."

I shaved the beard and began enrolling in a few classes—TV acting and commercials, makeup, voice and classes teaching the use of resumes, head shots and the proper compilation of a portfolio. I had some minor dental work done, arranged for some photography sessions and began putting my portfolio together. Then, in January, 1989, just after Mama's funeral, I made an all-out effort to bring myself to the attention of acting agents, submitting head shots of myself through the mail to the seven major talent agencies in Atlanta. Within a few days, a woman booking agent from the Serendipity Agency phoned me, exclaiming:

"We definitely want to represent you. I need twenty more head shots right away!"

I delivered the head shots pronto. Immediately I was thrown into action. While at the agency one of the booking agents queried:

"Can you go on an audition right now?"

"Sure!" I smiled, a wide, startling grin dancing with the excitement racing through my veins.

At the audition I discovered that the parties requesting it were looking for an executive type to photograph for a brochure advertising a real estate agency. I was promptly selected for the job.

From there things began to pop. Over the next two months, February and March, I was signed with six of the seven major talent agencies in Atlanta, and over the next five months, April through August, I auditioned for thirty different acting jobs, a mixture of TV commercials, movies and brochures, and was selected for fifteen of them, having to turn down five more because they conflicted with my other acting jobs.

At six, one, 185 lbs., my coloring healthy, halfway to a golden bronze, every one of my agents felt I had that strong executive look.

"You have the absolute perfect look for this business," one of them put it. "You can't miss! And at forty-five you're the right age. And you can play other roles besides an executive just as well—a doctor, lawyer, pilot. Most anything."

My other five agents were in agreement, emphatically offering similar views. And their views were born out by the number of job offers I received from my auditions. Getting in front of a camera and expressing myself proved to be sheer enjoyment, exciting, fun, a ball—expressing different moods, different personalities, different characters, with little vestige of my once southern accent.

In August, along with my other acting jobs, I landed a major role, that of a Confederate sergeant in the movie, WHIPPOORWILL, a Civil War story presently being filmed. From that involvement I came to know other enterprising professionals in the trade and a group of us formed a production company making our own movies and videos.

My new star was soaring.

But there was another endeavor I had to pursue. More important than the acting, the commercials, the movies, or the production company. Something I sensed clearly after Pea River Swamp. An undeniable obligation to give something to others in return for what had been given to me.

The revelation. The secret.

I had to publish my story. For that I needed a writer, a collaborator, the right person, one who could become attuned to my story well enough to help put it into the proper words.

CHAPTER 36

I ENTERED THE classy Chinese restaurant near Sandy Springs on my lunch hour from work. Inside, I was to meet with Gerald G. Griffin, a writer, waiting for me at a booth.

Decked out like some magazine fashion plate in my dark conservative-cut suit, I walked over to where Griffin was sitting, the author dressed more informally, slacks and shirt, a low-key tweed jacket, his manner seeming the icon of anchorman calm behind fashionable tinted glasses.

We greeted one another with flickering smiles and a hardy handshake, and after some words of amenity I seated myself, the waitress took our order, and I was ready for some serious discussion. "Well, what do you think?" I said.

"Why do you want to publish this story?" Griffin asked quietly. With the exception of the Shack 11 dream and the Pea River Swamp revelation, I had previously given him the written notes constituting my story for his review and opinion, and today he was to give me his feedback. "I can imagine all the pain and agony for you putting this together with me."

"That's not important."

"What is?" Youthful appearing for his 55 years of age—sensitive hazel eyes, high forehead, thick brown hair, ruddy complexion. Griffin gave the impression of a man at ease with himself. There was no paucity of outstanding writers in Atlanta but Griffin, in addition to being a mellifluous writer, possessed a Ph.D. in psychology, that extra sensitivity and professional savvy I considered so vital to the writing of my story.

"Preventing that pain and agony for others," I answered. "I want people to see that they shouldn't keep their emotions bottled up. They have to get help—from somewhere," I added cryptically. "Without that their problems only get worse. I don't want them to wait forty-one years, like I did, before they talk to someone. They should do it early in life. All their problems on the table. My story can help these people. Give them something vital to happy living."

Griffin's eyes were now keen and penetrating, already attuned. "There's more than what you've written here."

"Yes."

"Then let's give it a go. You could have something worth telling."

Though the reasons I gave Griffin for writing the book were hoped for by-products, they weren't the overriding reason. Griffin would discover that soon enough.

The real reason was the revelation. The secret.

The last chapter.

CHAPTER 37

THE REVELATION. THE secret.

To begin, after death there is heaven; there is hell. Before death there is life. Life can be heaven at times and hell at times. We have freedom of choice to make it what we want it to be.

This life on earth, in the living Universe we can see while alive, is but one small segment in the long totality of Nature-Supreme Nature existence. It is this totality, the elegant progression through it that offers the meaning of existence, not any one segment of the progression.

And since this life, living in the earth form of our bodies, is but one segment of this progression, its meaning is incomplete and thus inconclusive, though it should be enjoyed to the fullest while being accepted for what it is, and what it is is revealed through harmony with Nature.

But organized societies are so devised as to prevent this harmony, the government, the State, the politicians, the churches, the corporations, the heraldry of the ruling classes, and so forth, coconspirators in the brutal manipulation of the individual for their own purposes. But more damaging, organized technical societies are disharmonious, out of tune with the harmony of Nature. Thus the individuals in these societies become disharmonious outcasts in their own bodies, suffering varying degrees of misery preventing the enjoyment of life that harmony with Nature provides, these unhappy legacies of disharmony passed on from one generation to the next when they do not have to be.

The significant meaning of this mode of existence on earth, with its own particulars of perception, and its own unique means of procreation, form, enjoyment and expression, has little to do with the madding crowd's *faux pas* inventions of the meaning of life—the delusional myths, dogma, verisimilitudes, vanity and self-righteous contrivances—since this meaning is beyond its endowments to comprehend and can only be seen from the potpourri totality of progression. The question is not what is the meaning of life but what is the meaning of existence, which can only be answered after one has passed through all dimensions.

What meaning this particular mode of existence does have, and the secret of enjoying its breathing life, is discovered only when one becomes in harmony with Nature, then all else falls into place. Otherwise, it's a long, hard, meaningless road from womb to tomb, with no deliverance until one is released from the tomb into the next segment of Nature-Supreme Nature's progression.

What this all reduces to is that one should focus on his present mode of existence and not be concerned with the others, the other dimensions, since they are beyond one's ability to grasp and there's no way to prepare for them. And the saving focus of this present living breathing mode of existence is to come into harmony with Nature. Anyone can do this.

Within the realm of each person's mind, a realm deeper than the consciousness, there's an inborn current of energy identical to the energy flowing throughout the Nature-Supreme Nature continuum of progression. And it is this spark that tunes you in and harmonizes you with Nature, bringing release in this mode of existence before release into the next dimension of progression.

Before this spark can be released to achieve harmony with Nature, however, the conscious and unconscious minds must be brought into harmony with each other, meaning no contamination of the consciousness with crippling states of misery, agony or any of the other spirit draining mental-emotional stresses of living. Any of these will block release of this inborn spark of Nature's energy.

The first step, then, is to clear the mind so the spark can be released. This is crucial! Without it all else fails. Rather than being intellectual creatures who control our emotions, we are emotional creatures who control our intellect. And if our intellect is controlled by unstable emotions, that disharmony has to be cleared.

Psychotherapy is not necessary for this clearing, though for someone whose mind is so disharmonized with itself, it offers one effective means for achieving it. What's critical for this clearing is that you find someone with whom you can talk in a special way. Someone you trust. Someone you feel comfortable with. Someone who is nonjudgmental and not a gossip. Someone who will keep confidential what you tell he or she. Someone who is willing to help you with your sense of well being.

Then talk to them. Talk, talk, talk! Talk about your concerns, your worries, your frustrations, your parents, your childhood, your family, your friends, your enemies, anything troubling you.

Ventilate! Get it all out. Get all your problems out. Keep nothing to yourself. Hold no feelings or emotions back. The terrible price you pay within for doing so is not worth it. Such stifled inner life is disharmonizing—to your mind, your body, your whole being. It's ruining your life and your living, and your inherent capacity for enjoyment and meaning. Life is too short for that. Too valuable to concede even one second of it to pent up emotions disharmonizing your spirit.

Go for it! Loosen up. Let it out.

Of course, it will take some talking time to develop this kind of rapport with someone. Time before you're really bearing your soul and forcing the emotional disharmony out of yourself. This is not an overnight task. Not a matter of a few talking sessions. It may require months, even a year. Whatever, its the best use of your time you'll ever make.

Now, as you ease into this talking rapport with someone, begin keeping a written journal, noting on paper all the significant things you're talking about—feelings, emotions, stress, disappointments, despair, unhappiness, events and people and circumstances producing all of this disharmony. Keep adding to the journal, keep updating it, keep inserting things you left out but later remembered, until eventually you have your entire emotional life history on paper, from the time you first can remember to the present, something similar in emotional analysis and scope to this book.

Write your own book on yourself.

This writing and talking to someone will flush your mind; clear it; cleanse it; harmonize it. Keep this flushing-clearing-cleansing going by whatever other means seem helpful to you. Perhaps a book on self-hypnosis. It may aid your task to self-hypnotize yourself, with suggestions to your mind to harmonize itself. These additional means at harmonizing your mind may prove helpful once your talking to someone is finished and your journal is completed.

Once your conscious mind is harmonized with your mind's deeper layers—this doesn't have to be perfect, the main thing being you don't have any bottled up major disharmony, you are ready for the next step; communing with the exotic and sensuous mystery of Nature.

Again, this is not an overnight task. It takes time. It takes practice. It takes genuine appreciation of Nature and what Nature holds in store for you. There's a saying that the best things in life are free. This is correct because the best thing in life is Nature, and it's free. Get out among this gift.

Begin with any natural setting of Nature, any season of the year—lake, ocean, river, stream, mountains, woods, prairie, valley, orchard, even a yard garden. Then look at it. Really look at it. Feel it. Hear it. Touch it. Smell it. Sense it. Suffuse it into your being. Return to the setting as often as you can, repeating this. Find new Nature settings and do the same thing. Embrace Nature on a regular basis- see, listen, smell, touch, taste, feel, sense, over and over and over.

Wake up to a view of Nature, to the melodies of birds and the cool morning dew. Listen to the sea sounds on a beach and inhale the briny roar of the ocean. If mountains are the backdrop then marvel at them, at the sheer rock faces, the gray cliffs of rock, the slashing valleys of greenery in between. Then savor the magnificent sunsets over the mountains, the chilly purity of the air, the softness of the night, the misted stars, the ripple path of the setting moon.

Awe at the splendor of winter, the glitter of perfect white snow, the smell of winter's bare tree limbs, the smell of their bark, waiting, preparing, for the surge of new life. See winter's autumn gold through the trees. Marvel at the darkened majesty of leaden skies with wind-driven snow, listening to the wind building to a low-pitched scream, constantly changing the drifts of the snow's pure white flakes.

Smell the flowers, touch and see their endless beauty. Listen to the rumble of thunder and hear the patter of the rain and smell its freshness. Hear the soothing wild chatter of the forest, the harmony of its song. Taste the wild strawberries, the wild fruit. Watch the changing of the leaves and some other memorable aspect of your life. Go there alone. Commune. Then say aloud:

"Find the spring that controls your own Universe."

The spark of Nature's energy inborn within your mind will release itself, inexorably inviting all of the energy of outward Nature to fill you. At that moment you become harmonized with Nature, an expanded state of grace, a feeling of flowing into all things and sensing all things, an inexplicable sensing of Supreme Nature. A lasting harmony as long as you refresh it with periodic communing. A harmony slowly allowing you to begin sensing unbelievable things beyond your imagination. Things revealed to you through dreams, happenings, encounters, insights, changing your inner life and your outward life with others, filling you with humming and singing; filling you with tremors of new excitement and anticipation; laying before you what to do with your life to fully enjoy it, to get the most out of it, and to make the most out of it in a release of new found virtue.

A prodigious, inimitable wonder of living.

Then your life takes on a calmed euphoric gallantry; a bold, noble meaning for which it was intended.

Fantastic! Spectacular! Ecstatic! Vitalizing!

Find the spring that controls your own Universe. Then set it free. Supreme Nature is God. God is the spring that controls your own Universe.

Epilogue

I DIVORCED SANDRA in 1995 after 29 years of marriage in spite of her not wanting a divorce. She had a heart attack in 1997, a major stroke in 1999 that left her paralyzed on the left side, another heart attack in 2001 and another one in June 2003...She underwent quadruple bypass in June and is doing well under the circumstances...We remain friends and I was with her and other family members during the touchy bypass operation/recovery in Nashville, TN.

Donna lives in Nashville with her husband Francisco and 11-year-old daughter Kelly. Michelle lives in Lawrenceville, GA with her husband Scott and their 4-month-old son Dobbs (my first grandson). April along with her life-long partner Nicole also lives in Nashville.

My brother J.P. was killed in a train/auto accident in Alabama in Nov. 1990. My other brother, Red, died in the book of course...Ruby Lee, my oldest sister, died in 1992. My sister, Inez, lives outside of West Point, GA with her husband Norman "Lad" and their "large" family. Marilyn, my youngest sister, lives in Phenix City, AL with her husband Norman...Marilyn didn't have any more children other than the one mentioned in the book. Her name is Vanessa and she is married with one daughter. Her name is Amy.

During the fall of 1999, a friend and I were camping out in the North Georgia mountain wilderness in my camper. A large hemlock stump was located between the camper and our campfire.

We had our customary campfire and enjoyed our usual camp side meal before retiring for the night. It was unusually hot and humid in the mountains that night and I decided to take off my clothes in an attempt to cool off. It must have worked because I fell into a deep sleep.

In the wee hours of the morning, a fast flickering light bouncing off the glass startled me awake. I sat up in my bunk bed and looked out the window to investigate. In no time, my friend sleeping in the other bunk bed said quite alarmingly "What's going on?"

I exclaimed in a hurried remark "The Stump's On Fire And I'm Naked!" After jumping outside still in the nude and getting the fire under control which was blazing dangerously close to the propane tanks, I realized the significance of that statement. Most of my life I had faced numerous situations where I was ill prepared but got the job done anyway! I knew immediately that I had the perfect title for my book. ***The Stump's On Fire And I'm Naked.***